Acclaim for

The Little Way of Ruthie Leming

"A brother's lovely remembrance of his sister and tentative exploration of the road home—a road truly less traveled." —*Wall Street Journal*

"Beautiful, moving...emotionally gripping...[an] excellent memoir... It is these bracing reflections on place and community, ambition and happiness that transform the book into something far more than a tragic autobiography. Dreher has written a powerful statement about how we live today—and more importantly, about how we *should* live."
—*The Week*

"Excellent...[a] well-written memoir." —*Dallas Morning News*

"Gripping...surprisingly personal and, at times, painfully honest."
—*Tampa Bay Times*

"Pulls hard on the heartstrings." —*Vanity Fair*

"Ultimately, this is what makes Dreher's book so powerful. As Ruthie nears the end of her life, the prose is compassionate but remorseless...The book inspires, moves, and convicts."
—*National Review*

"Thumbs up...a lovely memoir." —*Baton Rouge Sunday Advocate*

"THE LITTLE WAY OF RUTHIE LEMING made me cry...It will do the same to you, because it's an honest book about family, home, loss, and the pain none of us can avoid forever."
—TheDailyBeast.com

"5 stars...If you need further convincing about the beauty of life in small places, you won't do better than to read THE LITTLE WAY OF RUTHIE LEMING."
—*Christianity Today*

"If you are not prepared to cry, to learn, and to have your heart cracked open even a little bit by a true story of love, surrender, sacrifice, and family, then please do not read this book. Otherwise, do your soul a favor, and listen carefully to the unforgettable lessons of Ruthie Leming."
—Elizabeth Gilbert, author of *Eat, Pray, Love: One Woman's Search for Everything Across Italy, India, and Indonesia*

"THE LITTLE WAY OF RUTHIE LEMING reminds us of the importance of love, faith, and family. And while it deals in death, this book shows us that it is, indeed, a wonderful life."
—*BookPage*

"This book will make you feel hunger pangs for what you didn't know you even missed. And then it will feed you, line upon line, soul bread. As the Israelites ate manna in the desert, Dreher's evocative prose gathers the unforgettable manna moments of Ruthie Leming's life."
—Ann Voskamp, author of *One Thousand Gifts: A Dare to Live Fully Right Where You Are*

"Dreher, writing in this tender memoir, learns compassion, gratitude, and to focus on the blessings of the moment."
—*Publishers Weekly*

"THE LITTLE WAY OF RUTHIE LEMING is *Steel Magnolias* for a new generation."
—Sela Ward, Emmy Award–winning actress and author of *Homesick*

"Emotionally complex and genuinely affecting."
—*Kirkus Reviews*

"This is an authentic and deeply touching memoir, which honestly asks many of the best questions about the things that matter. Interacting with this story will change you!"   —Wm. Paul Young, author of *The Shack* and *Cross Roads*

"A hard-eyed self-examination and a loving, but complex, portrait of filial love."   —*Booklist*

The Little Way
of
Ruthie Leming

A SOUTHERN GIRL,
A SMALL TOWN,
AND THE SECRET OF
A GOOD LIFE

ROD DREHER

GRAND CENTRAL
PUBLISHING

NEW YORK   BOSTON

Grand Central Publishing
Hachette Book Group
237 Park Avenue
New York, NY 10017
www.HachetteBookGroup.com

Printed in the United States of America

RRD-C

Originally published in hardcover by Grand Central Publishing.

First trade edition: April 2014

10 9 8 7 6 5 4 3 2 1

Grand Central Publishing is a division of Hachette Book Group, Inc.
The Grand Central Publishing name and logo is a trademark of
Hachette Book Group, Inc.

Lines from Charles Peguy's poem "The Portal of the Mystery of Hope" come from
a 1996 translation from the original French by David L. Schindler Jr. and are used
with the permission of William B. Eerdmans Publishing Company.

All photographs are courtesy of the Dreher family, unless noted otherwise.
The Hachette Speakers Bureau provides a wide range of authors for
speaking events. To find out more, go to www.hachettespeakersbureau.com
or call (866) 376-6591.

The publisher is not responsible for websites (or their content)
that are not owned by the publisher.

The Library of Congress has cataloged the hardcover edition as follows:
Dreher, Rod.
    The little way of Ruthie Leming : a southern girl, a small town, and the
secret of a good life / Rod Dreher.—1st ed.
        p. cm.
    ISBN 978-1-4555-2191-3 (hardcover) — ISBN 978-1-4555-4534-6
(large print hardcover) — ISBN 978-1-4555-2190-6 (ebook) — ISBN
978-1-61969-627-3 (audiobook) 1. Dreher, Rod. 2. Journalists—United
States—Biography. 3. Brothers and sisters—United States—Biography.
4. Sister—Death—Psychological aspects. 5. Country life—Louisiana.
I. Leming, Lois Ruth, 1969–2011. II. Title. III. Title: A Southern girl, a
small town, and the secret of a good life.
    PN4874.D73.A3 2013
    070'.92—dc23
    [B]

2012033741

ISBN 978-1-4555-2189-0 (pbk.)

To Hannah, Claire, and Rebekah
This is your mother; these are your people

What matters in life are not great deeds,
but great love.

—ST. THÉRÈSE OF LISIEUX

Contents

One   Country Mouse, City Mouse   1

Two   "Forever and a Day"   20

Three   A Family of Her Own   43

Four   Sweet Babies   51

Five   The Father, the Son, and the Holy Ghost   61

Six   The Peppers   87

Seven   The Bright Sadness   96

Eight   Standing in the Spirit of God   123

Nine   Expecting a Miracle   136

Ten   "I'm Scared"   166

Eleven   "The Choir Invisible"   185

Twelve   Lean on Me   204

Thirteen   The Narrow Path   218

Fourteen   One's Destination Is Never a Place   238

Acknowledgments   269

Reading Group Guide   273

The Little Way
of Ruthie Leming

CHAPTER ONE

Country Mouse, City Mouse

Here's the thing I want you to know about my sister.

A long time ago—I must have been about seven years old, which would have made Ruthie five—I did something rotten to her. What it was, I can't remember. I teased her all the time, and she spent much of her childhood whaling the tar out of me for it. Whatever happened that time, though, must have been awful, because our father told me to go lie down on my bed and wait for him. That could mean only one thing: that he was going to deliver one of his rare but highly effective spankings, with his belt.

I cannot recall what my offense was, but I well remember walking down the hallway and climbing onto the bed, knowing full well that I deserved it. I always did. Nothing to be done but to stretch out, face-down, and take what I had coming.

And then it happened. Ruthie ran into the bedroom just ahead of Paw and, sobbing, threw herself across me.

"Whip me!" she cried. "Daddy, whip me!"

Paw gave no spankings that day. He turned and walked away. Ruthie left too. There I sat, on the bed, wondering what had just happened.

Forty years later, I still do.

———

Ruthie would grow up to be a schoolteacher, a friend, a neighbor, and quite possibly the kindest person many people in our Louisiana parish had ever met. But our little town, St. Francisville, suffers no lack of kind people. There was something different about Ruthie, though. I didn't always see that, of course—and I didn't really see it until the end. Ruthie had always been my little sister, which, in our family, meant my frequent foil.

My little sister was born on May 15, 1969. My parents named her Lois Ruth Dreher, accomplishing the neat trick of honoring four elderly female relatives with only two names. As far as I was concerned at the time, the kid ruined my life as a two-year-old prince of the realm. When Mam and Paw brought her home from the hospital to our house in the country, I was appalled. Ruthie had a crib in her own room, across the hall from mine. That was too close.

When she had been home from the hospital for about two weeks, I told my parents, "I don't want her."

"Okay, we'll take her back," replied Mam. She loaded Ruthie in the car after making a show of packing up a little suitcase. Then Mam put me in the car and started to drive, wondering how far we'd have to go before I gave in. We got all the way to Highway 61 before I started crying and said that I wanted her. "My baby, my baby," I cried. Crisis averted, Mam turned the car around and headed for home. But I was still jealous and would remain so for some time.

This scenario or some variation of it should be familiar to anyone who has been a sibling or raised siblings. But as time went on—and not much time, either—it became clear that Ruthie and I were so different it was hard to imagine that we came from the same family.

The Drehers were country people. We lived in Starhill, a rural community six miles south of St. Francisville, a town of two thousand souls and the county seat of West Feliciana Parish. Though our little red brick house wouldn't have been out of place anywhere in late 1960s suburban America, it had the intimidating distinction of being smack in the middle of plantation country, a land of magnolias, Spanish moss, and architectural grandeur. West Feliciana is in English Louisiana, a southeastern region settled by people of Anglo descent, some of them Tories escaping the American Revolution. They built magnificent cotton plantations, and sold their goods at Bayou Sara, a trading port on the Mississippi, just below the bluffs on which the town of St. Francisville was built.

Growing up in St. Francisville you can't escape history. Every schoolchild goes on a field trip to Grace Episcopal Church, and stands under the moss-strewn oaks to hear the story of the time a cannonball from a Union gunboat on the river struck the church's bell tower. Our ancestor Columbus Simmons fought as a Confederate sniper in the battle of Port Hudson. For eleven days, he lived in a hollow tree, eating grubs, his legs peppered by shrapnel, until his capture. After the battle the Yankees let their prisoners go, and he limped back to his home in Osyka, Mississippi, and rejoined the Rebel army. Later Columbus migrated to West Feliciana, bought land in Starhill, and raised his family there. His children were George; Clint; my great-grandmother, Bernice; and her two younger sisters, Lois and Hilda. My sister and I learned about Columbus as a small boy at Lois's and Hilda's ancient knees. That's how close history was to Ruthie and me.

My father, Ray Dreher, was the first in our branch of the family to go to college, though against his will. He wanted to be outside, building things and working with his cows. But after returning from a stint in the US Coast Guard, my grandmother Lorena insisted that her son take advantage of the GI Bill and enter Louisiana State University. In 1958, while working on a degree in rural sociology, Paw bought sixty-seven acres in Starhill from his great-aunt Em—the asking price was forty dollars an acre—and began small-scale farming on part of the old Simmons place. He also started a job as the parish sanitarian, which, in a rural parish like West Feliciana, meant he was not only the health inspector, but often the public official who helped impoverished families get basic plumbing into their houses. To look upon my father as a young man—freckled forearms, sun-scorched face, chest the size of an oak trunk, fiery orange cowlicks blazing atop his head—was to understand immediately that he was a man who had no business confined to a desk. It wasn't in his nature.

Dorothy, Ruthie's and my mother, moved to town with her family from Mississippi at age eleven, when her father took a job at a sweet potato canning plant. She was nine years younger than Ray. One day in 1962 Paw walked into Robb's Drugstore, and was startled to learn that the beautiful young woman behind the counter, the one with the tender brown eyes, the sunshiny smile, and the way of speaking that made you feel like you had known her forever, was Dorothy Howard, all grown up. They began courting, and married in the summer of 1964.

Dorothy and Ray—Mam and Paw, as everyone calls them now—built their Starhill house when I was two years old. It sat in an open field at the edge of a pasture where Paw grazed his cattle herd. Paw would raise his children in the country, a mile as the crow flies from where he had grown up. His parents, Murphy and Lorena, still lived in the old cottage on Highway 61, and his brother, Murphy Jr., a real estate broker and world-class joker who once—no kidding—prank-called Ayatollah Khomeini, was raising his family across the road from them.

Starhill was where all the Drehers lived. There were fields and forests everywhere. For us, going to town meant driving the six miles north on Highway 61, in those days a two-lane blacktop, to St. Francisville. Baton Rouge, thirty miles in the other direction, was an exotic journey. New Orleans, an hour and a half farther downriver, might as well have been Paris.

From an early age Ruthie loved the country life. "Ruthie wanted to be with me whenever I was doing something outside," Paw says. "I never will forget the time when Ruthie was in diapers, and taking a bottle. I came in the house frustrated. It was in the wintertime, and I had planted sixty acres of rye grass back on the place. Old man John I. Daniel's cows kept tearing down the fence. His cows were getting in there eating all the rye grass I had for my cows.

"Ruthie heard me telling Mother that I was going to be back there a while fixing fence. She told her Mama that she wanted to go with Daddy, and she wanted Mama to fix her a bottle. She went herself, got her two diapers under her arm, and got in the truck. This was eight thirty in the morning. I was back there till eleven o'clock. That baby never said one time that she wanted to go home. She would kneel at the window watching me, or take a nap on the seat, or call me if she needed a diaper change."

Wherever Paw went in his pickup truck, Ruthie wanted to go too. Me? Not so much.

"If I didn't take her, she'd be mad at me. You? You didn't give a damn," he says, laughing. "You were watching TV or reading. Me, the kind of man I was, I wanted you to be outside, with me."

Most of all I preferred to be with Aunt Lois and Aunt Hilda, technically my great-great-aunts and the last of the Simmonses. The sisters, born in the final decade of the nineteenth century, were in their seventies by the time I came along. They lived together in a tumbledown shack at the end of a gravel road that ran through a pecan orchard near our house. That tin-roofed wood cabin, framed by sweet olive trees and enclosed by groves and gardens, was, like C. S. Lewis's enchanted wardrobe, a doorway into another world.

I now know that Lois and Hilda—whose father, recall, had fought in the Civil War—were the most extraordinary people I will probably ever meet. As a little boy, though, they were just Loisie—rhymes with "choicey"—and Mossie (Hilda married Ashton Moss, who died young). They had grown up in Starhill as strong-willed country girls who loved life on the farm, but who also yearned for adventure. When the United States entered the Great War, the sisters volunteered as Red

Cross nurses. They caught the train at the bottom of the hill near their family home and didn't stop their journey until they arrived at the Red Cross canteen at Dijon, France.

On many mornings in my early childhood, after Buckskin Bill, the Captain Kangaroo of Baton Rouge, told his loyal TV viewers good-bye from Storyland Cabin, my mother would give me a couple of diapers and let me walk through the orchard to Loisie and Mossie's place for the day. Sometimes I would stray from the pea-gravel path and walk under the pecan trees, with their faintly tangy musk. In the springtime a spray of white dogwood flowers hung high in a thick grove of trees opposite the pecans, a bunting celebrating the end of winter and marking the border of Loisie and Mossie's yard.

In that cabin I would sit with the two aged aunts, thin and frail as dried kindling, on their red leather couch and look through canvas-backed photo albums of their war years. There was the time, Lois said, when General "Black Jack" Pershing showed up at the canteen late one night and nobody could find the key to the kitchenware cabinet. Lois had to strain the general's tea through her petticoat. Hilda told of being in Dijon on the day the Armistice was announced, and slapping a giddy Frenchman when he seized her on the street, shouted, *"La guerre est finie!"* and tried to kiss her. She pretended to be scandalized by this, but what I heard was the excitement of someone who had had a grand adventure in a part of the world unlike our own, where nothing ever happened. Sitting on the couch beneath three rare Audubon prints, the sisters told me of their travels through Provence, the Côte d'Azur, Toulouse, and Paris, beautiful Paris. We tracked their route on the pages of a vintage Rand McNally atlas splayed on our laps.

Sometimes I would sit in Loisie's lap in the kitchen, not much bigger than a closet, and stir her pecan cookie batter by hand. We would pull sheets of those cookies out of the oven, each one buttery and crisp and about the size of a quarter, and eat them with cold milk on the front porch (or "gallery," as the old aunts called it, in the antique usage). Often we would sit by the fire and read the newspaper together. I loved the look and sound of those exotic words in the headlines. *Kissinger. Moscow. Watergate.* I could only intuit it at the time, but these elderly ladies, spending their final years in rural exile, were among the worldliest people I'd ever meet. Hilda, an eccentric Episcopalian, taught herself palm-reading. Scratching her bony finger across my soft pink palm one day, she said, "See this line? You'll travel far in life." I hoped it was true.

Lois was an accomplished amateur horticulturalist, and took me with her on strolls in her gardens. There was a large *Magnolia fuscata* tree in her front yard, with its pale yellow blossoms that smelled of banana. Loisie and I would walk, me holding her hand, past her camellia bushes, the stands of spidery red lycoris, King Alfred daffodils, and jonquils. There was a pear tree, a chestnut, cedars, live oaks, flowering dogwoods, and, towering over the backyard, an old Chinese rain tree, its podlike blossoms puffed like a thousand and one pink lanterns.

There was a king snake that lived in the bushes under the huge magnolia tree in Loisie and Mossie's yard. Loisie taught me that the old snake was our friend. If he was there, she said, he would keep rattlesnakes away. One day when I was eight, I walked with a friend to the aunts' cottage, and there was the king snake, black as night and marked by pale yellow runes, stretched across the pea gravel, sunning itself. My friend was paralyzed by fear, but I stepped right over the snake without bothering him. Loisie had said he was our friend, hadn't she, and inasmuch as she was the happy genius of this grove, who was I to doubt her?

This was my haven as a boy, a house and a garden a three-minute walk from my house, where I learned things that would shape the course of my life. But it was foreign territory to my sister. "Aunt Hilda turned Ruthie aside," is how Paw remembers it. "She was one of those women who dotes on boys. And she favored intellectual-type things. You were reading at three and a half. Ruthie wasn't. You liked books. Ruthie liked outdoor things. You were so interested in the lives those ladies had lived, and the places they had been. Ruthie wasn't, but it still hurt Ruthie badly that she would never be included."

Ruthie would have been bored stiff by parlor conversation and strolls through cultivated gardens. She wanted the woods, rough as it came. She loved it when she could prevail upon Paw to take her down to the hunting camp in Fancy Point swamp. I spent a fair amount of time there too, though the last place I wanted to be on a wet, frozen Saturday morning was standing in the woods with a shotgun—I was too young to handle a rifle—looking for a deer to shoot. For me the best part of those mornings was being with my dad and his friends in the warmth of the camp kitchen, drinking hot, sweet Community coffee, eating jelly cake, and listening to the crazy talk from Oliver "Preacher" McNabb, the old black cook who had once been in Angola State Penitentiary for murder. And then I had to go pretend to enjoy stalking deer, when I really wanted to be inside, cooking with Preacher and listening to his stories. Deer-stalking is what our culture told us young boys were supposed to love above all things.

Ruthie, she really did love all of it—especially the hunting. As soon as she was big enough to carry a shotgun, she did. When a hunter brought down a buck, the men took the carcass back to the camp to skin it. If I got too close, I would start to gag. Ruthie was right in the middle of it all, and in time, learned to skin a buck herself. "One time when she was a teenager, she and I went down on the edge of the swamp, down by Ed Shields's house," Paw says. "I put Ruthie on one hill, and I got up on the next one. After we sat there a while, we heard the dogs barking and coming. There were lots of leaves on the ground, and it was dry. We could hear the deer running in the leaves.

"As they got close, I heard Ruthie shoot that rifle of mine. I hollered, 'Ruthie, did you get him?' Her answer was, 'Hell yeah, I did!' That deer was running wide open, and that baby had hit him square in the neck. That was a difference between y'all. That time you killed that big thirteen-point in the swamp, you were torn up about it. But she was on top of the world."

Our family spent a lot of time outdoors, which was a normal thing around West Feliciana back then. In the spring, summer, and early fall, we fished in rivers, creeks, and ponds. When Ruthie and I were small, our dad had a pond built on his land and stocked it with bass, bream, and catfish. Fishing on that pond was what we did. It was great fun, especially when Paw gave us mini-cast rods and reels, which made pulling in those auburn-breasted bream, only the size of a man's hand, like landing a trophy bass. Fishing was our family's thing, and Paw's pond was our family's place. Though I was no fan of the outdoors, I would be lying if I said I didn't enjoy it.

But I would also be lying if I said I wouldn't rather have been in the city, at the movies, or better yet, at a bookstore. I loved science fiction, and novels, and books about space, and comics from *Richie Rich* to *Archie* to the *Green Lantern*. And best of all, there was *Mad* magazine, with its smarty-pants humor, and its snappy Yiddishisms. Nobody around here talked like that. I wanted to be where people talked like that.

"You were our dreamer," Mam says. "Ruthie wasn't. She was satisfied with what she had in front of her. You had your head in books all the time. She loved nature, and being outside."

If that's what you love, there is no better place to be on earth than West Feliciana. But if not, well, you've got problems, or at least you did if you were growing up in our house. I think the incomprehensible strangeness of her older brother brought out Ruthie's competitive nature, which manifested itself at an early age. She figured out soon enough that she was far more athletic than I, and that she could best me in most any physical contest.

She was a tough little strawberry blonde, barrel-chested like our father, with our mother's deep brown eyes. I was pudgy, weak, and embarrassingly uncoordinated. In third grade the playground fad was a toy called the Lemon Twist. It was a plastic lemon connected to a strip of flexible plastic rope, with a loop around the opposite end. You slipped the loop over your foot, and let it rest around your ankle. Then you spun the lemon around, leaping over it with your free foot. You might as well have asked me to dance the tarantella. My little sister was an instant ace on the Lemon Twist.

For me this was humiliating. It was a pattern that would repeat itself. Once Paw mounted a campaign to encourage me to build my upper body strength. I was on the floor in the living room, struggling to heave out a pitiful few push-ups. Paw tried to keep Ruthie out of the house when this was going on, because he knew she couldn't resist trying to outdo me.

"There she came up the hall, saw you on the floor, then flopped down and started pumping them out," he recalls. "That was the end of that ring-dang-doo. You just quit."

Ruthie was always a fighter. After we were both in school our mother took up driving a school bus. The drivers would line up outside the elementary school in the afternoon, chatting with each other until the final bell rang, letting the kids out.

"One day," Mam recalls, "Ruthie was probably third grade, I remember Clyde Morgan, one of the other drivers, sitting there with us saying, 'That boy better watch out.' Your sister was coming across the way to the bus, with her lunch box in one hand, and her book sack in the other. This little boy kept running by her, hitting her on the head. We watched her weigh the book sack in one hand, and the lunch box in the other. Clyde said, 'Look, she's choosing her weapon.' She picked up that book sack, and when he made the next round, she whacked him with the book sack, knocked that boy on the ground. Calmly picked up her book sack and got on the bus. Never said another word about it."

Ruthie was a hard little nut. But if that were all she was, she wouldn't have had so many friends, and no enemies. She was one of those rare people who had a natural talent for nurturing friendships with both boys and girls. And though sports, hunting, and fishing were her passions, she could be as feminine as she needed to be when the occasion called for it. Ruthie was probably our town's only homecoming queen who really did know how to skin a buck and run a trot line.

Our parents hadn't let Ruthie go to kindergarten, so when she started first grade, all the other children had already hived off into groups. Ruthie was left out. That was the year Mam started driving the school bus. Ruthie's first-grade class would be on the playground when Mam drove up for the afternoon bus run.

"I would see Ruthie sitting by the tree alone, with nobody to play with. It would break my heart, but she'd never complain about it. She never forced herself on anybody," Mam says. "I'd try to suggest to her ways of making friends, but she'd say, 'I'm okay, Mama; I'm watching them play.' After that first semester she was in the middle of everything. She was just kind of magical. She saw something good in everybody, even as a child."

In the summertime we'd all spend two or three nights each week in the baseball park in town, with either Ruthie or me playing on a team, or watching players from the older leagues compete. There were two ballparks—a little one and a big one—at Vinci Field, which had been carved out of the woods atop a hill near downtown.

The ballpark was the center of social life for us. Moms and dads whose kids played on the peewee teams would back their pickups against the chain-link fence at the little field and drink beer while their kids faced off under the lights. After the peewee games, most folks moved over to the big Babe Ruth League field nearby to watch teen-aged boys play serious baseball. Whether you watched the game or not, whether you played the game or not, the ballparks at Vinci Field were where you saw your friends and neighbors, made plans for weekend cookouts and fishing trips. You squared off on the diamond against boys named Tater, Booger, Sammy, and Allen Ray, and you hoped your umpire that night would be Tut Dawson, thin and tough as a razor strop, because he had an unerring eye for strikes and called them true.

For my 1970s generation of West Feliciana kids, summer smelled like neat's-foot oil, light beer in a can (you'd sneak a sip when your dad asked you to fetch him a fresh one out of the cooler), Off! mosquito repellent, the decaying wood of the big green Babe Ruth bleachers, and the smoke from our folks' Marlboro Reds. You'd go home at night worn out, sunburned, with a thin film of dirt covering your body, scratching fresh mosquito bites with filthy fingernails. Your belly was full of Cherry's Potato Chips and fountain Coke—free if you recovered and turned in a foul ball—and you'd barely be able to keep your eyes open long enough to take your shower.

The ballpark was also the place where many of us were touched by tragedy for the first time. In the summer of 1974, on my first team, the John Fudge Auto Parts Angels, a towheaded Starhill kid named Roy Dale Craven was the star pitcher. That might not have meant much in a league where the oldest players were, like Roy Dale, nine years old, but Roy Dale was a real phenom.

He was also a poor country boy with a million-dollar smile. His mother, Evelyn Dedon, and his father had divorced when he was very young. She raised Roy Dale and his brothers in a little brick house on the side of Highway 61, on the outskirts of Starhill. Roy Dale invited his father up from Baton Rouge one afternoon to watch him play his first game. The dad must have seen what a raggedy mitt his kid was playing with, and bought the boy a new glove. A week later that glove was as floppy and dirty and broken in as if Roy Dale had used it all season long.

Roy Dale and his glove were inseparable. One day Paw drove home to Starhill for lunch and saw Roy Dale and his brothers headed across a bottom for Grant's Bayou, carrying fishing poles. Roy Dale also had his glove. There was no one else to play with, but he couldn't bear to leave it behind. Paw, who was one of the team's coaches, remembers that Roy Dale was so passionate about baseball because he had so little, and grasped at every opportunity offered him. He was a sweet kid. The game was his life.

One night the coaches pulled Roy Dale from the mound after he completed the second inning because he vomited up his supper in the dugout. All he'd had to eat before the game was pickles. No one knew if he had eaten so badly because he had chosen to, or because that was all the food his family had in the house that day. No one wanted to ask.

On July 15, late in the afternoon, Roy Dale lit out from his yard to his cousin Allen Ray's, across Highway 61, hoping to catch a ride to the ballpark. He did not see the northbound car, which struck and killed him. The driver was not charged. I found out about the tragedy sitting in the back of Paw's pickup, headed to the game, when we were stuck in traffic backed up from the accident scene. Paw said later it was just like Roy Dale to be so excited about playing ball that night that he didn't pay attention to anything else.

That funeral was the first time most of us kids had seen death up close. At some point before the service started, one of the Angels found the courage to step into the aisle at the funeral home chapel, and go forward to pay respects to our teammate. A gaggle of six- to nine-year-old boys walked forward and saw that beautiful kid, Roy Dale, dead in his coffin. They buried that Starhill boy with his glove on his hand and his uniform on his back. This may have been the nicest set of clothes Roy Dale owned. That night I heard Paw and his friend Pat Rettig, the other coach, out on our back porch, talking. I stood by the screen door to listen, and realized these grown men were weeping in the dark. I didn't know how to take it, and went away.

The baseball seasons came, and the baseball seasons went, and the ballpark was the stage for other childhood dramas. One night, after a Babe Ruth game, Mam was helping a friend close the concession stand at the big field. "You kids were out on the field there running," she says. "Remember, Ruthie was competitive with you, but she wouldn't let anybody say or do anything to her brother. So we were in there

packing up chips, and Gerald Bates said, 'Oh my God, y'all, look.'
These two boys had jumped on you. Ruthie was a feisty little thing.
She ran through the gate, grabbed one of those boys by the neck, and
started whipping him while you turned to the other boy."

———

For all our sibling rivalry Ruthie and I got along most of the time and
enjoyed growing up together in Starhill. We played ball together in
the yard, often with some permutation of neighborhood kids: the Wil-
sons, the Morgans, the Rettigs, and the Shipps. We fished, worked
in the garden, rode our go-cart and Paw's Honda three-wheeler, and
swam in the town pool while everybody's mom sat under the shaded
benches, smoking and chatting away in the heat of the day. Sometimes
the grown-ups would load a mess of kids into the back of somebody's
pickup, and off we'd go to the creek.

We had cats and dogs and chickens, and cows for a time, and horses
too. We even spent a weekend one chilly autumn with a blind calf bed-
ded down by our fireplace. Mam took in every stray animal she could,
including a baby owl she and Paw found abandoned in the swamp
during the flood of 1973. When she was in elementary school, Ruthie
doted on Little Bit, an ugly little mutt that looked like a bleached hag-
gis with legs and a splotch of brown gravy. As far as I was concerned,
Little Bit existed to give me the opportunity to tease Ruthie.

Somehow I discovered that Little Bit hated it when anyone sang
"Happy Birthday." It made her howl. "Happy birthday to you-u-u,"
I sang, and the pitiful creature would sit on her haunches, throw her
head back, and bay.

"Dad-dee!" Ruthie yelled.

"Happy birthday to you-u-u!"

"Owooooooooooo! Owooooooo!"

"Dad-DEE!"

"Happy birthday dear Li-i-ittle Bi-i-i-it—"

"Owooooooo!"

"You stupid idiot!" she would say, and then her fat little fists flew.

This script played itself out a lot, only varying when she skipped the appeal to parental authority, and went straight for the pummeling.

Little Bit loved to follow the big dogs from the neighborhood when they tracked deer through the woods. But she was so short and stumpy that she couldn't keep up with them. Once she failed to return from running deer. Ruthie couldn't stop crying over it. Late one chilly night Paw and Mam put us into the cab of his pickup and we rode to the back end of the place to see if we could find her. Paw heard the dog howling in a creek bottom. While we waited in the truck with Mam, he went into the dark, rattlesnake-infested woods, climbed down a steep, twenty-foot embankment into the creek bed, picked up the cold, frightened, lost dog, and brought her in.

Ruthie was overjoyed. Little Bit almost certainly wouldn't have survived the night if Paw hadn't done that. She would have died of exposure, or more likely a coyote would have killed and eaten her.

Our family's social life revolved around neighborhood fish fries, crawfish boils, and barbecues. Our fathers hunted and fished together; our mothers traded stories as they made potato salad for the barbecues and fish fries. There was something particular about Mam and Paw that made our house a center of the community. They didn't have a lot of money, but there was always room for more at our table. People dropped by constantly, and stayed for dinner—and sometimes late into the night, even during the week. They wanted to be around Mam and Paw, who were boundlessly hospitable.

Our family was happy and secure. In the winter months Paw got up before sunrise to build a roaring fire in the living room fireplace. He went out and warmed Mam's school bus up, then came inside, unwrapped store-bought honey buns, topped them with a generous pat of butter, and slid them into the toaster oven. Ruthie and I would come in for breakfast to those gooey treats. Most nights when we were small, we crawled into Paw's lap, him sitting in his big recliner, each of us nestling into a crook of his arm. He smelled like tobacco and bourbon, if he'd had a drink before dinner. Mam brought him a cup of hot black coffee and we would lie there in his arms, talking about our day. I never saw any of my friends do that with their dads.

Ruthie and I knew we were in a special family. Paw was a strict disciplinarian, but he didn't have to do it often because we had such respect for him and for Mam. He was the kind of man you wanted to please because he seemed so strong, so wise, and so good. It seemed to us that there was nothing he couldn't do, or didn't know.

We hero-worshipped him, Ruthie and I did. And this became a problem for me when everything in my life fell apart in the summer of 1981, not long after I turned fourteen. A group of kids from our school, including Ruthie and me, took a trip to the beach. Before this vacation I had been one of the most popular kids in my class, from the time I started school until then. But for some reason, a handful of kids a year older than me decided that I was going to be the mark on this trip.

I wandered one afternoon into a hotel room where the kids were hanging out with two of our adult chaperones. Before I knew what was happening, several of the older boys, including football players, had me down on the hotel room floor, threatening to take my pants off in front of the girls standing on the beds giggling. The girls, especially two popular ones at the center of the preppy clique, egged them on. I thrashed and flailed and begged them to let me go. I called out to the chaperones, the mothers of classmates, and begged them to help me.

They stepped over me, lying pinned to the floor, and left the room.

The gang let me go without stripping me naked—they probably only intended to give me a good scare—and I fled down the hall, into my room. I wanted to catch the next flight out, but had to endure the next few days, hoping that it wouldn't happen again. Ruthie, who had been off at the beach with one of her friends, never knew what had happened, and wouldn't have understood what it meant to me if I had told her. I made it home without further incident, but the world looked very different to me after that. To this day my mother remembers a sea change: "I knew something had happened on that trip. I didn't know what, because you wouldn't tell me. It was in your eyes."

When school started that fall, word had spread that I was now untouchable. Boys who had been my friends since elementary school now wouldn't talk to me in the hallway. Older boys shoved me on occasion. The preppy queen bees made a point of insulting me every day. By no means was I the only one they treated like this. There was nothing that anybody could do about it, or so it seemed. The thing that killed me, though, was how my best friends literally dropped me overnight. Cutting a boy who had been their close pal most of their lives was the price required to join the cool kids' club, and gain access to their booze, cigarettes, and social status. It felt like the end of the world to me. I doubt it troubled them one bit.

School became little more than a daily opportunity to confront what a piece of stinking garbage I was, and how powerless I was to make any of it stop. The misery continued throughout my tenth-grade year. None of this made sense.

During this time I fought often with my father. I honestly can't remember what we argued over, but I remember him being frustrated with my outcast status. Both he and my mother worried about me, but they didn't know what to do, and panicked. It was especially hard for my strong-willed father, who could not empathize with a son whose way of seeing the world was increasingly alien to his own. In one of our yelling matches Paw accused me of bringing all this on myself for being so obstinately strange. And that's when I knew how alone I was.

I turned at the time to the woman who had been my ninth-grade English teacher, Nora Marsh. With her tightly braided curly red hair, her Yankee accent, and fondness for rock and roll, Nora stood out among the teachers. Descended from an old West Feliciana family, she had grown up in Chicago but moved to the parish to live in and care for

Weyanoke, her family's antebellum plantation house, and spend week-ends at her place in New Orleans. She was fun, smart, and—catnip to a teenager like me—had a "Question Authority" bumper sticker on her Chevy Citation. She became a mentor to several of us bookish out-casts. Nora knew how hard we had it in school, and served as a cheer-leader for us, and a messenger of hope. What she told us, mostly by her example, was that we were okay, that we were normal, that loving books and ideas was nothing to be ashamed of, and that, honest to God, things weren't always going to be like this.

One Friday in the autumn of 1982 several of us were hovering around Nora, waiting to go to a pep rally when we heard an announce-ment on the school intercom. Representatives from a new residential high school for juniors and seniors were going to be in a particular classroom if anybody wanted to meet them. What was this? We had to check it out.

The idea behind the new Louisiana School for Math, Science, and the Arts was to bring academically gifted juniors to a refurbished high school in Natchitoches, a town in north-central Louisiana, put us up in unused college dorms, and teach us college-level courses. It was to be a state-funded public boarding school for Louisiana gifted and talented students. An escape! Only two could be accepted from West Feliciana; three of us wanted to go. Nora helped us all take the tests and gather our transcripts and recommendations. As exciting as the academics were, I wanted more than anything to leave, to get out, to put as much distance between my hometown and myself as I could.

One day, near the end of the spring semester, I stopped by the post office in my old blue Chevy pickup before heading to my after-school job at the grocery store. I went in, opened the box, and there it was: a fat letter from the Louisiana School. I took it back outside, sat in my truck, and trembling, opened the envelope to learn my fate.

I was in.

Paw was against my going. I had no business leaving home at

sixteen, he thought, and God knows what kind of nonsense I could get into up there. There was nothing wrong with me that more effective discipline couldn't fix. Mam did not want me to go away so early either. But she could also see how broken I was, how lost, and how miserable. She fought with Paw for his permission to let me go. She finally got it.

And so, in August, the day finally came for me to leave home. With our pickup full of my worldly goods, we met my old friend Jason McCrory, the other kid from our school to win a slot in the inaugural LSMSA class, and boarded the car ferry across the Mississippi together. Jason and I stood on the bow of the boat, saying nothing. I thought about what I was leaving behind. The intolerance, the social conformity, the cliquishness, the bullying. At sixteen this is what I thought small-town life was and always would be. There, on the far side of the river, was the rest of my life, straight ahead. I had no intention of looking back.

CHAPTER TWO

"Forever and a Day"

When I set out for Natchitoches, I left my little sister behind in St. Francisville. This was the fork in the road for us, the moment in our lives in which we diverged. Neither of us could have known it then, because each of us had begun a joyful new chapter of change that would determine the courses of our lives. I was finally among my tribe now in Natchitoches, and gaining the confidence that comes with knowing that one has a place in the world. For Ruthie the world brightened because of a boy from Texas they called Blue Eyes.

Mike Leming moved to town in 1980, when he was twelve. Ruthie, then a fifth grader, came home from school one day to say there was a new boy in school. Mike was a year older than Ruthie, which meant they didn't see a lot of each other until they were in high school together. When we were growing up, kids in the first through sixth grades attended Bains Elementary, a flat-roofed, one-story red brick building on the Bains Road, three miles north of St. Francisville. It was one of those desultory 1970s modern schoolhouses that might have been designed by the architect dad on *The Brady Bunch*, and which looked like 1966's idea of the future. Mike came to town the year West Feliciana High School opened just up the low, sloping hill from Bains. It too was a flat-roofed modern building, but it was built into the side of a hill, and after Bains, this shiny new school imparted the approximate euphoria of new car smell. What's more every single classroom was air-conditioned. Every one! No more scheming to get assigned to the desk that was closest to the classroom wall fan. In the West Feliciana school universe, this was what it meant to move up in the world.

We children didn't understand this at the time, but ours was a poor parish; the fancy-pants new school came courtesy of tax receipts from the River Bend Nuclear Generating Station, construction on which began in the mid-1970s. There were few rich kids in West Feliciana schools. The student body was evenly divided between black and white, but the white kids—almost all middle or working class—were generally much better off than the black kids, most of whom were very poor. There wasn't much palpable tension between the races, but there weren't many deep cross-racial friendships, either. We went to the same school, but lived in different worlds.

The social universe of white kids was roughly divided into three cliques: preps (middle class to upper middle; drug of choice: alcohol); potheads (working class; drug of choice: marijuana); and nerds (every-body else; drugs of choice: anxiety, Dungeons & Dragons). There was overlap, of course, and a number of kids—like, well, Mike and Ruthie—who wouldn't have identified as preps but still hung out with them. To be sure, despite the fact that some of them wore argyle socks and Izod shirts, none of the kids we all called preps would ever be mistaken by actual preppies as one of their tribe. Plenty of so-called preppy guys drove pickup trucks and listened to country music. No small number of girls in those preppy circles had bows in their big hair. "Preps" was the day's catch-all term for socially engaged white kids who didn't smoke dope (or at least much dope), some of whom thought of themselves as elites.

It was common in those days for teenagers to have after-school jobs, and there was no question that Ray Dreher's kids would work to make their spending money. Ruthie spent part of the salary she drew as a clerk at Boo Bryant's pharmacy on Hank Williams Jr. cassettes. One year she had tickets near the front row for a Hank Jr. concert in Baton Rouge. Wound up and possibly under the influence of Tennessee's finest sour mash, Ruthie took off her bra, whirled it around her head several times like a lasso, taunting the chortling band members, and threw it onstage. Hank put the garment on the neck of his guitar, raised hell, and tossed her a drumstick after the song.

If there wasn't a concert or something else going on in Baton Rouge, teenagers didn't have much to do on the weekends. In the seventies there was a local pool resort called Bikini Beach, and a burger-and-pinball place called the Redwood Inn (which boasted the first Pong game in town), but by the early 1980s, when Ruthie and I were teenagers, both places had closed. The only fast-food joint in town was the Chicken Shack (the sun-bleached yellow plastic sign out front said "Log Cabin Fried Chicken," but nobody called it that), in a gravel lot off Highway 61 next to Choo-Choo Bennett's Gulf station. There was no place to sit at the Chicken Shack; you'd drive up, wait for the cashier to open the mosquito screen on the right side, order a hamburger or box of fried chicken, then wait in your truck until the mosquito screen on the left side opened, and someone barked out your name. It was a great day when the Chicken Shack installed a bug zapper the size of a mop bucket from the overhang in front; it meant you had something to do while you waited for your order.

It was that kind of town.

For a couple of years Boo Bryant, the pharmacist, spun records at Catholic Hall for Catholic Youth Organization dances, which were a lot of fun, and gave awkward seventh and eighth graders, smelling of Sea Breeze, Love's Baby Soft, and Brut by Fabergé, practice in the art of slow dancing.

With nowhere to hang out, West Feliciana teenagers took their partying to wherever they could park their pickup trucks. In Ruthie's high school years that place was typically the parking lot of the new Sonic Drive-In on 61 or down by the Mississippi River.

Sometimes the gang gathered down by the ferry landing where Bayou Sara empties into the Mississippi. There were rusted hulks of cranes and other abandoned heavy equipment. On other occasions teenagers drove down a gravel road that ran along the riverbank and parked in a semicircle in a clearing in the woods two miles out of town, overlooking the water. It was secluded and far from adult eyes. Unless they built a bonfire, the only lights were the moon, the stars, and the glow from the Big Cajun coal-fired power plant on the opposite bank. The river was where you went to drink, to listen to country music, and to be with your crowd.

The river wasn't the only place to go, though. Somebody was always having a party, either at their house, their parents' camp, or at a barn. Teenagers were often on the road to Baton Rouge to the movies, or bowling. A lot of teenage social life centered around the West Feliciana Saints, the high school football and baseball teams. If the CYO scheduled a dance for the same night as a Saints football game, a win meant the priest would let the kids dance till one in the morning, but a loss meant the music stopped at midnight.

In those days teenagers in our town didn't really go on formal dates. Instead you'd either go out with your friends, or you'd "go with" someone—which meant you were seeing that person exclusively. If a boy and a girl liked each other, the boy would screw up the courage to ask the girl to go with him. That typically meant they would hang out with all their friends anyway, but would be off-limits to the romantic attentions of others. It was easy to tell which girls were going with which boys: if you got behind them on the highway, the girl would be riding in the front seat of his pickup as close to him as she could be without actually sitting in his lap.

Mike Leming was a year older than Ruthie and began noticing her in the hallway when she moved up to ninth grade, and therefore over to his side of the high school building. He liked the way Ruthie carried herself. He had never seen anyone like her—tomboyish and girly at the same time. She had lots of friends and never talked about anybody, nor did people gossip about her. When kids were changing classes in the hallway and huddled to talk in groups, he was struck by how she had a way of making people comfortable by the way she talked to them.

Ruthie's social ease was especially attractive to Mike. Though he was tall, blond, handsome, and athletic, Mike was painfully shy. He couldn't figure out how to approach Ruthie.

One April night in 1983 Ruthie convinced Paw to let her attend a creek party. She was two weeks shy of her fifteenth birthday, and couldn't believe he had let her go. She saw the Leming boy there, and they got to talking, and laughing with each other, and the next thing you know, he kissed her. Ruthie had a midnight curfew and made it home with only three minutes to spare. That Monday at school everyone teased her for kissing Mike Leming at the party. What was the big deal? It was just a creek party. "Mike and I are just friends!" she protested.

The next weekend the Saints baseball team played John Curtis High, a suburban New Orleans school, in a regional playoff. John Curtis was well known around the state as an athletic powerhouse. Squaring off against them was a David-and-Goliath moment for the West Feliciana country boys. Mike played right field for the Saints. Ruthie rode the fan bus to New Orleans for the game.

To everyone's great surprise the Saints played the hell out of John Curtis, and reached the bottom of the ninth inning ahead, six to two. Victory seemed so certain the West Feliciana fans finally answered the city team's pregame taunts by singing "When the Saints Go Marching In." But then John Curtis rallied, coming within one run of tying the game.

Bases loaded. Two outs. The John Curtis batter had struck out every time he had come to the plate that night.

Strike one.

Strike two.

And then, on the next pitch, the batter connected. The ball struck a high, hard arc over right field, like an incoming mortar round, right through the heart of West Feliciana's season. Mike ran for the chain-link outfield fence and started to climb, hoping to lift himself high enough to catch the ball and win the game. There was no catching this ball, glory-bound for a grand slam. Sammy Patrick, the West Feliciana pitching ace, collapsed on the mound in shock and disbelief. Mike hung on the fence for a few seconds, then let himself fall to the ground, spent and defeated.

Ruthie, like every other West Feliciana fan there that night, was shattered. She and her friends held each other, wailing and sobbing. *Our boys worked so hard all year,* she thought, *and had this game all but won!* The Saints' gruff coach gathered his team behind the dugout, and with tears in his eyes told them how proud he was of them.

Heads bowed, the boys gathered their gear and loaded back onto the team bus. The fan bus followed close behind. The buses pulled over at a McDonald's on the way out of town. Mike sat next to Ruthie in the booth and they ate hamburgers and fries together. This left her giddy, and almost redeemed the disastrous night.

The following weekend Mam and Paw let Ruthie have a birthday party in Paw's old barn, just up the gravel road from their place. They promised her they wouldn't stay back there, watching the kids, but they trusted her to make sure her friends wouldn't drink alcohol. A big crowd turned up that night in Starhill, parking their trucks in Paw's field, and beckoned by the sound of country music, joining the party under the tin roof. One Starhill kid turned his truck lights on and captured Ruthie and Mike making out by the fence row.

"What's the matter with him?" Ruthie fumed. "Hasn't he ever seen anybody kissing before?"

In the aftermath of the evening Ruthie and Mike had to pick up several trash bags' worth of empty beer cans and whiskey bottles. Mam and Paw were furious. Ruthie and Mike were disappointed in their friends. That's how these parties usually went, though. That next week Ruthie turned fifteen and got her learner's permit to drive. Paw let her take his big white Lincoln Continental, a wedding cake on whitewalls, to school.

Ruthie and Mike were crazy about each other, but couldn't quite move to the scoot-across-the-truck-seat phase of a West Feliciana teenage courtship. Were they just friends, or weren't they? Mike adored Ruthie, but couldn't believe a girl like her wanted to be with a guy like him. His self-doubt and natural timidity caused him to hang back. Ruthie took this for disinterest. They were at an unhappy stalemate.

One July day Mike was riding a lawn mower, cutting grass outside the Bank of St. Francisville. He saw Ruthie drive by four or five times with Mam in the car, and wondered what she was up to.

"Ruthie," said Mam, "if you don't pull over and ask that boy, I'm going to do it for you."

Ruthie stopped the car, got out, and walked over to Mike. He powered down the mower.

"Hey," she said.

"Hey."

"You know that Junior Babe Ruth championship tournament they're having this month at the baseball park?"

"Yeah, I'm playing in it."

"I know. I'm going to be on the court. Some kind of queen thing. The girls on the court have to have one of the baseball players escort them. I was kind of wondering if, um, you would escort me. You think you might be able to do that?"

Mike only managed to say, "Yeah, I reckon I could." Ruthie thanked him, got back into the car with Mam, and drove away. Mike started the mower again, and glided across the Bermuda grass. And that was all it took. Ruthie Dreher took her place on the tournament court, on the arm of Mike Leming. They were never again apart. Years later, in fact, they would both say it was hard to remember a time when they hadn't been together. Ruthie and Mike just knew this was how it was supposed to be for them—a conclusion all their friends quickly drew.

With Ruthie at his side, and not a paper's width between them, Mike would drive them to Baton Rouge on dates. They would go to the movies, and then to eat at Wendy's, Ruthie's favorite. When the Greater Baton Rouge State Fair was on in the fall, they would drive into the city to the far end of Airline Highway, and step out into the colored lights of the midway, with all its funnel-caked, cotton-candied, Tilt-a-Whirled glory. Ruthie was the fearless one. She would ride every ride. It didn't matter. She just wanted to do it. Not Mike. She'd ride them, and he'd wait for her, tickled and proud that she was his girl.

Most weekend nights, though, they would ride in Mike's truck into town to see what their friends were up to. Creek parties, barn dances, and in the fall, football on Friday night. There wasn't much going on in St. Francisville, but for Ruthie and Mike, it was enough. The main event was each other—it didn't matter where they were or what they were doing, as long as they were together.

"I don't care about my friends," Ruthie told him. "I just always want to be with you. You're not only my boyfriend, but you're my best friend. I can tell you anything and you understand me."

Their devotion deepened throughout the fall of Mike's senior year. One night they went to a party on the sand dunes at Thompson Creek. Late into the evening they lay with each other under the stars, in each other's arms, staring at the full moon.

"I love you, you know," Ruthie said.

"I love you, too."

And that's when they knew this was for keeps. A year later Ruthie wrote Mike a letter in which she called that moment "the best night of my life."

"I've been happier than I've ever been," she wrote, "and it's all because of you. I'll love you forever and a day."

Ruthie began wearing Mike's blue football and baseball letterman jacket. When his senior class ring came in, Mike never put it on his finger; he gave it straight to Ruthie. Because Mike's family lived a long drive away, at the northern end of the parish, Mam and Paw invited him to sleep on the couch on weekend nights. That worked to Paw's benefit too. On Saturday mornings Paw put Mike to work cleaning fence rows, cutting trees, removing brush, chopping firewood, and doing other chores.

At first Mike was intimidated by his girlfriend's father, but the intimidation eventually gave way to respect and affection for Paw. Because Mike didn't have a lot of spending money, Paw bought him several steel traps, and taught him how to snare raccoons by placing the traps underwater in the creek. Mike set a trapline in the hollows behind Paw's place, and caught two or three coons each night. Ruthie sometimes helped him run his traplines. Paw taught him how to skin the coon to keep the hide intact. Every couple of weeks the buyer came through and paid Mike fifteen dollars per hide—enough to buy gas for his truck and burgers and Cokes for him and his girl. Paw called him "Trapper."

During her junior year Ruthie's crowd began hanging out at the river, where they could build bonfires and drink beer without adults hassling them. But Mam and Paw had forbidden Ruthie to spend time there. After a local boy died in a drunk-driving crash, parents were scared. They had reason to be. Still, if you weren't a social outcast, and you wanted to be with your friends from school on the weekends, you went to the river. Mam and Paw, however, would not yield on their conviction that it was no place for a girl to be.

After a while some of Ruthie's friends began taunting her for her absence at the river. You think you're better than us, they said. That got to Ruthie, who hated elitism above all else.

One night Mam and Paw went to a ball game in town. As they left the stands Mam told Paw she had a strange feeling Ruthie was down at the river. They drove to the ferry landing, took a left, and motored in the darkness to the bonfire site. And there was Ruthie. She had come there with Mike.

Furious and hurt Mam parted the crowd and took her startled daughter by the arm.

"Sister, I can't let you come down here," Mam said. Ruthie knew instantly that she had been caught, and that she was in the wrong. She put her head down and, through scalding, humiliating tears, let her mother lead her away. She wept and didn't say a word all the way home. Mam was crying. Paw was crying. It was the worst thing they had ever had to do to their daughter.

Ruthie went silent around our parents for several months—not from anger, as they suspected, but from shame that she had hurt them. "It just about killed her that she had caused them pain," Mike says. "She had this deep sense of not wanting to hurt other people, not to be a burden to them."

My sister's sensitivity and her loyalty to our parents only strengthened her bond with Mike. Mike was a deeply shy, introverted young man whose upbringing had been difficult, in part because of family finances, in part because his workaholic father was so emotionally and physically remote. Ruthie's love built his confidence. "I knew I could trust her. She was so loyal. How can a person do that, especially at such a young age? But that was the kind of heart she had. Pure. It didn't really matter if I saw her talking to another guy. It never bothered me, because I knew she was loyal to me. I never had to worry."

This purity of my sister's heart gave Mike peace of mind when he joined the National Guard as a senior and, after finishing high school, shipped out to boot camp in Fort Jackson, South Carolina, for four months of training. She wrote him every single day to encourage him, to tell him how much she loved him, and to keep him up on news from home.

Ruthie spent that lonely summer working in our cousin's law office in St. Francisville. "I'm making seven hundred dollars a month!" she told Mike. "Can you believe it? That's a lot of money."

By that time I was between my freshman and sophomore semesters at LSU in Baton Rouge, and was home working a summer gig at the nuclear plant. There was no place I wanted to be less than stuck in Starhill. So I checked out. I'd come home from my nine-to-five job, make myself a tall glass of Tanqueray gin, grapefruit juice, and soda, and retire to my room to drink, read Hemingway, listen to ska, and marinate in self-doubt. To the rest of my family I looked like a self-centered, uppity layabout. There was no doubt some truth to that, but it was also the case that I was confused and drifting.

Ruthie, though, may have been lonely, but she was rarely bored, and she doubted nothing about life. Everything she had, or could have, sufficed. She was the kind of person who would never grow up to write a memoir about her life because she was too happy and involved in living it. I didn't want what Ruthie had, but I was jealous of the way she had it. How did she do it? She made everything look so effortless. On some mornings she would wake up at daylight and get a couple of hours in fishing for bass and bream on the pond before she went to the law office. On weekends she played golf with her and Mike's buddies, babysat for extra money (she was already saving for her and Mike's future), or went bowling with friends. She went to parties every now and then, but it didn't feel right without Mike there.

Ruthie and I got along surprisingly well that summer, no doubt because I stayed out of her way. One Saturday afternoon we drove into Baton Rouge to go shopping, and I told her about the dream I had the night before.

"I dreamed that you and Mike got married," I said. "Is that weird? Are y'all thinking about it?"

"We've talked about it," she said nervously, "but I think we're going to wait until we get a few years of college behind us."

"Did I tell him the right thing?" she later asked Mike in a letter. "That's one dream that I wish would come true! What I want most in life is to spend it with you. I love you more than anything in the world. I always daydream about what we're gonna do on our honeymoon and what our house is gonna be like. I sure hope we can make my dreams come true....I'm ready to start school and get it over with so we can hurry up and start our life together. It is gonna be a damn good one too! I can't wait!"

Though Daddy's little girl had lost her heart to Mike, Ruthie and Paw grew even closer that summer. They spent many afternoons on the pond together after work, casting for bream. On Father's Day weekend Ruthie washed and cleaned out the inside of Paw's Bronco, as his gift. Meanwhile I had promised to mow the grass for Paw that day, but instead holed up inside the house watching the live MTV broadcast of the eleven-hour Amnesty International benefit concert from Giants Stadium, starring the Police, U2, and Peter Gabriel.

"Rod says it's great music, but I don't know," Paw wrote to Mike. "That still don't get the grass cut. Maybe tomorrow."

I had no interest in going fishing with Ruthie, so she often went up to the pond with Billy Lawton, a neighbor kid. One afternoon Billy and Ruthie floated in the middle of the pond in Paw's aluminum boat, their lines dangling in the water.

"Ruthie, look!" Billy whispered.

Billy thought he was looking at a cow standing at the water's edge at the pond's other end.

"Billy, that's a buck!" Ruthie gasped.

The big deer, antlers coated in velvet, studied them closely. A fish took Billy's cork under and ran with the line, but Ruthie quietly ordered him to ignore it. She was afraid he would scare the deer away.

The buck dipped his head to drink, then raising it, concluded that the people in the boat were no threat. He ambled down the raised levee that was the pond's west bank, marching toward them. No fear. He finally found his way into the cornfield, and was gone.

"All I could think about was how you would have fainted," Ruthie told Mike, in a letter. "Maybe you can get him this winter. I can't wait!"

She was overcome by excitement at the buck spotting. Me, I would have had to see Elvis Costello in the car next to me at the Sonic to have registered similar glee. No surprise then that I declined to accompany Paw, Mam, and Ruthie on a weekend trip to Holly Beach, a rustic Cajun coastal community in southwest Louisiana, near the Texas border. Some family friends had a camp in the remote and fairly desolate stretch of sand and invited them to make the four-hour drive down. Mosquitoes, alligators, heat, humidity, and no girls? Could there be a more dismal way to spend a weekend? I chose to take my chances at home with gin, air-conditioning, and the English Beat.

Ruthie had a blast. She fished, sunbathed, and learned how to use a throw net to catch crabs in the surf. They ate a fish stew called court bouillon over rice, crawfish crepes, boiled crabs, T-bones, and leg of lamb. She took a drive with Mam and Paw down the Holly Beach main drag to eyeball the gators living in the ditches on either side of the road. She was shocked to see a pickup passing the other way nearly run over a four-foot gator on the asphalt. Paw stopped the Bronco to see if the gator would move. Ruthie leaped out and chased the big lizard out of the road.

"Ruthie!" Paw said when she climbed back in. "You would have *died* if that thing had started chasing you!"

"I didn't think about that, Daddy," she said. "I was just worried that somebody was going to run over the poor little thing."

On the long drive home that Sunday, Ruthie wrote to Mike to tell him about the glories of Holly Beach. "That place would make a great honeymoon spot, hint hint," she said. "It was so relaxing and romantic."

Paw and Mike also grew closer that summer, despite the distance. Mike wrote a couple of letters that grabbed the older man's heart. Mike told Paw that he was a good man, and a special one who had been like a father to him. Ruthie wrote Mike to praise him for his sincerity and thoughtfulness.

"You couldn't have gotten to his heart in a better way than this," she said. "You really let your feelings flow and it really made him feel good cause he feels the same way. He loves you like a son. After he read it, he got up and went to the back because we had company and he had to go wipe the tears off his face."

Paw wrote Mike too, addressing him as "Trapper," and tried to keep his spirits up amid the rigors of basic training.

"There is nothing they can do to you that you can't take. Just keep your mind in order, your spirits up as well as your strength," Paw counseled. "Do not be misled by those who don't care, and be the best damn soldier possible. You will end up the winner, and a better man for it. We are all mighty proud of you and what you are doing."

In late July Ruthie rode to South Carolina with Mike's parents for his graduation from basic training. She would have only a day or two with him before he began advanced training. They didn't have much time together, but for Ruthie it was the highlight of her summer. She and Mr. and Mrs. Leming had not even checked out of the Fort Jackson–area hotel that Sunday when Ruthie put pen to La Quinta Inn telephone pad notepaper and began her next letter.

"I just thought I'd write you before we left here so you would get this quick," she wrote. "I want you to know how proud I am of you. I can't wait to get home and brag on you. You just look so sharp and handsome in your uniform. It just made me want to cry every time I looked at you. You make me feel so good inside when you compliment me and look at me with those beautiful eyes.

"I'm sorry I cried so much today, but I just couldn't help it," she continued. "I didn't want to embarrass you but I just love you so much and you make me so proud that I have to cry. It felt so good being in your arms and kissing you. You make me feel so secure. You have really matured and are a man now! I love your muscles—they're so sexy."

She ended by assuring him, as she often did, that she was his girl, "forever and a day."

"I can't wait to get our life started," Ruthie wrote. "I want to spend the rest of my life with you."

———

In the fall of 1986 Ruthie began her senior year of high school. Mike came home later that autumn and prepared himself to start classes at LSU that spring. It didn't take long for Mike to discover that college wasn't for him. After a difficult semester he went to work at the local paper mill.

Ruthie was the class of 1987 valedictorian and left her graduation ceremony that night with her college education already paid for with scholarships and awards. Nearly all of the ninety-three graduates in her class announced plans that night to go to college, or to some form of career training. At the end of her freshman fall semester, Ruthie phoned Mam and Paw from her dorm at LSU, and told them she had something to tell them when she came home for Sunday dinner that weekend. They were afraid of what she would say, guessing she was planning to break the news that she and Mike had eloped.

That Sunday, after Paw said grace, Ruthie declared: "I've got something I want to say. That group that I graduated with? Only three of us are left in school now. And I want to thank y'all for what you did for me. I know it wasn't easy to be tough."

Recalls Mam, "You can't imagine what hearing that meant to us."

When Ruthie started LSU that fall to work on an education degree, she lived in the dorm next to mine. I was a junior. We saw each other only in the cafeteria behind our residence halls. During the week she stayed buried in her books, worked hard, and made perfect grades. I was studying journalism, philosophy, political science, and considered long, beery arguments over existentialism with my fellow young scholars to be time well spent. My college transcript, while respectable, does not support this generous interpretation.

At LSU Ruthie thought I was getting away with something, and not only because I managed to ace tests even though I had stayed out late drinking beer and barely studied. She may have experienced on campus the same frustration and envy I felt when Ruthie triumphed on every front back home with so little effort. Worse, Ruthie could not understand what I studied, and what engaged me intellectually, and therefore she regarded it with suspicion, even loathing.

One evening she shared a table in the cafeteria with my best friend Paul and me. Paul, a political theory major, and I, minoring in philosophy and political science, loved to talk about big ideas. That evening we got off on something about Nietzsche and the death of God. Ruthie listened patiently, but finally lost her cool. She told us she thought that was the "stupidest bunch of you-know-what" that she had ever heard.

"What is wrong with y'all?" she said. "Listen to you. You sit here for hours talking about this crap, and it doesn't mean anything. You're just talking; you're not *doing* anything!"

We thought she was putting us on, but Ruthie wasn't joking.

"I'm serious, y'all," she said. "I don't understand the two of you. I really don't. What good is any of this y'all are talking about going to do anybody? Do you really think you're going to support yourselves with this stuff? What does any of it mean in the real world?"

She wouldn't listen to anything either of us had to say in defense of philosophy or philosophizing. At the time I thought Ruthie's prickly anti-intellectualism was funny. Ruthie wanted to get as far away from people like us as she could. As soon as she finished her student job on Friday afternoons she pointed her big blue Crown Victoria north, left campus, and lit out for Starhill.

Halfway through her undergraduate career, Ruthie and Mike decided to marry. They had been together for over four years and did not want to wait until she finished her degree. Ruthie expected Mike to do the traditional thing and ask her father's permission to marry his daughter. He sat down with Paw three days in a row, but couldn't muster the courage to speak his mind.

Ruthie finally lost her patience.

"I've had enough!" she declared. "Daddy, Mike's been coming over here because he wants to tell you that we want to get married. And he won't do it!"

Mike's abashed cowardice amused Paw. That the high school sweethearts would one day marry was a foregone conclusion. Though he wasn't happy with the idea of Ruthie marrying while still in college, Paw knew it was bound to happen. Ruthie had put him on notice earlier. Standing in his living room during her freshman year, Ruthie told Paw that she and Mike wanted to get married at some point between semesters.

"Well, honey, your grades are good now, but do you think you'll be able to keep that up if you're married?" Paw said. He spitballed a number of rational arguments against early marriage at her.

Ruthie leveled her gaze at her father, stepped to him, put her finger in his face, lowered her voice, and growled: "Daddy, don't you make me choose, because you aren't going to like the choice I make."

That was that. On the Mike question Paw knew better than to cross Ruthie.

All her life Ruthie had trouble making decisions. Once she started pricing wedding packages, Paw saw the potential bill growing ever longer. Intending to cut his costs early, he gave Ruthie five thousand dollars to pay for her wedding, saying it was all he could afford, and told her she would have to work within that budget. What she didn't spend, she could keep.

Ruthie found that flummoxing. "But, Daddy," she said, "when it was your money, it was different. Now that it's my money, I don't know what I'm going to *do*!"

The girl was naturally, reflexively frugal. Ruthie found a less expensive dress than she would have chosen otherwise, and got on with it. By the time she and Mike married on December 30, 1989, Ruthie had the wedding paid for, and two thousand dollars in her purse to pay for the honeymoon. The weather was cold and wet in St. Francisville that day, but the rain stopped before the ceremony. Mike stood with the pastor at the front of the Methodist church, nervously glancing at the plain white walls and at friends and family gathered in the aged wooden pews. And then the music began, the old wooden French doors at the rear swung open, and there was his bride, luminous, on Paw's arm. He thought: *This is my life now. She chose me. How can I be so lucky?*

After a formal cake-and-punch reception in the church hall, the wedding party moved down the street to the Red Horse tavern, a saloon in an old two-story wooden building. Ruthie and Mike were having so much fun dancing—especially to Van Morrison's "Brown Eyed Girl," which was their song—and drinking beer under the neon lights with their friends that they were late leaving for their honeymoon.

The newlyweds motored north in the Crown Vic to Natchez, Mississippi, to start their wedding trip. After a couple of days there they looked at each other and said, *Where do you want to go?* They took off driving west, not knowing where they were headed, and not caring. They were married, and that's all that mattered. The dream had come true. Mike and Ruthie. Ruthie and Mike.

Back home Ruthie moved into Mike's trailer in Starhill, and got ready to start the spring semester at LSU. She also threw herself into being a housewife. Ruthie loved making food for her husband. She was already an accomplished Southern cook, laying a nightly feast for Mike of hearty country fare like pork chops, roast, rice and gravy, meat pies, snap beans, and corn on the cob. Mike felt cared for as he never had been.

"Ruthie was always thinking about what she could do to help Mike. And he was all about, 'What can I do to help Ruthie?' Each one only thought about the other one. They were how marriage is supposed to be," recalls Stephanie Toney Simpson, Ruthie's childhood friend and a bridesmaid at her wedding.

My sister graduated from LSU in 1991 and began teaching sixth grade in the West Feliciana public schools. Meanwhile my career was taking off. After graduation I landed an intern job on the Baton Rouge *Advocate*, covering the police beat and drinking after deadline at the Thirsty Tiger, a dive bar across the street from the paper's downtown office. True, there was a sense that newspapering's rascally glory days were behind it. Many of the older journos had been through alcohol rehab; an oft-repeated story from the *Advocate* newsroom concerned a photo lab technician who nearly drowned after passing out drunk in the darkroom sink. I had no doubt, though, that I had chosen the right line of work. This was *fun*.

After three months the newspaper's longtime film critic, a gifted writer whom I had grown up reading, resigned to move to New York. The paper offered me his job. I was an inexperienced writer and was terrified of the responsibility, but I didn't dare turn down a break like that. In the spring of 1992, as Ruthie completed her first year leading a classroom as a teacher, I got another break: an offer from *The Washington Times*, DC's conservative competitor to the *Washington Post*, to become its television critic.

Washington! I had done a political consulting internship there during my junior year of college, and had fallen in love with politics and the city. Now, at the age of twenty-five, I would make my return. When I stood in Mam and Paw's yard telling them good-bye, Paw's face began to tremble all over, as if it were about to fly to pieces. He grabbed me hard and held me tight. This time I was going far away, and almost certainly for good.

It nearly killed him to watch me go. But it felt to me like I was starting the life I had always wanted, answering the call I had been hearing since I crossed the Mississippi almost a decade earlier. I found a third-floor walk-up apartment on Capitol Hill, and jumped into my job and life in the city with both feet. On the morning Bill Clinton was first inaugurated, I watched the TV coverage of the ceremony from home. When the outgoing President George H. W. Bush stepped onto the military helicopter to fly away, I heard the rotors behind the Capitol a few blocks away. I heaved the window open and leaned out over East Capitol Street to watch the chopper rise over the Hill. I glanced back at the set, to see on network television the same scene I was watching from my window. As far as I was concerned, I was now living at the center of the world.

That's not how Ruthie saw it. In her eyes I was living in Siberia.

"I don't understand what he's doing," she told our parents. "He's way up there in the big city where we can't help him. What if he gets sick?"

This bothered her. This bothered her a lot. It concerned her too that I was, as she put it, "throwing money down a rathole" by renting an apartment. I ought to be saving to buy a house, putting down roots, living a respectable life.

At Thanksgiving I made my first trip back home. Ruthie and Mike were talking about building a house on some land Paw had given them across the gravel road, a long stone's throw from his own house. Ruthie sketched the kind of house she wanted, and gave it to an architect. The house reflected Ruthie's priorities. She planned for the two children's bedrooms to be close to the master bedroom, so she could be near her kids at night. The kitchen and breakfast space was large; she wanted her friends to be able to gather there and drink wine while she was cooking for them.

Late on Thanksgiving afternoon I left Mam and Paw's to walk over to see the house site. The cleared plot took in most of what had been Aunt Lois and Aunt Hilda's orchard. Their cabin itself sat on land that belonged to cousins who lived far away, and with whom we didn't get along. Standing where the new house would be, near a barbed-wire fence marking the property line, I could faintly see the outline of the cabin through a thicket. I decided to take a look.

I crawled through the barbed wire and navigated slowly through the overgrown brush. Brambles, briars, and overgrowth had consumed the camellia bushes Loisie had so carefully tended. The orchard and her gardens were a ruin, and so too, I now saw, was the old cabin, which predated the Civil War. I had not laid eyes on it since Loisie died and Mossie moved to a rest home some fifteen years before. The front porch was so overgrown by bushes and vines that I couldn't reach it. A tree had fallen on the roof over Loisie's bedroom, on the downstairs level, cracking open a window frame. I climbed through.

The cabin was vacant and musty, but it still held the faint aromas I remembered from my childhood. The damp charry clay smell from the fireplace. The cracked corn dust from the bin in the pantry where they'd kept bird feed. That peculiar scent of their enameled cast-iron washbasin in the kitchen. If I closed my eyes I could recall absent smells: cut jonquils and paperwhites in a Mason jar; the Keri lotion Lois kept by her rocking chair to keep her hands moist; the nutty, buttery pecan cookies baking in the kitchen, or golden cupcakes from Loisie's 3-2-1 recipe. I would sit on her lap at her table in the kitchen and stir the batter in her pale green 1940s Fire-King mixing bowl. *Batter.* Loisie taught me that word. I loved saying it, and licking the spoon when we were done mixing, feeling the grains of sugar with my tongue against the roof of my mouth.

As a grown man, I stood in the dark, cobwebbed kitchen, wondering where it all had gone. There, on a board above the washbasin that served as a shelf, sat Loisie's mixing bowl. I held it in my hands, this priceless relic I had thought lost forever. My emotions overwhelmed me, and I felt the strong urge to leave. I took the pale green bowl in hand, went down the back steps into the bedrooms. Out the French doors in Loisie's bedroom was the tiny side porch where I fed Loisie's cats with her, and where, after she was taken to the hospital in her penultimate illness, a wicked cousin came one Sunday afternoon, lured all the cats out with their dinner, and killed as many as he could with a shotgun. The rest ran away and lived wild in the woods. Hilda had asked the no-good cousin to get rid of the cats because she was tired of caring for them for her sister. And that's what he did. My mother, my father, my sister, and I sat in our backyard that day, hearing what was going on, crazy with grief, powerless to do anything to stop it.

When we saw the cousin's truck leave, Mam hurried through the pecan orchard to the cabin and ran to the side porch, where the cats were accustomed to getting their food. She saw spattered blood, empty shotgun shells, and saucers of milk. He must have taken the dead cats with him.

Lois died not long after that, never knowing what had happened to her cats. Before she died I went to Aunt Hilda and told her I knew what had happened, and that she had ordered it. "Darling, please don't be angry," she said, but I was, and told her I hated her, and ran home. After Loisie died that side of the family dispatched Mossie to the nursing home and looted the cabin of all the art objects and relics of their lives. I visited Mossie a few times, but her mind was starting to go in a serious way, and given what had happened with the cats, my heart wasn't in it. Mossie died in 1988. I didn't go to her funeral because I was backpacking around Europe with Paul, my college buddy.

I put those thoughts out of my head, climbed back through the bedroom window, slogged through the thicket, squeezed between the barbed wire of the fence, and was once again in the sunlight. I looked across the yard at Mam and Paw's brick house in the near distance, as the evening began to fall. Suddenly it struck me that one day their house would be as Hilda and Lois's cabin was today. I could hear people inside, our Thanksgiving guests, laughing and talking, but they would all be dead one day. Perhaps some great-grandchild yet unborn, or one of his children, would come in through a back window and search for relics of a barely remembered past. I tucked Loisie's mixing bowl under my arm and walked on back to my mother and father's house.

CHAPTER THREE

A Family of Her Own

In the late spring of 1993 Ruthie and Mike had their first child, a daughter they named Hannah Ruth. They brought their baby home not to an old trailer, but to their new place in what used to be the great-aunts' orchard. Ruthie called it her "dream house."

"She was so content," Mike says. "This was the way things were supposed to be. We wanted a family more than anything, and now we had one."

Six years later Ruthie gave birth to another daughter, Claire Elizabeth Leming. If Hannah, by nature high-strung and eclectic, would become the melody among the Leming sisters, then Claire would turn out to be the steady bass line. She was an ornery baby with a cry that could bring down the walls of Jericho.

In 2002, during the birth of Ruthie and Mike's third daughter, Rebekah Ann, Ruthie's uterus ruptured. Doctors saved her and the baby on the operating table, but it was a chillingly close call, and the end of her childbearing.

As the girls grew older their personalities began to express themselves. Because of her age, Hannah—six years older than Claire, and nearly a decade older than Rebekah—considered herself an outsider in relation to her sisters. She was the restless one, the sister full of nervous energy, impulsive, extroverted, and eager for adventure—especially in the city. Outwardly more solemn, Claire, who most physically resembled Ruthie, was the homebody, the caretaker, the hunter, and true-blue country girl who decided early on that she wanted to live in Starhill all her life, and teach school, just like Mama.

When Claire turned thirteen she and Hannah fought over fashion. Hannah needled Claire about her disinterest in trendy clothes and cosmetics; Claire, who felt most comfortable in a T-shirt and blue jeans, and who thought it was ridiculous to cover her glowing skin with makeup, pushed back, and pushed back hard. Rebekah was the peacemaker between her sisters. Though she shared her father's taciturnity, at least around people she didn't know well, she was in truth a merry trickster.

Bekah, as they called her, inherited both her mom's and her dad's talent for athletics, playing team softball in the summer and cartwheeling across the lawn and down the hallway at home all year round. Like her mom and Claire, Bekah loved nature and going barefoot outside, but she hated the idea of hunting. "Why would anybody want to be so mean to animals?" she asked Claire one day. Claire has long suspected her younger sister will grow up to be a veterinarian.

In 1999, when Claire was born, Mike was working full-time for the Louisiana National Guard. He also served as a volunteer firefighter for the Starhill squad, which was founded in 1988, with Paw as its chief. Now people in Starhill wouldn't have to wait for fire trucks to come all the way from St. Francisville—but only if enough men in the community agreed to give time and labor to fighting fires. Paw asked Mike, who was Ruthie's boyfriend at the time, to consider joining the crew. Mike agreed, because doing something hard like this to take care of the community seemed like the manly thing to do.

One hot and humid summer day the Starhill Volunteer Fire Department received its first-ever call: a house on Paper Mill Road was burning down. Like the other Starhill men Mike converged on the burning house in his pickup. He saw flames roaring from the windows and doors of the wooden house, and felt a shot of adrenaline course through his body. He didn't have time to think about fear. The fire was burning wildly, consuming a family's home. He quickly dressed out in his fire-fighting gear and presented himself to Paw, the fire chief, for duty.

"Put this air pack on," one of the men told Mike. "We're going in."

Carrying hoses gushing water from the pumper truck, Mike and the others forged ahead into the burning house. The blasts from the firehose knocked the flames off the walls. In minutes the fire was out. Mike was awestruck by the power of the men of the community, working together, to bring that raging fire under control.

Hot, sooty, and exhausted the Starhill men took off their gear, stood in the yard by their trucks, and talked about what had just happened. They had heard the alarm and dropped everything to run into a burning building on a scorching day, risking their lives to save the house of a family from the community. They didn't do it for money; they were volunteers. They did it because this is what a man does.

Mike walked away from the charred and smoldering house a changed man. In the flames and amid the camaraderie, he had seen a vision that would guide the rest of his life. "For me," he would say later, "there was no turning back."

Mike started thinking about firefighting as a vocation. In 1990 he took the test to become a Baton Rouge firefighter. He aced it, but couldn't get hired. He took the test three more times in ten years, scored one hundred percent each time, but he wasn't called. He decided that it just wasn't meant to be.

In 2000 Mike was out of town on National Guard business when Ruthie phoned him to say she had just watched a TV news report saying the Baton Rouge Fire Department was starting a new recruiting drive. She thought he should take the test again. By department rules no rookies over age thirty-five were allowed, and Mike was getting close to the line. He wasn't sure he should bother.

Besides, because he was at Fort Polk, the US Army base in north Louisiana, Mike couldn't get the job application. Ruthie drove down to Baton Rouge and filled it out on his behalf. She knew how important the dream of being a firefighter was to Mike. This time Mike got the call. With the firefighting job, the hours would be irregular, the commute from Starhill longer. Worse, the cut in pay over his Guard job would be steep: he would lose over one-third of his annual salary, a big blow to their family. Could Ruthie stand to tighten their belts even more?

"She didn't hesitate one bit," Mike says. Ruthie's willingness to support her husband's vocation was a gift. She gave Mike a second family, for he would grow inextricably close to his fellow firefighters over the next few years. While on duty the men lived with each other in the firehouse, which usually meant hours spent together, just talking. Firefighter families would come by the station to visit during downtime, allowing the men to get to know each other as more than work colleagues. Weekend camping trips knitted the ties among the men and made their families even closer.

"Being a fireman, you knew you were going to put yourself in harm's way, and take more of a risk than in any other job," he said. "I enjoy serving. I guess it's just something innate. I try to help somebody out when they're down, or at their worst. It feels good to at least try."

Fresh out of rookie school Mike met a firefighter who would become one of his, and his family's, closest friends: Steve Shelton, a tall, burly man with a chiseled jaw, a laidback demeanor, and eyes that sparked with merriment. Everybody called Steve "Big Show," a nickname he earned in a charity boxing tournament in 1998. It was a cops versus firefighters contest billed as Guns and Hoses. Each boxer had to pick a stage name; someone stole the moniker of a professional wrestler and christened Steve "The Big Show."

The nickname might not have survived the day if not for a startling turn of affairs. Steve is a big man, but he was puny compared to the muscle-bound behemoth of a Louisiana state trooper they pitted him against. Not too long after the first bell, Steve somehow connected with the big bruiser's jaw, cleanly cold-cocking him. Down went the giant for the TKO!

Steve has been Big Show ever since.

After they became close Mike invited Show to come up to Starhill from his home in the nearby town of Zachary and hunt deer on Paw's place. Show readily accepted, and quickly fell in love with Mam and Paw. When Mike had to leave town for an extended period of Guard training, Show started helping Paw, who had an ailing back, take care of his land. This is how he became tight with the Starhill crew.

"Your mom and dad never meet a stranger," he said. "Once they get to know you, you become family right off, especially if you help them with something. Whatever's theirs is yours."

Whatever's theirs is yours. That's the first thing John Bickham noticed about Mam and Paw when he moved with his wife and two girls to Starhill. John, a trim, unassuming man of average height and build, and thinning salt-and-pepper hair, does not stand out in a crowd. He doesn't speak loudly or forcefully, but when he does you realize that he sees a lot more through his wise, observant eyes than you might have thought. John Bickham—or J.B., as Paw calls him—is intensely conscientious, and never talks about or draws attention to himself. He works as an operations controller at the ExxonMobil Refinery in Baton Rouge, one of the largest petrochemical complexes in the world. He sits at a bank of computer screens all day keeping things moving in the synthetic rubber unit. When you find out from someone (never J.B.) how much responsibility for the life-and-death safety of refinery workers rests on his shoulders, you think, "Of course; that's the quiet man you would absolutely trust with your life."

Growing up in Baton Rouge John had always longed for country life. In 1990 he and a pal bought a piece of land in Starhill, split it between them, built houses there, and moved north out of the city with their families. John's father had always wanted to live in the country too, and his son talked his folks into making plans to move to Starhill with them.

Within a month of John's relocating to West Feliciana, his father died. His mother chose to remain in Baton Rouge to be close to her church. At the time John, who worked with the fire department at the Exxon refinery in north Baton Rouge, also served on the Starhill Volunteer Fire Department. That's how he got to know Paw. In his grief over his father's loss, John drew close to the older man.

John saw that keeping up Paw's barn, mowing the grass around the pond and Paw's pastures, and maintaining the tractors, was too much work for Mike to handle alone. So he pitched in. Besides John enjoyed working alongside Paw, even as age and infirmity diminished Paw's ability to do for himself.

As Big Show and John, both deer hunters, found out, to be part of Mam and Paw's circle is to gain access to good hunting grounds on Paw's fifty acres. It also meant access to the bass, bream, and catfish in the pond. Hunting and fishing in "the Back," as we called it in our family, was a passion for Ruthie that lasted past childhood.

"She always wanted to go fishing," Mike says. "She would go buy crickets, or she liked to use a plastic worm. She'd fix lunch, and drinks, and we'd just go to the pond. Because she loved hunting and fishing so much, she never begrudged me a chance to go off somewhere with my friends to do it."

It's not uncommon for women raised in West Feliciana to accustom themselves to their husbands' hunting and fishing habits. It is less common for them to share those interests. And then there was the way Ruthie did it.

When Mike killed a deer, Ruthie dashed to the skinning rack in Paw's barn to clean the deer herself. She wasn't content simply to slice the hide off the deer's carcass and butcher it. She approached the task like an amateur forensic scientist, examining the deer's entrails for clues.

When Mike came in from a fishing trip, Ruthie instructed him to leave the stringer of slimy fish in the kitchen sink for her to take care of. She would whip out her electric knife, gut the fish, debone them, and freeze the fillets or prepare them straightaway for dinner. If the girls were around, she would enlist their help, and take the opportunity to give them a biology lesson about fish anatomy. Mike's buddies found it hard to believe that his wife not only gave him no guff for stinking up her kitchen with fish, but that she also demanded to process them herself.

In fact it's hard to overestimate the part fishing, especially on Paw's pond, played in the Leming family's life. "When did we start going to the pond? Well, how old are you when you start walking?" Claire Leming, now a teenager, asks rhetorically.

Fun for the Lemings often meant summer afternoons down at Thompson Creek, near Ronnie Morgan's camp. They call it the Starhill Riviera. Ronnie is a longtime neighbor and contemporary of my parents, but perpetually youthful in his crackpot joie de vivre. With a heart as big as his head is bald, Ronnie is the kind of good ol' boy who lives perpetually poised between his third beer and the question, "Hell, what could it hurt?" As Starhill's version of Jimmy Buffett by way of Hunter S. Thompson, he would get the Margaritaville vibe going down at his camp in the late afternoon. Ronnie cooked potluck—gumbo, jambalaya—and all you had to bring was cold beer, a bottle of whiskey, and, if you liked, something to put in the pot. In cool weather, folks would build a bonfire. David Morgan, Ronnie's son and a country singer and guitarist, would play solo, or sometimes get his band together. Starhill danced. That was a Louisiana Saturday night.

"All the kids would be playing outside, and nobody would care," Hannah says. "It was a carefree life. Nothing but good times and good friends." The sisters remembered too how affectionate their mother and father were with each other. When Mike would work an overnight shift at the fire station, Ruthie would stay up late talking to him by phone. "Like a couple of teenagers!" says Hannah. "I would be like, 'Mom, come on!'

"They were so silly and sweet," Hannah says. "It was cool to me that they always seemed to fall more in love with each other each day. Some married couples, you can tell that they just get to this point where they're done with love. It wasn't that way with them. And their love radiated to us. What they loved they wanted us to love too."

CHAPTER FOUR

Sweet Babies

When Shannon Nixon Morell met my sister, she was eleven years old and one of eight African American children living in a troubled home. Her father was an alcoholic. Her mother worked three, sometimes four, jobs to keep the family fed. There was intense poverty, and chaos. Shannon never told her new sixth-grade teacher about what was going on in her house, but Ruthie knew. Shannon was ashamed of her circumstances, and felt trapped and angry.

Ruthie smiled at her and said her name. That was enough for Shannon, who came from a home where nobody smiled, or seemed to care what happened to her. Ruthie saw promise in Shannon, and would sometimes spend their lunch hour in a field next to Bains Elementary, trying out strategies to help the struggling girl master her schoolwork.

"Shannon," Ruthie would say, "your life is hard, but you can do better than this. I can't let you feel sorry for yourself. If you feel sorry for yourself, you're going to give up."

Shannon liked that. It made her believe that she had within her the power to change her life.

One day she said to Ruthie, "Mrs. Leming, I want to be a psychologist when I grow up."

"Why not?" Ruthie said. "If that's what you want to be, go for it!

You can do it, baby. Just put your mind to it, and don't let go of your dream."

After finishing sixth grade Shannon moved up to the nearby high school building, but she kept in touch with Ruthie. When she was old enough for the cheerleading squad, she told Ruthie she wanted to try out, but wasn't sure that she was good enough.

"Shannon, you're awesome at this," said Ruthie, who had been on the pep squad in high school. "You have the talent. I know you can do it. Believe in yourself. Don't ever settle for being just okay when you know you have it in you to do better."

Because Ruthie believed in her, Shannon started to believe in herself. She tried out for cheerleader, and made the squad. This caused some of her black girlfriends who hadn't made the cut to turn on Shannon, accusing her of trying to be white. Shannon couldn't talk about this with her family, who shared those racist views. So she went to Ruthie.

"Don't listen to them, Shannon," Ruthie said. "You know what you're really worth. They're just trying to tear you down. Be strong, sweet baby, and keep on going."

Shannon left West Feliciana after graduation and joined the Navy. Today Shannon is a married mom who lives in southern California and works in, yes, psychology, at UCLA's Semel Institute for Neuroscience and Human Behavior. She lives with her husband and children far away from her hometown, and, given her difficult relationship with her Louisiana family, she doubts that she will ever return. She is thriving in California, both personally and professionally, and thinks of Ruthie as the woman who midwifed this beautiful life—a gift she tries to share with others.

"People say when your life is constantly miserable you either keep fighting or you give up and fall into the misery around you," Shannon says. "Ruthie was a source of strength to me to get me through all that.

In the work I do, it's always my goal to make people feel like they're important, that they're worthy. That's how she treated me.

"I came from a place where I didn't feel important, and nobody missed you when you were gone," she continues. "I always felt like I was important to Ruthie. She gave so much to us kids from a small town."

During my sporadic visits home from Washington, I was struck by my sister's deep empathy for her students. One night, sitting at her kitchen table, I helped Ruthie grade papers. The kids in her class seemed to miss easy questions. As we sat at her kitchen table, I asked my sister what was wrong with them.

"I'll tell you what's wrong with them," she said. "See this worksheet? This little boy's mother dropped him off one Christmas Eve on his grandmother's doorstep, and disappeared. Pick out a bad worksheet, and I can tell you something terrible going on. You can hardly imagine how hard some of these kids have it."

The hard cases among her students held a special place in her heart. It became a running joke among her fellow teachers that when they would get together to confront a student with a disciplinary problem that Ruthie would always take the student's side. Her fellow teachers would be ready to come down hard on the errant kid, when my sister, by no means a bleeding heart, would chime in, "Sweet baby, what can we do to help you?" She always called them "sweet baby."

And then when the team meeting was over she would ask the chastened child, "Now, how's your mama and them? Is your baby sister feeling better?"

Ruthie's teaching day consisted mostly of standing in front of twenty or more students and lecturing at a blackboard, the old-fashioned way. At first she taught her classes nearly all their subjects. Later in her career, when she was moved to the newly built West Feliciana Middle School, she specialized in math. One of her techniques became something of a signature. When a student had trouble with a math concept, Ruthie would go to the student, kneel by his desk, and, side by side, help the child work through his difficulty. The emotional intimacy and humility of that physical gesture touched them.

There was little Ruthie wouldn't endure to fulfill her duty to the kids in her classroom. Early in her teaching career, she had intense pain in her abdomen. She ignored it for days, but the pain only got worse. Finally Mike forced her to go to the doctor, who sent her straight to the hospital for emergency surgery. Ruthie had an ectopic pregnancy, which caused one of her Fallopian tubes to burst. She could have died from internal bleeding. Ruthie's doctor told Mike he had no idea how Ruthie even stood at the chalkboard.

That was Ruthie, though. She never thought of herself, only of others, and what she could do for them. Many of Ruthie's former students have stories of how Ruthie made them better students and better people. Given the widespread poverty and chaotic family life among some communities in West Feliciana, no small number of Ruthie's students came to school undisciplined and unprepared to learn, to put it charitably.

And yet Ruthie abided with them. Her former students remember her as calm and soft-spoken, the kind of teacher who did not have to threaten, or even raise her voice, to establish authority.

"Children had a love and respect for her because we knew she loved and respected us," says Ashley Jones, who was a student in one of Ruthie's first classes. "Ruthie wasn't there for the paycheck. She was there because she saw this as her calling in life. That is why she had the effect she had on us kids."

Years later Ashley spent time as a substitute teacher at West Feliciana Middle School where Ruthie was then teaching. She was astonished to see that Ruthie was the same patient, tender teacher that she had known as a child.

"I'm thinking, twenty years she's been in this school system, and they've never gotten to her," Ashley says. "They're wild and disruptive, and ADD, and ADHD, and everything else they diagnose kids with these days. And this tiny lady came in with the softest voice, and put them all in line. It was the craziest thing to see."

Kendrick Mitchell, another of Ruthie's early students, came from a strong home and made good grades. His problem was bullying. A self-described nerd, Kendrick loved Greek mythology and Sherlock Holmes mysteries—unusual tastes for West Feliciana sixth-grade boys, especially so for African American kids. Kendrick took loads of taunting from classmates for his love of reading. Ruthie phoned me one night in Washington to tell me about this kid in her class who was smart and bookish, but whose spirit was being broken by bullying. This was the first time she had a student like this, and she wanted my advice.

"The thing he can't see now is that the rest of his life is not going to be like the sixth grade," I said. "You need to let him know that there's nothing wrong with him for liking books. You need to let him know that he shouldn't give up, and that once he gets out of school, life is going to be great."

"Would you write him a letter?" Ruthie asked. "I think it would mean a lot."

I told her I would. I sent it off the following week.

For her part Ruthie took Kendrick aside and told him he reminded her of her brother when he was younger.

"My brother is a reporter for a newspaper in Washington, DC, now," Ruthie told him. "You can do anything you want to do if you put your mind to it. Don't let these kids get you down."

Today, working in human resources for a Fortune 500 company in Houston, Kendrick says that the patience and encouragement Ruthie gave him—"She always, *always* had time for you, no matter what," he says—was even more important than the knowledge she imparted.

"Mrs. Leming taught me that it was okay that I didn't want to be on the football field or in the streets doing bad things," he says. "She would even go as far as recommending books to me. She watched the type of books that I liked to read, and when we would go on library trips, she would hand-pick books from the shelf and say, 'I think you might like this one.' That's how she was. We weren't just names and faces to her. She *saw* us."

———

I didn't see my sister let her hair down as much as I would have liked. That side came out when she was with her girlfriends. Many were her fellow teachers in West Feliciana schools. Ashley Harvey, Jennifer Bickham (no relation to John), Karen Barron, Jodi Knight, and Rae Lynne Thomas were her running buddies. Leading the pack was Abby Temple, who had become Ruthie's closest friend not long after she arrived as a teacher in 2002.

In high school Abby was a freckle-faced beanpole a year behind Ruthie. They didn't know each other well. Abby left St. Francisville, but came home after a painful divorce. When a job teaching sixth grade opened up, Abby took it—and became best friends with Ruthie.

Because Abby was the temperamental opposite of Ruthie, theirs was a somewhat improbable friendship. Abby was tempestuous; Ruthie was serene. Abby was restless and questioning; Ruthie was content and accepting. Faith came hard to Abby; believing was easy for Ruthie. Abby loved the exotic and wanted to travel the world; Ruthie craved the rustic and the familiar. Abby was always in a hurry; Ruthie had time for everyone. Abby loved to argue; Ruthie sought harmony above all.

They adored each other.

What Abby loved most about Ruthie was her genuine nature. Ruthie wasn't the kind of Southern woman who would tell you something honey-dripping to your face, then wield the stiletto when you weren't looking. And Ruthie was wise. She had strong convictions, but if you went to her for advice, she listened, really listened, and withheld judgment until she had thought hard about your problem. Abby took her pain and confusion over her divorce, her loneliness, her dating life, and her anxiety about the future to Ruthie. Whatever the particulars of her advice, Ruthie never told Abby to write somebody off.

"A lot of people would say, 'You shouldn't be around that person,' " says Abby. "That wasn't Ruthie. She was always, 'Let's think about this, let's see how we can make this work.' Her advice was always so wise. You don't find that often."

At the beginning of their friendship, Abby and Ruthie spent most of their time together at Ruthie's house in Starhill. They sat in Ruthie's kitchen for hours, drinking wine, with Ruthie cooking. The rest of her house was a mess, but Ruthie let it go. Her friend Abby was there, and Ruthie never put anything ahead of spending time with someone dear.

They talked about God a lot. In the wake of her divorce at thirty, Abby was angry at Him. Other people got second chances at love; why not her? She wanted to have children; why wouldn't He want that for her too?

Theology was not Ruthie's strong suit. She rarely if ever read spiritual books, did not attend adult Sunday school classes, and shunned systematic inquiry into the ways of the Lord. What she had to offer was a sympathetic ear and simple faith: Ruthie believed God existed, and loved us, and wanted the best life for us, though not necessarily the easiest life. That was all Ruthie knew about God, and all she wanted to know.

"Abby," Ruthie would say, "I pray for you every night, and I know God is going to help you find someone."

Abby got that a lot, and she usually hated it. It was the kind of thing women who already had husbands and children said. But Abby knew that those words were not cheap, feel-good clichés when they came from Ruthie. Abby could see how troubled Ruthie was by her sorrow and fear, how much Ruthie ached for her best friend's sadness, how much she wanted Abby to be at peace.

"Abby, I just trust," she would tenderly say. "I just believe."

It wasn't all merlot and misery for Abby and Ruthie, not by any stretch. It was hard to coax Ruthie out of the house—she preferred to be at home with Mike and the kids, maintaining her nest—but sometimes Ruthie could be talked into taking a night, or at least an afternoon, on the town.

One Sunday after lunch Mike, Abby, and Ruthie took a drive across the Atchafalaya Swamp to hit Angelle's Whiskey River Landing. Angelle's is a Cajun dance hall on the riverbank that holds a big zydeco dance on Sunday afternoons. Abby and Ruthie ended up dancing atop the bar that afternoon.

More often Abby and the girls from school would convince Ruthie to join them at Que Pasa, a Mexican cantina on the outskirts of St. Francisville, for Friday afternoon margaritas on the porch. Sometimes the teachers would go to Baton Rouge to cut loose. After her divorce, Abby met another man and became engaged, but the suitor lost his nerve. When her fiancé canceled their wedding at the last minute, Ruthie and the teacher crew took Abby to the city for a therapeutic night of beer, karaoke, and derring-do. These excursions usually ended up with everyone back in Ruthie's Starhill kitchen, with Ruthie making breakfast for the gang.

Ruthie, as always, had a knack for making friendships easily. Take the way she met Ashley Harvey. Ashley's parents owned a pharmacy in St. Francisville, where she grew up, but Ashley lived and taught school in a town across the river from Baton Rouge. She was thinking about transferring to West Feliciana Middle School, but she wasn't sure it was a good move. One day she ran into Ruthie at Rebekah's day care.

"Here she was, just running in to pick up her daughter, and she spent twenty minutes talking to me about how this was the best place in the world, this was such a great school, that we'd be working together, and how she would look forward to teaching with me," Ashley recalls.

"I thought, 'Okay, it's done, I'm going now.' She's the reason I live and teach here."

One year at homecoming Ashley rode with Ruthie from school to downtown St. Francisville for the parade. Ruthie had Mike's truck that day. When they parked on a side street, Ashley struggled to change out of her work clothes into something more comfortable for parade watching. She told Ruthie it felt weird to get undressed in a pickup truck.

Ruthie cocked an eyebrow at her and smirked, "You think yours is the first naked body to be in this truck?"

On a road trip with the gang to a beach in Florida, Ruthie gave them another glimpse of her saucy side. One night Ruthie drank beer a bit past the point of cheerfulness, then slyly announced to the ladies, "I *love* me some Mike Leming. I *love* me some Mike Leming in the shower."

"We were like, *Lord*!" Abby snorted. "After that we would all say, 'We *love* us some Ruthie Leming.' "

Until a few years ago you had to take a car ferry to cross the Mississippi River between St. Francisville and the town of New Roads. Once Jennifer Bickham complained to Ruthie that she had missed the ferry returning to St. Francisville and had to wait for it to slowpoke back across the river.

"Ruthie said that if she had been delayed like that, she would have used that time to make out with her husband," Jennifer says, laughing. "That changed my perspective on being delayed."

Even though she was a stickler for rules—she once chastised Ashley for opening a beer in the car within sight of their Florida beach hotel—there was one phrase that could make Ruthie, as long as she was with Abby, defy convention: *I double-dog dare you.*

Down on the Starhill Riviera a sixty foot sand bluff overlooks the water and the sandbars of Thompson Creek. At the top big trees with exposed roots from erosion perch precariously on the edge, one heavy rainstorm away from losing their grip and plunging into the bottom below.

"I threatened all the kids, and the parents too, that I damn sure didn't want to see anybody climbing that bluff. It was just sand," says Ronnie Morgan, the host of those creek party weekends.

"I went to the camp to get some more beer, and when I got back, there's Ruthie and Abby about twenty feet from the top. Somebody had made the mistake of double-dog daring them to climb up and touch the roots. I told them to get their asses on down, or I'd whip 'em both," he recalls, laughing. "You get Ruthie and Abby together, no telling what would happen."

One year the Women's Service League, the parish's most socially prestigious philanthropic organization, held its annual gala at a large, historic home. Everyone came in formal attire. The house was old and peculiar, and had tunnels honeycombing it. Abby; her father, Tom; Mike; and another partygoer decided to explore one of the tunnels. They got on their hands and knees, and crawled through, single file, with Tom bringing up the rear.

"The tunnel came out in a bedroom," Abby says. "We saw a woman and two men in the bed!"

They skittered out backward. It was that kind of night.

At the end of the party Abby, who is in the Women's Service League, was supposed to help clean up.

"My sister Amanda was ticked at me because I was drunk, and was supposed to be helping," she says. "It was cold, but somebody double-dog dared me to jump into the swimming pool. I was in my nice dress, but I looked at Ruthie and said, 'Come on.'"

"She took her shoes off, and in we jumped. Next thing you know, here comes Mike and my date, right behind us."

That was Ruthie Leming: good, but not goody-goody.

CHAPTER FIVE

The Father, the Son, and the Holy Ghost

I have not always been a tourist in my sister's life. Once, while I was still a young man and wrestling with some big questions, I considered returning home to Louisiana for good. Though I had been living and working in Washington for only a year when my niece Hannah was born, I wanted to be a part of this new family that Ruthie and Mike were creating. I also wanted to be at peace with my father.

My life in Washington was, for Paw, the ultimate expression of rejection, for if I loved him, surely I would want to stay near him. He couldn't credit the legitimacy of my professional ambition and personal desire to experience the world beyond our place. Nor could he understand my need to test myself and my abilities as a writer in ways that I could not if I stayed close to home. Rather he saw my decision to leave for the East Coast as a decisive statement that I loved myself more than I loved him and the land and the patrimony he had reserved for his children. What he could not see, what he would not see, was that he could, at times, be so overbearing in his expectations that he made it difficult for me to live around him without feeling crushed.

In 1993, when Ruthie and Mike had Hannah, I lay awake in my Capitol Hill bed at night and reconsidered my position. Maybe Paw had a point about the importance of family. I certainly had not expected to feel the gravity of that newborn babe, pulling me out of my comfortable faraway orbit. I hoped that maybe my absence had made him reconsider his relationship with me, and what he would be willing to concede, so we could live together peaceably. Surely.

Our arguments had started comically small. When I was a teenager he liked to rib me about my music.

Paw: "Why do they call 'em the Thompson Twins if there's three of 'em?"

Me: (Silence. Slow burn.)

Paw: "Why's that one call himself Boy George? Duddn't look like a boy to me."

Me: (Silence.)

Paw: "What the hell's a Talking Head, anyway?"

By college, the subject matter and the temperature of our disagreements had escalated. One night we had a bitter argument about something, probably a political matter; politics had been an especially sore spot since I came home in the spring of my freshman year and said, nitwittishly and with the kind of smug ardor only undergraduates can muster, "Daddy, I think you should know that I'm a socialist."

Yes, I said that.

Anyway the key part of that night's argument went something like this:

Me: "I don't agree with you."

Paw: "Are you calling me a liar?"

Me: "No, I'm just saying that I don't think you're right about this."

Paw: "But I'm telling you the truth!"

Me: "It's not a matter of factual truth. You are giving me your opinion. I don't share it."

Paw: "Do you think your own father would lie to you?"

I well remember the confusion and anger on his face that night, and my despair at the conclusion that there really was no way to bridge this gap. My father is one of the most intelligent men I've ever known, but this wasn't a matter of intellection. This was emotional. To my father for me to disagree with him on important matters was not simply to be mistaken. It was to reject him and what he stood for. You can imagine the hurt he suffered. You can imagine the frustration I endured.

And yet the only way for me not to hurt him would be for me to yield to his unreasonable demands. Hadn't he sacrificed his own wishes, and his own vocation, out of an overwhelming sense of duty to his mother and father? Paw had not wanted to go to college; he thought he belonged at trade school, where he could improve his mechanical skills, which were his passion. More than that, though, he didn't want to disappoint his family. They came first, and to live otherwise would be an abdication of duty, a vice. In his mind that was the way things ought to be.

So in the autumn of 1993 I quit my job and moved back to St. Francisville, and house-sat for my old teacher Nora Marsh in Weyanoke, her antebellum house, far out in the West Feliciana countryside. The plan was that I would live off my savings, spend time with my family, read, and look into applying to graduate school. I was looking forward to living alone in the big old house, with no television, no newspaper, and no neighbors, as the setup would afford me long stretches of silence and contemplation and prayer. I was in a far more spiritual state of mind in those days than I had ever been. I had recently completed a period of spiritual exploration that had led me from the Methodist faith of my father to Roman Catholicism.

Three weeks before Hannah was born I had been formally received into the Roman Catholic Church, completing a journey of conversion that began nine years earlier. You could say that my mother inadvertently put me on the road to Rome. Back when I was seventeen years old and happily ensconced in boarding school in Natchitoches, Mam phoned my dorm to give me spectacular news: I was going to Europe that summer! She split the cost of a raffle ticket with a friend, and won the grand prize: a trip for two to Europe. I was to take Mam's seat on the tour bus.

This is how I put my feet on the Champs-Élysées for the first time, with Aunt Lois and Aunt Hilda in my heart. Believe it or not, though, that is not what stayed with me about this holiday. On the way to Paris from London, the coach stopped in a town around sixty miles southwest of the French capital. Our group was going to see a famous Gothic church, they told us. Fine by me. By then I had shed the small-town faith in which I had been raised. Being a seventeen-year-old man of the world, I was fairly confident that God did not exist, but I was pleased, of course, to look at beautiful churches.

This is the untutored boy from the sticks who ambled unaware into Chartres Cathedral, one of the great architectural treasures of Western civilization. The complexity, the beauty, the sheer genius of the thing staggered me. I moved past the huge statues of biblical patriarchs, carved into the jamb of the west portal door, and into the narthex, staring gape-mouthed at the soaring arches in the church vault. Who had built this? How had they done it? And in the thirteenth century! It looked like those thin ribs held aloft tons of limestone, and, miraculously, those vast stained-glass windows, great sheets of reds, greens, blues, and golds, glowing in the sunlight like rubies, emeralds, and sapphires in the firmament, forming portraits of Jesus, His mother, the prophets, and the saints. Nothing in my experience had prepared me for the glory of this building, and the overwhelming scale and intensity of its beauty.

I walked out of that cathedral a different man, though I wouldn't understand what Chartres had done for me until years later, when I completed a religious conversion that began the moment I first stood outside the west entrance and beheld the stone Christ Pantocrator, the Ruler of the Cosmos, blessing the pilgrims who passed beneath him through the doors of a kind of paradise. The bus drove on to Paris, but I recall not one thing about the first time I saw the Eiffel Tower, ate a real French baguette, or much else about my maiden voyage to this city that figured so prominently in my boyhood imagination. I only remember Chartres. It was, to me, a message from another time and place, and a mystery. I did not know what it said, not yet, but I wanted to find out. What kind of religious vision can inspire men to build a temple like that to their God? What is God saying about Himself through the stone and the glass of that cathedral? What is he saying to *me*?

To be sure I did not become more religiously observant on that trip, or back home for my senior year of high school. What happened was that Chartres put me onto something. I was still a teenage boy full of himself and longing to drink beer and chase girls, but in Chartres I had encountered something that for all its stony mass and solidity, seemed to me a thin veil over a higher reality. It sounds strange but I felt... *judged* by Chartres. I had seen it; I couldn't unsee it. Chartres haunted me, principally because having been there, I could no longer say with any conviction that Christianity was nothing more than middle-class social conformity or a con game for nitwit followers of TV evangelists.

It took almost ten years of running away from Chartres—which is to say, of course, from God—and a prayer answered with such unusual precision and directness that I could not call it a coincidence, before

I accepted in full the call that had been placed on my life in Chartres. I began formal instruction in the Catholic faith during my last few months in Baton Rouge, but completed the process at St. Matthew's Cathedral in Washington, DC. There Cardinal James Hickey received me into the Catholic faith on Easter Vigil, 1993. My parents, generously, did not mind; they were only happy that I was going to church.

A few months later, back in West Feliciana and living at Weyanoke, I said the rosary often, asking Mary to pray that I would know God's will, and do it. Things were going well with my family too. I loved seeing them all again, and participating in the joy and togetherness the baby occasioned. As fall gave way to winter I spent evenings visiting with Ruthie and the baby, holding the next generation in my arms, listening to Ruthie's dreams about motherhood, and resting in the warm glow of family togetherness. Hannah's advent awakened in me a surprising longing for home, and a sense that I wasn't fated to live far away, after all. Hope, it is said, is memory plus desire. If that's true, then the nostalgia those nights at home with my sister and her child evoked for our own childhood, when we lived with a greater sense of harmony, and the yearning to recapture it, kindled a new hope within me—a hope that my wandering days were over.

And then one night in December Paw and I were riding down a country lane when he said something shocking, even life-changing. He said it casually, in no way triumphantly. Understand, his was an expression of gentle gratitude, not mockery: "I'm so glad you came back home, son. You realize now that I was right all along."

I froze. *Nothing had changed after all.* I had given up a good job in Washington, and left behind a rich life with a community of friends who loved me, to return to a town and a family in which my duty was to know my place. The lesson my father had learned from the tumult of the last ten years was that I had finally surrendered. Maybe he didn't mean that, exactly, but I was too shocked to ask, afraid that the bond of peace we had known between us since I'd moved to Washington would be sundered.

That night I tossed in my bed, eaten alive by anxiety. To stay here, I now knew, would mean no peace absent constant surrender to him. Around two I gave up on trying to sleep, dressed myself, and drove my old blue truck into Baton Rouge. I sat in an all-night diner near the LSU campus drinking coffee until it was time for the first mass of the morning at St. Agnes Catholic Church downtown. It was December 8, the Feast of the Immaculate Conception, devoted to Mary. I slipped into the church in the darkness before dawn.

I could hear a priest moving around in the back, but otherwise I was the only one there. I slipped into a pew, folded down the kneeler, and began to pray. This wouldn't do. I left the pew, walked up the center aisle as close to the altar as I could get, knelt at the marble communion rail, and once again prayed.

"You have shown me what I needed to see," I said. "I know now what I needed to know. Please help me get out of here. *Please*."

I stayed for mass, then drove back north, toward home. I stopped off in Starhill to see Ruthie. I let myself in the front door and called her name. "I'm back here," she answered. She and the baby were still in bed.

I sat down on the bed next to where my sister cuddled with Hannah, and told her about my conversation with Paw. And then I broke down in tears, telling her that I was afraid I had thrown away my big chance to make it as a journalist, chasing a dream of family harmony that could never be. I cried hard. When I wiped my eyes, she was crying too.

"I'm so sorry," she said. And that was all she could say. It was all she needed to say.

I prayed a lot that December, especially my rosary. During two especially cold days I worked in Paw's barn painting a wooden high chair for Hannah to use when she was older. I decorated it with stars, planets, cats, and squiggly lines of color that looked like confetti. On Christmas morning I gave the chair to Baby Hannah, and wondered if I would be around to see her use it for the first time.

Early in the new year I received a letter from the managing editor of *The Washington Times*, my old employer. They were creating a position for a culture beat reporter, she said; would I be interested in returning to the paper? Please let me know by the last Friday in January, she said.

The easy thing to do, the most rational thing to do, would be to call the editor and say, "Yes! How soon do you want me?" Hadn't I prayed for a way out? Yes, but somehow I believed that God was going to send me an unmistakable sign confirming that I should return to DC. I had three weeks in which to make up my mind about the job. I prayed my rosary and waited on God.

During this time I heard an awful tale about the parish's Rosedown Plantation, one of Louisiana's most beautiful antebellum houses and gardens—a story that had the town buzzing. The new owner of Rosedown, an investor from Dallas, had announced plans to make a housing development out of a large portion of the two thousand acres attached to the big house. As part of his scheme he ordered the congregation of the Rosedown Baptist Church to leave the premises. Folks were scandalized.

The Rosedown Baptist Church congregation had been present continuously on the plantation since the slaves were first evangelized in the early nineteenth century. The current congregation was composed mostly of descendants of the original slave families who founded it. Their modest brick church on the plantation grounds' edge was not historically significant, but the congregation was. Besides it was their church. They did not, however, own the land on which it sat.

The congregation was small, it was poor, and it had no one to help them. Like everyone else in St. Francisville, I was outraged. I started making phone calls. A few days later, the Baton Rouge *Advocate* pub-

lished on its front page my freelance story reporting on the contro-
versy. A local movement to save the church grew. Days later, CNN
sent a crew to town to report on the congregation's fight. The *New York
Times* did a story. There were rumors that Oprah Winfrey was coming
to town with her program.

Finally the beleaguered plantation owner relented. The church, a
community institution for almost two hundred years, was saved. My
mother and father told me how proud they were of what I had done for
the cause. They saw how passionate I was about this story, and how
much good I could do with my journalism.

"Son," said Paw, "if you want to go back to Washington, go with
our blessing."

The easy thing to do, the rational thing to do, would be to take my
parents' unexpected benediction as the extraordinary sign from God I
was waiting for. But that wasn't my way. I still had a few days before
I had to let *The Washington Times* know of my decision. Maybe God
had something else to show me.

On Friday morning I was at home at Weyanoke, and received my
college friend Kim, up from Baton Rouge for a weekend in the country. She was going through a tough divorce, and needed to get away
from things. We sat in the kitchen, lingering over lunch, talking about
how hard things were, and where God was in all this.

"Oh, Kim, look," I said, pointing to the clock. "I have to make a
phone call to Washington. End of business today is the deadline for
this job offer, and they're an hour ahead on the East Coast."

"Are you going to take it?" she asked.

"Yeah," I said. "I was hoping for a sign from God, but I didn't get
one. I think it's the right thing to do, though."

I excused myself and went into the hallway where the phone was.
I called Washington, accepted the job, and told them I'd report in two
weeks. So it was done. I was going back. I nearly wept with relief.

I took my rosary, slipped into the nearby downstairs bedroom, and shut the doors so Kim wouldn't see me. I sat on a chair next to the four-poster antique bed and prepared to say my beads. But first a word with the Blessed Mother.

"Mary," I said, "I didn't get the sign I was hoping for, but I know you were praying for me all along. I know God helped me make this decision through your prayers. I want to offer this rosary in thanksgiving. And you see how much Kim is suffering; please hold her hand through this divorce."

I began to pray the beads. When I rubbed the bead between my right thumb and forefinger, starting the second decade, the room, which had been gloomy in the overcast January gray, suddenly filled with sunlight—and the aroma of roses. What was this? I slowed my prayers to a crawl, and began inhaling in deep drafts through my nose. This cold bedroom, in the dead of winter, smelled like a rose garden in full bloom. I eked out the prayers of those ten beads, savoring the intense rose aroma for as long as I could, then said the "Glory Be," ending the decade. At that moment the clouds returned, and the rose scent faded away.

I hurried through the last three decades of the rosary, then searched the bedroom for clues. There were no flowers in that room. There was no perfume, no scented soap. There was nothing that could have produced what just happened.

Finally, after I had made the decision, I had my sign.

Kim wasn't in the house when I emerged. In a daze I went upstairs to make up the beds. As I pulled the covers up over my bed, I heard the thwack of the screen door downstairs, and the padding of Kim's feet up the stairs. She hurried through the door holding her right hand out, palm up, her eyes wide.

"Smell this!" she said.

Her hand smelled like roses.

"Did you put perfume on?"

"No."

"Did you wash your hand with soap?"

"No! I was just outside walking around. When I came in, I came up the stairs to get something out of my room. I rubbed my nose, and for some reason, my hand smells like roses."

I swallowed hard.

"Oh my God, this is amazing," I said. "I was downstairs a few minutes ago praying the rosary. In the middle of it the room filled with sunlight and the aroma of roses. There's no way to explain it. There's nothing in that room that smells of roses.

"Kim, here's the thing: when I started my prayer, I asked the Virgin Mary to hold your hand through this trial you're going through."

Her jaw dropped. The rose scent vanished.

Two weeks later I entrusted all my belongings to UPS, and on my twenty-seventh birthday, I flew north toward what I was certain would be my everlasting home. A couple of weeks later I had dinner with a wise old Catholic priest, the man who had prepared me to be received into the Catholic Church, to tell him the rose story. He said that mystical literature is full of similar accounts of the Virgin announcing her presence with the aroma of roses. She had given me a gift that day in Louisiana, he said. She had confirmed the decision I had made to return to Washington, and showed me by her timing that I didn't need an obvious sign to trust in the leading of the Holy Spirit. Be less skeptical, she seemed to say. Have more faith.

————

Even though our lives were moving in different directions, Ruthie and I shared a spiritual side. Prayer came naturally to her. When she prayed, she prayed silently. Many times she would write things down, things that would happen during the day, or during the week. She'd have her little notes—it could be a scrap of paper—where she'd written down who to pray for, or what to pray for. People that she knew, if they were in need. Kids in her class that she knew were struggling.

For Ruthie a plain, abiding faith sufficed. You experienced God by doing godly things, she believed, and anything beyond that is frivolous. For me, the self-tormented Platonist, I couldn't make a single move without having a theory. If we were each given a chocolate ice cream cone, Ruthie would say thank you and eat it happily. I would say thank you, then lose myself in contemplating the ontology of ice cream, the geometric properties of the cone, the relative merits of chocolate versus other potential flavors, and, if it hadn't melted by then, I would eat it happily, then spend twice as long contemplating having done so. As with Häagen-Dazs, so with Almighty God.

Despite these very different approaches to faith, we had independently developed interests in the patterns that God uses when He communicates to us. We both believed strongly in meaningful coincidences, which the psychiatrist Carl Jung called "synchronicities." Ruthie called them "seven-oh-nines," after a remarkable set of coincidences that happened to her after Mike went off to war, an event that tested Ruthie's faith.

After the war in Iraq started in 2003 all Louisiana National Guard soldiers and their families prepared for the day when they would get the call to deploy. It worried Ruthie and Mike for years. Mike was in the 769th Engineering Battalion. If they received orders, it would not be for combat duty, but rather construction and logistics. Still they would work in a combat zone. Mike was concerned about having to leave his family to spend a year in such a place, but he loved his Guard work, and advanced to the rank of warrant officer.

In 2007 Mike was installing a gate for someone in Zachary when one of his sergeants buzzed his mobile phone to give him the official word: the 769th was headed to Iraq in September.

Mike waited till he made it home that day to tell Ruthie, but she knew it was coming. It was hard breaking it to the girls that their father was going to war for four hundred days, especially because Hannah would be starting high school and was more aware of the kinds of things that can happen to soldiers in a combat zone.

As his battalion's movement officer Mike had to track the unit's equipment from Baton Rouge to Camp Victory in Baghdad. He left for training in April. When he returned home, he and Ruthie made plans for paying the bills and taking care of household responsibilities. John Bickham and other Starhill neighbors joined Big Show and Mike's firefighter buddies in promising him he wouldn't have to worry about his family while he was in Iraq. They had his back.

As the date of Mike's departure approached, John Bickham worked harder around Paw's place to stay on top of chores, trying to give Mike more free time to spend with Ruthie and the kids. "Any hour he could get before he left, that's what we tried to give him," John says.

Mike's friends and neighbors, including David Morgan and his band, honored him with a farewell community dance called the Starhill Stomp before he left. Then the dreaded day finally came. After a prayer service the Louisiana soldiers told their loved ones good-bye at the Baton Rouge airport, and boarded their transport plane for Baghdad.

Communication between Starhill and Camp Victory was spotty. Mike and Ruthie e-mailed or spoke by phone once or twice each week, and Skyped later in his deployment, when the service became available on base. He didn't have much time to talk anyway. His job was maintaining construction equipment for a company of soldiers. The sand and blistering heat of Iraq, to say nothing of the IEDs (which killed one of Mike's battalion members), made for an exhausting deployment.

Ruthie began training for the Reindeer Run, a 5K foot race held during the Christmas season. Though she had never been a runner, Ruthie wanted to lose weight before Mike came home. Jennifer Bickham, another running rookie, joined her, as did Abby.

"We were training three days a week for that. Ruthie and I didn't run very fast, but we ran. Ruthie didn't have any quit in her, but I wasn't like that," Jennifer says.

"In the race, we get on the last stretch, and it's about four blocks long. It's a straightaway. My ankle hit the uneven concrete, and I hit the ground. I thought screw it, I'm done. She was like, 'Jen, get up. I'm going to finish this race with you. You've worked too hard.'"

Ruthie and Jennifer limped across the finish line together. She would not let her friend give up.

An eerie thing happened in that race. Ruthie ran wearing Mike's 769th Battalion T-shirt and his dog tags. Her official race number, printed on her paper bib, was 709.

Months later Mike learned he would be sent home for an R&R break at Easter. He sat at the kitchen table in Starhill unpacking the small bag he had brought with him on the plane and took out the bib numbers he had saved from the 5Ks he ran in Iraq.

"Ruthie said, 'What are you doing with my number?' I didn't know what she was talking about," says Mike. "She said, 'That's mine.' I said no, I just took it out of my backpack. She took off running to the back of the house, and came back with hers. They were exactly alike, with the number 709."

She thought these kinds of things were like God winking at us, letting us know that there is a hidden order running deeply beneath the surface of the world.

"My car died after Mike went back," Abby says. "I had to buy a new vehicle so she let me borrow Mike's truck while I was shopping. I was headed out to her house one day and she was headed into town. We passed each other going opposite directions. In front of me was a van from the penitentiary with the number 709 on the grille."

Adds Mike, "The weird thing was that my rotation in Iraq was officially called OIF—for Operation Iraqi Freedom—07-09. In her mind, that meant something. And believe it or not, I just happened to arrive back home in the US from Kuwait on July 9—another 07-09."

After a few days of demobilization Mike and his men made the last leg of their journey home, to the Baton Rouge airport. Dignitaries and the media awaited them on the tarmac, but more important, so did their families. A photographer from the *Advocate* shot the moment Ruthie and the girls embraced Mike. It would be on the front page of the next day's newspaper.

Because Mike was an officer the Lemings lingered at the airport for an hour, until he had seen all his men off safely home. Meanwhile Abby was frantic. They had planned a surprise party for Mike in Starhill, but Abby's flight home from a Florida vacation had been delayed into New Orleans. She threw her luggage into her car and flew north, hoping to beat the Lemings to Starhill.

As Abby sped past the on ramp near the airport, Mike and his family were at that moment pulling onto the interstate.

"That's a 709 moment right there," Mike said. Then they looked at the truck's digital clock.

It read 7:09.

As the Lemings reached Starhill, Mike beheld yellow ribbons tied to trees lining the country road on the last mile home. A sheriff's deputy had parked his car at the top of the gravel driveway, which struck Mike as odd. Seconds later Mike saw a pair of fire trucks on either side of the driveway, firing their deck guns to create a triumphal water arch for their returning hero—Mike had been awarded the Bronze Star for "exceptional meritorious service"—to pass under in his glory.

"The whole community was in the yard, waiting for us to get home," Mike recalls. "They took time to come out for me and my family. It gave me an incredible feeling."

Mike made it home in time for a serious community crisis, but one that, by Ruthie's lights, turned into an unexpected blessing. On September 1 Hurricane Gustav made landfall in Louisiana. New Orleans was not hard hit, but the Baton Rouge area, which had come through

Katrina without big problems, was devastated. In Starhill the power went out for days. Everyone pulled together to help each other remove fallen trees and make food, ice, and gas runs into Mississippi.

Naturally everyone got together on those hot nights at Mam and Paw's.

"They had two generators going, and the fans were blowing at your mom and dad's house," John Bickham remembers. "Good company and moving air, let's go. It was a good time. There was no TV. Nothing to do but sit in the dark with everybody else. We all just focused on each other. When you take distractions away, you realize that other people, that's what's important. It's not what you have in life, it's who you have."

About two grueling weeks later the lights came back on in Starhill. When she called me to tell me the power was back, Ruthie confessed that she was almost sorry to see it happen. "It was so nice to be with each other every night, just sitting around the grill, drinking beer and telling stories, just being together. Now we're all back in our houses, watching TV. It's kind of too bad."

––––––

My return to DC, the city I thought would be my new home, did not last. I moved again, in 1995, to Fort Lauderdale, to take a job as a film critic with the South Florida *Sun Sentinel* newspaper. The job was great, the people wonderful, but my romantic life was a desert. One autumn weekend in 1996 I flew to Austin to meet my writer friend Frederica Mathewes-Green, who had just published a book about her conversion to Eastern Orthodoxy, and was giving a couple of talks in the Texas capital. My friend Jason McCrory, whom I'd grown up with and then gone to boarding school with, lived there as well.

That Friday night, at the Logos Bookstore in northwest Austin, Jason introduced me to an undergraduate journalism student who had come out to hear Frederica speak. Her name was Julie Harris. She had read and admired Frederica's writing, and considered her a professional role model.

The college girl Jason escorted over had large, lively eyes, high cheekbones, impossibly full lips, and thick brown hair cut in a stylish bob. There I stood, wearing faded olive chinos, a *Trainspotting* T-shirt, and scuffed combat boots, suddenly feeling like the biggest fake hipster nerd in Austin.

After the reading Julie and I had dinner with Frederica and a group from the bookstore. Funnily enough Julie paid no attention to her journalism idol, only to the gabby Florida journalist on her left hand. The next night, a Saturday, we met with Frederica under the live oak tree at the Shady Grove restaurant. On Sunday, after church, Julie and I met again, and spent the afternoon together before my flight back to Florida. In the parking lot of Waterloo Records, I kissed Julie Harris, and we fell in love. On Monday, halfway across the country from each other, we were trading delirious e-mails. Four months, several visits, and countless letters later, I flew to Austin with a ring in my pocket and proposed. We decided to marry that December in New Orleans, after her college graduation.

Julie and I met in Louisiana one weekend that spring and spent a day driving around the city looking for a Catholic parish to book for our December wedding. We finally found one at the far end of Esplanade Avenue, near City Park. As soon as we walked in, we knew in our bones that this must be the place. It was free on the day we needed it, so we made our reservation. Four-year-old Hannah would be our flower girl.

Shortly after we returned to Florida to begin our lives as husband and wife, the *New York Post* offered me a job as its chief film critic. In the spring of 1998 we moved to Manhattan and became New Yorkers.

We were newlyweds in Manhattan during the city's best decade of the twentieth century, and we were deliriously happy. I worked for a New York City tabloid, the most purely pleasurable newspaper job I ever held. There was the nutball editor Vinnie Musetto, author of the infamous "Headless Body in Topless Bar" headline, three desks over. I could tipple with the tabloid god Steve Dunleavy at his perch at Langan's, the Midtown bar across the street from the *Post*. Mafia goddess Victoria Gotti kept a desk at the paper, where she alighted once a week to write her column. Julie, meanwhile, worked as an editorial assistant at *Commentary*, a magazine she had read and admired in college. There she worked with a number of the leading intellectual polemicists and essayists of our time.

Every week or two a cable news channel would phone asking me to be a guest. The phone rang off the hook in Starhill when that would happen. "Dorothy, Ray, turn on CNN, Rod's on!" My new job took us both to premieres and film festivals, and to cocktail parties with movie stars. The film producer Ismail Merchant once taught us both how to cook shrimp in a mustard dill sauce, and invited us to his country house for the weekend (alas, we had other plans). Weekends meant dinner at trendy restaurants, drinks at cool bars, and wandering, hand in hand, around Central Park or wherever our curiosity took us. Once I spotted Woody Allen on the Upper West Side, and thought, *well, there you go.* This was the urban paradise a younger version of myself dreamed of finding.

What I did not perceive was that something over that exciting year for me had taken root in Ruthie's mind, a seed of resentment that I was unable to discern, much less fathom.

The thing showed itself over the Christmas break in 1998, when Julie and I came south for our first holiday visit as husband and wife. Eager to do something nice for my family, and to show them that we had taught ourselves how to cook, like a responsible couple, we had asked if we could make them a bouillabaisse. It was simply a French-style seafood soup, something I figured they would appreciate as

Louisianans. Had I called it a court bouillon, the Cajun version of bouillabaisse, maybe none of it would have happened.

But it did happen. Julie and I spent all day buying various kinds of fish for the bouillabaisse, cooking it in the garlic, tomato, and herb broth, making the special red pepper sauce that goes on the baguette, and setting the table for a big family dinner. When the soup came to the table, no one reached for the ladle in the bowl.

"What's wrong?" I asked

Nobody said a word. Finally Paw asked for a coffee cup, into which he ladled a taste of the soup, but only that. His bowl sat empty.

Mam wouldn't taste the stuff. Neither would Ruthie. This beautiful tureen of saffron-colored stew, fat with shrimp and chunks of halibut, catfish, and red snapper, sat untouched in the center of the table.

"Mama, do you know who I ran into in town the other day?" Ruthie said, then mentioned the woman's name. "She's a good cook. A good *country* cook."

So that was it: we had insulted them by coming down with our New York attitudes and making some uppity French soup that they had never heard of. Never mind that it tasted exactly like the kinds of things people in south Louisiana eat all the time. Never mind that we had asked before we bought the first ingredient if they would be interested in having this for dinner. Never mind that they had let us work all afternoon on this dinner, knowing that they wouldn't even taste it.

It was rude and it was hurtful. It was also the first moment I became aware that something had gone seriously wrong between Ruthie and me. That kind of behavior was uncharacteristic of her. After the New Year we returned to Manhattan, angry and confused. What I only learned many years later, when Mam and Paw told me, was that Ruthie and Mike were struggling at tough jobs that didn't pay much, while I was making twice their salary combined (at least on paper) to go see movies all day, write reviews, and sometimes get on national TV to talk about them. Ruthie had no idea how high taxes and the cost of living were in New York, and how I actually made less than it seemed. Nor did she have much understanding of or respect for the idea of being paid money to write.

To her my New York adventure was the most galling instance yet of everything coming easily for Rod.

I didn't grasp any of that then, nor did Ruthie ever talk to me about her feelings. That wasn't Ruthie's way. I might have pushed harder to confront her on this, and to resolve our differences, had I known that some version of that bouillabaisse scene would play itself out on visits home for years to come. As it happened I contented myself with tolerating the tension on those short visits home, and never pressing too hard to resolve them, for fear of disturbing the peace on those brief interludes when we were all in the same geographical place as a family.

After a year and a half of living in an Upper East Side studio apartment, Julie and I swam across the East River to Brooklyn to spawn. We took an apartment on Hicks Street, in the brownstone Cobble Hill section. Our front door opened onto an unobstructed view of the skyscrapers of lower Manhattan. Coming home from work at night, the last thing I would see before going in were the glittering towers, especially the twin spires of the World Trade Center. Once, when Mike and Ruthie came up to visit, we stood on the Brooklyn Heights Promenade taking in the view of the Manhattan skyline. I asked Mike what he thought about it. He was quiet for a moment, then said, with awe in his voice, "What has man created?"

Despite the physical distance I stayed in close phone contact with my folks and with Ruthie. For most of my adult life rarely three days will go by without my speaking to Mam and Paw. Ruthie and I touched base every week or two. Though I spoke far more often with my family back home than any of my peers seemed to with their relatives, the emotional insufficiency of telephone calls became clear to me when our first child came into the world. Matthew was born in 1999. Mam and Paw came to Brooklyn to see their first grandson not long after we brought him home. Because air travel was expensive, we could only visit Louisiana twice a year, but I would lull little Matty to sleep at night by telling him stories of Paw's adventures as a young man.

We would lie in our bedroom above the Brooklyn-Queens Expressway and I would tell my boy about the time his Paw roped calves and wrestled steers in the rodeo. There was the time Paw was in the Coast Guard and rode out a hurricane in Mobile Bay, lashed to the wheel of his cutter. Then there was the time during my childhood when I saw Paw find a chicken snake stealing eggs from our coop, grab it by its tail as it was trying to get away, whirl it around his head like a lasso, and crack the snake like a whip. Its head went flying across the yard.

One night, as Matthew lay sleeping next to me, I wondered where his life's journey would take him. *Please God*, I prayed, *never let him live too far from his daddy. Please let me be a part of his life.* Then it hit me: that has been my father's prayer every night since I had left home for school eighteen years ago.

———

Like many other New Yorkers, we were deeply affected by the 9/11 attacks. On that September morning, Julie stood in front of our apartment holding Matthew in her arms, watching the smoke billow over Brooklyn from the World Trade Center. "Get back in the house with that kid! You don't know what's in that smoke!" a doctor yelled at Julie as he ran down the sidewalk to the nearby hospital.

I was on the Brooklyn Bridge that morning, running toward the disaster, gathering copy for my *New York Post* column. "I'm going to get as close as I can," I had told Julie before rushing out the door. When the first tower collapsed I had had plenty of time to make it into lower Manhattan on foot. My mobile phone did not work, so I couldn't let Julie know I was okay, that I had stopped to interview people fleeing the fire, and was still on the Brooklyn Bridge. My wife had no way to know if I was alive or dead.

Back in our Brooklyn waterfront apartment, Julie fielded frantic phone calls from family down South. She put on her most artificially cheerful Dallas-girl voice to assure Mam that I was on my way home, and would be back any minute. In truth Julie struggled to stifle the fear that she was a widow at the age of twenty-six.

Meanwhile, in Ruthie's middle-school classroom, the phone on her desk rang. It was Paw, calling to tell her what was going on in New York.

"We turned on the TV. I remember the expression on her face when we first heard it. I cannot express to you the fear I saw in her face," says Karen Barron, the teacher who was with Ruthie at that moment. "That fear never left her face until she finally heard that y'all were okay."

When the first tower collapsed I knew I had to make a decision in an instant. The massive cloud of smoke and pulverized glass rolled through the canyons of downtown Manhattan, and would momentarily reach the foot of the bridge. Police would close it to incoming foot traffic any second. If I was going to be there for the most important story of my career, I needed to run forward, and I needed to run forward now, while the bridge was still open.

Go! said my journalist's instinct. Hadn't I always wanted to be at the center of the world? Here I was. I did not know exactly what had happened that morning, but I knew that this was probably the most important story of my career. I was a witness. All I had to do was make a short run for it, and I could be physically present, notebook and tape recorder in hand, at what I figured would be a turning point of world history. Moments like this are what every journalist lives for. All I had to do was run three hundred feet, past the end of the bridge, and into the electrifying chaos and terror of lower Manhattan.

But then I thought about Julie and Matthew back home in Brooklyn. I had not believed either tower would fall, but I had been wrong once. If the other one collapsed, would it pancake, or would it topple over like a falling tree? Did I have the right to risk my life for the sake of a story? How could I leave my wife a widow and my son fatherless because I found the danger exciting and wanted to write a better column for the next day's paper?

It came down to this: is it more important to be a journalist, or Julie's husband and Matthew's daddy?

The massive white cloud was now at the foot of the bridge, moving toward me. The path into Manhattan was still open. I turned my back to it and walked back to Brooklyn, and my family.

I made it home with only a dusting of ash on my clothes. My mobile phone finally rang only steps away from my front door on Hicks Street. When I said hello, Julie screamed, then opened the front door. There I stood, wondering what the fuss was about. I was in a mild state of shock, and was carrying a croissant from a Brooklyn Heights bakery; I had stopped to get Julie breakfast. Back inside the apartment, before filing my column, I sat down at my desk in the basement, and wrote the following e-mail to friends and family, including Ruthie:

> I'm not going to tie up the phone lines long, but I wanted to tell you that we're okay. My dad phoned this morning to say, "The World Trade Center is on fire. Go look out your front door." You can see them clearly across the harbor from our front door.
>
> "Oh my God! Julie, come see!" I said.
>
> I ran down to grab my reporter's bag, knowing I'd have to go over to the fire. At that point, we didn't know what caused the fire. Then, while downstairs, I heard a tremendous explosion and screams.
>
> I ran out to the street. "A plane just hit the second tower!" a man screamed.
>
> I knew the subways would be out, so I decided to walk across the Brooklyn Bridge to get to the scene. There was a steady stream of

people sobbing, coming out of downtown over the bridge boardwalk. I interviewed several of them. They told absolutely horrifying stories of seeing people jump out of windows from high floors, their ties and coats flailing as they plunged to their deaths. One woman's knees were bleeding from having been pushed down by the terrified crowd.

"The Pentagon has been bombed!" a man screamed.

I made it to the last pillars of the Brooklyn Bridge before going into downtown. I ran into a colleague of mine. She said, "We better not go over there. Those towers are going to blow up."

One minute later, the south tower fell in on itself. I nearly fainted. It... well, I can't describe it now. I'm too shaken. Everybody on the bridge screamed. Some collapsed in tears. A woman started to vomit. My knees went weak, and a huge plume of soot and smoke barreled toward us. I decided to turn around and go home.

A stout black woman, covered with sweat, screamed to no one in particular, "Every knee shall bow and every tongue shall confess! It ain't over, people!"

An F-16 fighter flew overhead. The cloud of soot reached us, and it was like being in a volcanic eruption. Everybody had to breathe through their shirts. Cell phones didn't work. I rushed home to see Julie. When I opened the door, she was sobbing and shaking.

Now I'm learning that the second tower has collapsed, and the Pentagon has been bombed. The sky outside is black with soot and smoke.

There is no World Trade Center anymore. I can't believe we're seeing this.

It's war, you know.

Ruthie attempted to read that e-mail aloud at a school assembly to memorialize the dead. She broke down before she finished, and asked a principal to complete the recitation. My sister printed a copy of that e-mail and kept it in a safe at home. Every year on September 11, she would take it out and read it to her class. She never told me this.

In the days and weeks that followed, Julie and I—indeed, the entire world—learned about the extraordinary heroism of the New York City Fire Department on that day. We saw the selflessness of those men, their sacrifices, and the sacrifices of those they left behind, and the solidarity of a grateful city rallying around the bravest in their grief. I covered a funeral in Brooklyn Heights for one of the men from the local station. I stood outside silently watching the man's wife and small children leave the church, say their good-byes, and walk back to their minivan at the end of the street to drive back to the rest of their lives.

That fall Julie and I thought a lot about what our brother-in-law did for a living. And we were so proud, and grateful. The September 11 catastrophe also made us think about being closer to family, especially now that we wanted more kids. Besides, we couldn't afford New York much longer. Walking home from dinner on Smith Street one night, Julie observed, "New York is a lot like Disneyworld. Everything is much more intense than normal, and it costs five times as much." True. New York was the best time in our life, but we couldn't pull it off any longer.

We eventually moved to Dallas, Julie's hometown and driving distance from St. Francisville. I started a job as a writer and editor at *The Dallas Morning News*. Everybody in Starhill was thrilled. We were back in the South, more or less, and now lived an eight-hour car drive from Starhill. They all thought—Ruthie foremost among them—that Starhill was the only truly safe place in the world. We could all be together there, with our family, and our community, at home. Starhill meant comfort. Starhill meant security. You knew folks, and were known by them. You could count on people, and you could count on things never changing much. Seen from this place, the world was ordered, fixed, still. The world made sense. History, suffering, tragedy—these things happened to people in lower Manhattan, in New Orleans, and other faraway places where people were strangers. The sooner Rod understood this, they thought, the better off he'll be.

Or as Paw so eloquently put it, "Son, you're finally moving in the right direction!"

CHAPTER SIX

The Peppers

Everybody agrees it started with the jalapeños. In the late summer of 2009 Paw brought Ruthie some freshly picked jalapeño peppers. As she stood in her kitchen chopping them, she inhaled the vapors, and began coughing violently. She never really stopped.

Throughout the fall Ruthie coughed. She described its genesis as a perpetual tickle in her throat. My family and I drove down from Dallas in October for a visit, during which Ruthie hacked constantly, and seemed slightly short of breath. "You should get that checked out," I said. So did everybody else.

She dismissed our concern. Said not to worry, that her doctor in Zachary was on top of it.

Julie, the kids, and I were back in Starhill after Christmas, for what we knew would be our last long visit for a while. I had taken an editorial job at the John Templeton Foundation, a Philadelphia-based philanthropy, and we would be moving there from Dallas in mid-January. It was a sad time because everyone knew family visits would be less frequent, given the great distance and the cost of air travel. Mam and Paw told me how worried they were about Ruthie's cough, and how stubborn she was about her condition. They were frustrated with her doctor, who, in their view, wasn't taking Ruthie's sickness seriously enough. He thought it might be asthma, and gave her an inhaler, which did no good. A chronic cough lasting four months isn't normal. Besides Ruthie's hip had begun to hurt.

As the fall semester at the middle school wore on, Ruthie's struggle to breathe normally became critical. Teachers were not supposed to leave their cars in the parking lot next to the school building but were told rather to park in a lot farther away—a rule that was commonly flouted. Not by Ruthie. It wouldn't be fair for her to take what she considered to be a privilege, she reasoned. Coughing the whole way, she would walk the extra distance to the school building. By the time she reached her classroom upstairs, she would have stopped several times to catch her breath. And she would be exhausted.

To be fair Ruthie made it easy to believe that her illness was no big deal. She never slowed down. Ruthie's big black Ford Excursion rolled up and down the streets of West Feliciana constantly, ferrying the girls to school, music lessons, ball games, and social events.

Still her friends grew increasingly worried. By year's end they frantically tried to shake Ruthie out of her complacency. She had been hacking steadily since August, and had been to see her Zachary doctor only twice. Ruthie simply didn't want to be a bother to the man.

Finally Abby snapped. "Look, Ruthie, this is not getting better," she said. "You have got to take care of this."

Abby kept pushing, but got nowhere. Ruthie grew irritated and impatient. Her friends insisted that she get a second opinion, but Ruthie said that she didn't want to hurt her doctor's feelings by appearing to second-guess him. Besides, she argued, going to see a brand-new doctor would just be a big inconvenience for everybody.

Ruthie finally hit the wall, literally, when school reconvened in January after the Christmas break. By that point in her career Ruthie had left the sixth-grade classroom and started teaching eighth grade. Both Rae Lynne and Abby were also eighth-grade teachers, with classrooms directly across the hall from Ruthie's. The three teachers stood in the sunlit corridor talking to each other as eighth graders swirled and eddied around them, headed to their next class. Ruthie began coughing again, but this time her back hurt so bad that she had to press against the wall to ease the pain.

Abby had seen enough. She could not imagine what was wrong with Ruthie, but she couldn't take Ruthie's passivity any longer. She was tired of seeing Ruthie so exhausted, and of hearing her say she couldn't go for margaritas with the teachers because she wasn't feeling well.

Abby wanted the old Ruthie back. Maybe Tim Lindsey, the young family physician in town who had been so good to her dying grandmother, would be more engaged with Ruthie's case than this clueless Zachary doctor. She felt the blood rush to her face, and took charge.

"I'm telling you now," Abby growled. "Either you make an appointment with Tim Lindsey, or I'm doing it for you."

This time Abby wasn't taking no for an answer. When Ruthie protested that she couldn't do that because her Zachary doctor had all her X-rays, Abby shot back, "Then he can send them to Tim, or Tim can take his own set."

She set her jaw and stared Ruthie down. Ruthie blinked.

Defeated and resigned, Ruthie said, "I'm going to do it right now." She went back into her classroom, picked up the phone on her desk, called Dr. Lindsey's office, and scheduled an appointment.

———

It was on his thirteenth birthday that my sister's new doctor, Tim Lindsey, decided what he wanted to do with his life. When Tim should have been home having cake and ice cream, he lay in a bed in the West Feliciana Parish Hospital, waylaid by pneumonia. He was scared and he was miserable. But he knew he was going to be okay when he saw Dr. Patricia Schneider, a familiar face from church. To Tim's young mind, she was not a technician; she was a friend. She told him he would be fine, and she made him well.

As he recovered Tim thought about how much it meant to him to see a familiar face when he was so sick, and to put his trust in her hands. He thought about how the doctors whose children attended Wilkinson County Christian Academy, the religious school in nearby Woodville, Mississippi, where Tim was a student, helped out in the school community. How they would be on the sidelines at football games. How they could be ordinary dads as well as doctors.

He decided then, in his hospital bed, that he was going to be a small-town doctor. And he resolved that he was going to do this in St. Francisville, his hometown.

Tim doesn't remember the first time he met Laura Seal, but it must have been at WCCA. He was in first grade when Laura started kindergarten. WCCA was so tiny they knew each other throughout their childhood. They began dating during his senior year. Their first Christmas together Laura gave Tim a silver ring engraved with a cross. Two decades and five children later, he still wears it.

After graduating from high school in 1993, Tim enrolled at LSU, less than an hour from home. Laura, who comes on her mother's side from a big West Feliciana family, joined him the following year. They became engaged in 1997. Tim graduated from LSU that December and applied to medical school. Laura finished her degree in elementary education the following May. She was a June bride. They were both twenty-two years old.

In August they moved to New Orleans so Tim could start LSU Medical School. Laura took a job teaching first grade in a public school. He and Laura decided together that learning to be a good doctor was not the same thing as making the best grades in the class. They were not going to miss a family event, a vacation, or an LSU football game so Tim could study. Nor would they miss having dinner together every night. If that meant he wouldn't be at the top of his class, Tim was prepared to make that sacrifice. It was a matter of priorities.

After graduation and a three-year residency in Chattanooga,

Tennessee, Tim returned to St. Francisville to practice medicine. It was 2005; Tim and Laura were starting to have children and were eager to return home. Tim worked out an agreement with Dr. Chaillie Daniel, a young physician who had started a successful clinic in town five years earlier, to join his practice. Tim would also have a certain salary guarantee from the West Feliciana Hospital for two years, but not beyond.

It was a risky move, Tim thought. West Feliciana isn't a big place and there might not be enough business to go around. Tim quickly discovered that he enjoyed being a country doctor because he was able to get to know his patients personally before they became his patients. Treating people he knew as a baseball coach or a Sunday school teacher allowed him to practice medicine in a personal, emotional, and even spiritual way. For Tim healing was not only about fixing the body; it involved helping patients discover how they could bring their emotional and spiritual lives back into balance. He found that at times he anticipated that particular patients would be coming in to see him, simply because he had heard through the community grapevine what was going on in their lives.

———

Tim did not know Ruthie well. She was older than he, and had gone to a different school. Ruthie's and Mike's paths began crossing Tim's and Laura's when my youngest niece, Rebekah, and Mary Margaret Lindsey, their daughter, became best friends in first grade.

There were other connections. Tim and Laura were leaders in Young Life, the teenage parachurch Christian fellowship, whose meetings Hannah started attending when she was fifteen. But for the most part the Lemings and the Lindseys were little more than acquaintances until Abby succeeded in convincing Ruthie to walk into the Daniel Clinic.

Ruthie showed up there at the end of the workday. Her shortness of breath startled Tim. She could barely complete her sentences without gasping or succumbing to her raspy cough.

Her previous doctor had called it allergies. Then he said it was bronchitis, or maybe asthma. Nothing he prescribed had worked. Given Ruthie's shocking degree of physical distress, Tim knew something critical had to be done for her.

He ordered a chest X-ray. The results came back on a Friday, and they were grim. Splatters covered her lungs. Fearing cancer, Tim ordered a CT scan for early the next week. He phoned Ruthie at home to tell her the news.

"I'm not going to lie to you, it's not good," Tim said. "We have to rule out cancer. I'm not saying it's cancer, but I am saying we have to rule it out."

Ruthie took the news calmly. But when Abby called to hear the results, she found Ruthie in tears.

"There are spots on my lungs, and they don't know what it is," she cried. Mike was overnighting at the fire station and she didn't want to deliver the news by phone. She swore Abby to silence and said she wasn't going to tell anybody else just then. She didn't want to worry them.

"I've got to pull myself together," Ruthie said. "I've got to go pick up the girls."

"Do you want me to get them for you, Ruthie?"

"No, I can do it. I'll be fine."

"Ruthie, we're going to figure this out," Abby said. "We're going to get through this. Okay?"

"Okay."

Ruthie climbed into her SUV to head out to pick up her children, but the burden of this news paralyzed her. She realized that she couldn't, after all, keep it from Mike until he finished his shift on Saturday. She sat in the Ford under their carport, and dialed his number on her mobile.

"I have some bad news, Michael," she said, and began to cry. "Tim called and said they found spots all over my lungs. I'm so sorry. I know you didn't need to hear this."

Mike swallowed hard. This was worse than they had anticipated. A lot worse.

"Try not to worry too much," he said to his wife. "It might be nothing serious. They still have to do more tests. I love you. I'll see you tomorrow." Ruthie kept the news from Mam and Paw.

Days later the radiologist called Tim to discuss the results. "It's crazy, but I don't know what this is," he said. "It could be fungal, it could be an infection. She doesn't have a defined mass, and her lymph nodes are fine. This one has me stumped."

That's when Ruthie disclosed her condition to me. I was driving home from work at dusk and called her as I motored home along the wooded road headed for a ridge along the Schuylkill River. As I sat in traffic waiting for the light to change, I heard my sister say: "There are spots on my lungs. But listen, don't worry about it. If this were cancer, my lymph nodes would be messed up. They're normal. This could be some sort of fungus from those peppers I inhaled. You can't tell Mam and Paw, though. You know how they worry."

This really is cancer, I thought. But I dropped that notion like a pie tin of hot coals. Ruthie's tone was so matter-of-fact and reassuring that it was easy to trust her. Besides her lymph glands were fine, and we all knew that forty-year-old women who have never smoked don't get lung cancer. Anyway there's crazy stuff in the subtropical air in Louisiana; maybe a hurricane or a storm kicked up something last fall that got stuck in her lungs. It was probably a fungal thing.

It took three weeks for Ruthie to get an appointment with a pulmonologist. The doctor examined the first CT scan, found it puzzling, then ordered a second scan. This one was dramatically worse, and her lymph glands were enlarged. It looked for all the world like an extremely aggressive form of cancer.

"The truth is, it was a terminal illness from the moment I saw her." Tim sighs. "I know that. But in my mind, as a doctor who wants to fix things, I thought about that three weeks, and wondered if we could have found this earlier."

The pulmonologist ordered a bronchoscopy, a procedure in which surgeons snake a tubelike instrument through the mouth or nose into the lungs to examine the condition of pulmonary tissue and retrieve tissue samples for biopsy. It did not go well. Ruthie's lungs were in terrible condition, and hemorrhaged badly.

"I've never seen one like this," the pulmonologist told Tim. "The only thing we can do is figure out what kind of cancer this is so we can treat it."

Ruthie's doctors scheduled surgery for February 16—Mardi Gras, 2010. Fat Tuesday, the high holy day of south Louisiana revelry. They would go into her lungs to excise and biopsy the growth near her heart. In the days leading up to the operation, Tim tried to comfort Ruthie and Mike, but he was discouraged by how rapidly her health was declining. Meanwhile Ruthie was quietly researching medical possibilities.

Was she frightened? Yes. But she stayed calm. She knew that Mike and the girls were watching her closely, and taking emotional cues from her behavior. If she kept her head and stayed upbeat, maybe they would too. She had to be strong, she figured. She couldn't let Mike and the children be afraid.

The annual Spanish Town Mardi Gras parade rolled on the Saturday before her surgery. Though Carnival celebrations are more common in New Orleans and Louisiana's Cajun country, Baton Rouge's funky Spanish Town neighborhood held its own popular parade, which had become a Capital City tradition. Ruthie and Mike joined their friends in a krewe—a Mardi Gras parading club—called the Krewe of Updog ("What's 'Updog'?"—get it?) in the parade. Ruthie rode an Updog float, tossing beads and doubloons into the crowds below. She told friends who asked about her health that she was going to have a little outpatient procedure done on Tuesday, but it was no big deal.

Ruthie and Mike awoke at five on that morning, dressed, and drove to Baton Rouge for the surgery. All the girls knew was that Mama was going to the hospital to have some kind of operation done to determine what was causing the cough. Ruthie had kept all knowledge about the severity of her condition and the seriousness of the surgery from the three children. Because it was a school holiday in Louisiana—Ruthie, for whom the universe was south Louisiana, had been surprised to learn that schools elsewhere didn't have Mardi Gras off—Mam took the girls to Laura and Tim's house for the day.

Mam stopped off in Starhill to pick Paw up, then drove on to Our Lady of the Lake, the big Catholic hospital in south Baton Rouge. As the waiting room at the Lake filled with friends and family, the lead surgeon made an incision above Ruthie's breastbone and began to burrow into her chest cavity.

CHAPTER SEVEN

The Bright Sadness

What the surgeons found that February morning was so frightening that one of them telephoned Dr. Gerald Miletello, a veteran Baton Rouge oncologist, directly from the operating room. The surgeon's voice was shaky and scared as he described what he had seen in the patient's lung. It was a large, angry tumor that gripped the superior vena cava, the vein that carries deoxygenated blood from the upper half of the body to the heart. They had tried to cut the tumor out, but found it impossible.

The surgeons were upset. Ruthie should not have had this tumor. She was young. She had never been a smoker. She had no family history of lung cancer. Nothing about this diagnosis made sense.

Still in scrubs, one surgeon gathered Mike, Mam, Paw, and Abby into a small room adjacent to the waiting room. He began to tell them what he had seen inside Ruthie. Everyone was tense and afraid.

"It's cancerous," the surgeon said. "It's a malignant carcinoma."

Mike buried his head in his hands and heaved with sobs as Abby threw her arms around him, as if to keep him from flying to pieces. Mam and Paw collapsed into tears. Trembling, Paw looked with desperation around the room, as if looking for cover. Mam thought, *My God, I've got to call Rod.*

Julie and I knew Ruthie was having exploratory surgery that morning and had been up for hours, praying and worrying. At half past nine my iPhone rang. The screen told me it was Mam. Julie and I hustled into the bathroom, where our children couldn't see our reaction, in case the news was bad. I answered the call.

"Baby, it's cancer!" Mam shrieked. "It's cancer! It's malignant. Sister has lung cancer."

My stomach tightened. *This is really happening,* I thought.

To us.

To our family.

Julie, who could hear Mam's frantic voice through the phone, gasped and threw her arms around me. I steadied myself against the sink, swallowed hard, and told my mother I would be on the next flight I could book.

"Mama, don't worry," I said. "God will take care of us."

I ended the call, held my wife, and with my head buried in the crook of her neck, felt hot tears pour down my cheeks.

"We have to tell the kids," she said.

Our children—Matthew, Lucas, and Nora—knew that Aunt Ruthie was going in for an operation to figure out why she had been coughing so much. They did not know what this meant. They had never dealt with serious illness in a close family member. We dreaded breaking this news to them.

At eleven, Matthew was the one we were least worried about. Wry and unusually mature, Matthew was already adept at using ironic humor to distance himself from strong emotion. Four-year-old Nora—named for the high school teacher who helped me leave St. Francisville—was too young to appreciate the gravity of this news.

But Lucas? The news would tear him to bits. Blond, athletic, and buoyant, Lucas, age six, was easily the most spirited of our children—and by far the most emotional. He was especially close to Aunt Ruthie, who saw a lot of herself in him. She adored Lucas's sweet nature, his eagerness to be outdoors, and, despite his physical toughness, the way he would tear up over sentimental things. From the time he was four Lucas cherished waking up early on visits to Mam and Paw's, putting on his shoes, and running over to the Leming house. Sometimes he would crawl into the bed and snuggle with his aunt, who doted on him and gave that sweet baby Pop-Tarts even though his daddy said he couldn't have them.

And now we had to tell him that Aunt Ruthie was very sick and might die.

Julie and I gathered the children around the Jesus icon on the mantel. It was where we said our bedtime prayers. The night before we had prayed as a family for Aunt Ruthie's peace, and for God to guide the hands of the surgeons the next morning. Now we would pray for her again.

We sat together on the edge of the coffee table, with the children standing in front of us. They were visibly nervous, eyes wide and mouths tight.

"Kids, we have some bad news," I said. "Aunt Ruthie has cancer. It's a bad disease. She's really sick."

They stood stock-still.

Lucas was the first to speak, saying in a tiny voice, as if he were peeking out from under a blanket, "Is she going to die?"

"She might, baby," I said. "The doctors are going to do all they can, and we're going to pray for her. But she might."

His fists shot up to his eyes, pressing them hard and rubbing vigorously. The harder he dug and twisted, the more wild tears soaked his cheeks and hands. It looked like he was juicing a lemon.

Nora and Matthew, their faces blotchy and distressed, stepped by instinct toward me. Julie swept them and Lucas into my embrace. We collapsed into each other and cried for Ruthie, for Mike, for the girls, and for ourselves. After a minute of this, I stood and asked everyone to face the icon. We crossed ourselves and prayed for Ruthie.

I told the children I would have to go later that day down to Louisiana to be with Aunt Ruthie. Lucas ran to his room and threw himself facedown on his bed. He pulled his pillow down tight over his head and tried to hide from the worst day of his life.

I phoned my manager at the John Templeton Foundation, told him the news, and said I needed to go. I had been an employee there for exactly six weeks.

"Take as much time as you need," he said. "Don't worry about it. We're thinking of you and praying for you all."

In those days I wrote a blog for the faith and culture site Beliefnet .com. Because of the intimate rapport I had developed with my readers, I felt that I could tell them what was happening with my sister, and to allude to a sadness I felt about a piece of unfinished business that lingered between us.

Since that "good country cook" remark over the uneaten bouillabaisse over a decade earlier, Ruthie had found more than a few occasions to sink a similar claw into me on visits back home. By then it was undeniable that Ruthie harbored anger at me, even though most of the time we got along well. It would usually come out in arguments over food, or the different ways we raised our children. Ruthie plainly loved me, but she just as plainly thought that I was a snob and a fraud.

I knew this was how she felt, but I also did not know how to address it. Like our father Ruthie was not one to let facts or contradictory opinions get in the way of emotional truths she had settled on. That was her nature. And it was my nature to investigate, to dissect, to analyze. Ruthie did not want to talk about it. Had I been living in Louisiana, we would have had to talk about it, because the tension was hard to bear. But I wasn't living in Louisiana; I only visited for a few days each year. Why stir up trouble? We could work it out someday.

On our last Christmas visit home to Louisiana before we moved to Philly, Ruthie made an offhand remark about me at the dinner table that cut me deeply. As we gathered at the table to pray before Sunday dinner, Ruthie said, "Rod, why don't you say the blessing, since you're so holier-than-thou."

I held my tongue, but was furious. Still seething after the meal I told Paw privately I was fed up with Ruthie's behavior toward me.

"What is her problem with me anyway?" I asked him.

He looked hurt. "I don't know, son. There's something there, but I don't know what it is." She later told him that she had mistaken the spiteful phrase "holier-than-thou," which means "religiously self-righteous," for the benign term "prayerful." I wasn't convinced.

This episode was on my mind as I waited for the car to arrive to take me to the airport. I just had time to post this message on my blog:

> Folks, my presence on this blog will be light in the days to come. I've just received terrible news of a critical family medical emergency, and will be getting on a plane for Louisiana this afternoon. I'm not at liberty to share details right now, out of privacy concerns, but I do beg your prayers for us. I will share more information as I am able.
>
> To be sure, I'm not at odds with my stricken family member, but let me beg something else of you: right now, on this very day, ask forgiveness of those you've offended, and offer it to those who have offended you. Be reconciled, if you can. Don't live as if you have all the time in the world, because you don't. None of us do.
>
> Change your life. Repent. Love. It's urgent. You have no idea how urgent until you get a phone call like I received this morning.

Within two hours my plane lifted off from Philadelphia, headed south.

———

Back at the hospital Abby snapped into crisis manager mode.

"Do you want me to call Tim?" she asked Mike. He said yes. She left the room to use her mobile phone. Mike stepped into the bathroom, knelt down next to the toilet, and, overcome by anxiety and horror, vomited. Abby punched Tim's number into her phone, and told him everything.

"Do you know people?" she said to him. "What do we need to do?" Tim told her he would take care of everything.

As the day wore on the waiting room filled and emptied with more friends and family. News of the diagnosis devastated each new arrival. By late morning everyone was shattered, scared, sobbing, holding each other. Fear paralyzed Mike. Paw stumbled to a private alcove down the hall to be alone. Mam joined him and prayed silently: *Why, God? She has always done the right thing. She has always been such a good girl. She has those three babies. Why her?*

———

When Ruthie awoke from anesthesia one of her surgeons was sitting at her bedside.

"I have cancer, don't I?" she said.

"Yes," the doctor said. "You do."

Then she met Dr. Miletello, a wiry, middle-aged physician with short salt-and-pepper hair and a generous smile. He would be her cancer specialist. His soft voice and tender demeanor made his manner more pastoral than clinical. For twenty-five years he had been having these bedside conversations with new cancer patients. It never was easy.

Yet Ruthie's response to the news shocked the veteran oncologist. "She was almost like 'thank you.' No hostility. She was just very accepting," he remembers.

A short time later Mike and Abby found Ruthie in the recovery room. She was alone and slightly groggy. A nurse let them know Ruthie had been told she had cancer, but Ruthie wasn't aware that Mike and Abby knew.

"I'm sick," she told them. "I'm really sick."

"We know," Abby said. "And we know you know what this is."

"We're going to figure this out," Ruthie said. She was trying to help them find their footing.

Abby was full of questions. What's the next step? What do we do now? She was trying to tame the chaos by imposing structure on it. Mike, though, sat silently next to his wife, trying to figure out what this thing was that had them in its jaws.

Mam and Paw came into Ruthie's room, having resolved to be brave, no matter what. They saw Mike and Ruthie sitting in chairs side by side, with their heads bowed, speaking quietly to each other. Mike, lost in contemplation, did not notice them enter. Ruthie lifted her head and smiled.

Like Dr. Miletello before them, Mam and Paw were astonished by Ruthie's reaction. This malignant tumor had destroyed their sense of order and calm, but there was their sick child, beaming. They were so frightened, but she was so brave.

The news hit the West Feliciana community like a cyclone. As the day wore on a hundred or more friends mobbed the hospital. Some offered to move in with the Lemings to care for the children while Ruthie fought this. John Bickham told Paw that he would sell everything he had to pay for Ruthie's medical bills if it came to that. At the middle school the teachers did their best to get through the day, but kept breaking down. All over town people prepared food and took it by the Leming house, which, this being Starhill, sat unlocked.

"We were surrounded by so much love," Mam recalls. "It was the most horrible day of our lives, but we could feel the love of all these good people. There was nothing we could have wanted or needed that wasn't done before we asked. And they were there. Do you know what that means? People were *there*."

The worst part of the day was over. The second-worst part—telling Ruthie and Mike's children—was yet to come. According to the plan made before Ruthie went down for surgery, Laura and Tim were to bring the girls down to Our Lady of the Lake to see their mother at day's end. Earlier in the day Tim spoke to Ruthie and Mike about how they would break the news to the children. They agreed Tim would be the one to do it.

That afternoon Laura loaded the Leming girls into her SUV. They stopped by the clinic, picked up Tim, and drove south to Baton Rouge.

Mam met the girls and the Lindseys as they stepped off the elevator on Ruthie's floor of the hospital. Mam tried to act normal, but her red eyes and puffy face gave her away. Hannah sensed that something was wrong. Tim and the children went into Ruthie's room. Laura remained outside with Mam and Paw. The girls' grandparents knew that in a few minutes the Leming girls' safe, serene childhood would abruptly and cruelly end. Mam and Paw had absorbed so much already, and didn't think they could bear to witness any more suffering that day.

Behind the closed door of Ruthie's hospital room, Mike's pale, shell-shocked comportment startled Tim. As the girls quietly filed into the room, Mike said not a word to his children, only hugged them.

Mike sat with Hannah and Bekah on the couch. Claire took her place on the bed next to Ruthie, holding her hand. Abby stood by. Tim sat across from them all in a chair. And then he began.

"You know, girls, Mama's been very sick," he said. "We have been trying to find out what's going on with her. We know that she's been feeling really bad, and we've been wanting to know what's wrong so we can make her better. Today we found out that there is cancer in her lung."

Hannah and Claire screamed, sobbed, wailed, and keened. Bekah, though, sat silent; at seven, she didn't understand what was happening. Mike said nothing, only leaned forward with his chin quavering, his swollen and bloodshot eyes somehow producing more tears. Ruthie had tears in her eyes too, but worked to stay strong for the girls. The children clambered onto the bed with their mother.

"Now that we know what it is, we're going to do what we can to treat it," Tim continued, addressing the children. "We're going to try to do everything in our power, but this is a very bad disease."

Then Ruthie spoke. With as much resolution as she could muster, Ruthie commanded, "Girls, we are not going to be angry at God."

Tim was floored. Here was Ruthie, hours after receiving an unimaginably vicious blow, taking charge of her family and declaring that rage and doubt will have no quarter in her household.

One of the children asked Tim, "What does this mean? Can she die?"

He responded that this was a harsh diagnosis, but only God knew how long any of us had. The road ahead was going to be very tough, he said, but Mama was strong. She had a lot to live for. We were going to help her battle this.

And then they prayed.

Tim and Laura took the girls to eat dinner and then back to Starhill. As Tim drove north up Highway 61, past the tank farms, the chemical plants, the cow pastures and battered trailers outside the city's fringes, he thought about all the different times that he had to deliver bad news to a patient or a patient's family. This time was different. This was a new side to being a country doctor. The Lemings were friends. He had never had to say something so crushing to little girls whom he knew personally. *How would I tell my own children news like this?*

On the drive home that night Hannah, who was in her junior year of high school, talked about how she would not allow herself to go to college, that she would stay home and take care of her mother and her sisters. It didn't last. The pain and terror of her mother's situation quickly overwhelmed her, and she threw herself into school and extra-curricular activities—things that kept her out of the house and on the go. "After that night," Tim says, "she started running, and she never stopped."

My flight from Philadelphia touched down at the Baton Rouge airport after dark. Our Starhill neighbor John Bickham was waiting for me. He drove me to the hospital. In his quiet, steady way, John briefed me on the events of the day, methodically preparing me for the scene at the hospital.

"They've been hit pretty hard, I'm not going to lie to you," he said. "But Ruthie's holding them together. It's something to see, I tell you."

We walked along the hospital corridor toward Ruthie's room in silence. I prayed quietly and crossed myself before I opened her door. There I saw my sister, lying in her bed, visibly wrung out, her hair greasy and her face tense, with an ugly black incision at the base of her throat. She smiled at me.

"Well, this is a fine mess," I said.

"Isn't it though?"

I kissed her and tried not to cry. I stayed only a few minutes. She was clearly exhausted, and needed to sleep. I rode back to Starhill with John. I found Paw in his chair at home, looking feeble and forlorn.

"Hello, my boy," he mumbled. I bent and kissed him on his wet cheek. He held me close for longer than usual. Mam was across the way at the Leming house, spending the night with the girls. They were all in Ruthie and Mike's bed, trying to comfort each other. Mam held Bekah. Hannah and Claire held each other.

Suddenly Hannah sat upright. "Oh my God, Mam, our Mama is your *baby*!" A rogue wave of emotion washed over the family. They wept for a long time.

———

Ruthie's doctors wanted to keep her in the hospital for more testing. Meanwhile an endless flood of visitors flowed through her room. Mam and Paw parked their car in the lot across from the hospital entrance that second morning, and saw Baton Rouge Fire Department trucks jamming the semicircular driveway. Said Paw: "You'd have thought the hospital was burning down."

Mike's firefighter colleagues were upstairs in Ruthie's room and in the hallway, rallying to the Leming family's side.

"They were just offering themselves," Mike says. "If we needed anything, they said, they were there to help us. And it was just nice to have them around then, because we are so close, working the way we work."

No small number of Ruthie's visitors wanted to pray with her—a kind gesture, to be sure, but a cumulatively exhausting one for a woman as physically and emotionally strained as Ruthie was then. There was a particularly pious man who had a reputation for long prayers. Word reached Ruthie that he was coming to see her. Several of us talked outside Ruthie's room, and decided she was too tired to endure this that day. We would intercept Ruthie's friend when he arrived, and politely ask him to come see her at home, when she had more strength. I stepped into Ruthie's room to tell her not to worry, that we would handle him.

"No, Rod, let him come," she said. "He needs to do this." And then she told me a few things about her friend's private suffering that I had not known.

"If it makes him feel better to pray over me in his own way, then that's okay," she said. "It's something I can do for him. And I'm not going to turn down anybody's prayers."

While my sister seemed to be at peace with her situation, her husband was not. Mike would steal away to the hospital chapel, and sit alone with his thoughts, and his God. It was the only place he could find silence. *I don't understand this,* he told God. *I don't understand this at all.*

But God was silent. Mike stayed with Ruthie at the hospital, sleeping on a cot the hospital provided for him. Back home in Starhill I volunteered to stay at the Leming house with the girls so Mam could sleep in her own bed. Hannah and Claire slept in their rooms, but Bekah wanted to be in her mother and father's bed, where I was sleeping. It had nothing to do with me. Bekah had always been quiet and remote around me. She was the Leming girl who was the most like their father—which is to say, shy and by nature silent. Plus I was a virtual stranger to this child; she had seen me only three or four times a year, and on those visits, she was polite but distant. Truth to tell, I was a little scared of Bekah that night. She was so small, and she had to bear so much now. All she knew was that her mama and daddy were gone from home, and there was a man she barely knew sleeping where Mama was supposed to be. I was as hapless in my anxiety that night as I had been the first time Ruthie passed baby Hannah to me to hold.

What if I drop her?

Bekah saved me from my helplessness by quickly falling asleep. I lay in Ruthie's place in the bed with the lights off and began to pray.

Till that point I hadn't allowed myself to give in to my emotions, but there, in Ruthie's bed, under cover of darkness, I let go. I wept convulsively, and wordlessly demanded that God justify what He had allowed to happen to my sister and her family. I knew that God could not by His nature will evil, but He let this happen for some reason. *Why?* I screamed silently, tears rushing out of the corners of my eyes.

Then, suddenly, I became aware of a presence in the bedroom, hovering over the bed. It instantly sobered and quieted me. I had my eyes wide open, staring at the ceiling dimly illuminated by the security lights outside the window. Nothing was visible there. But something—someone—was there. Was it God? Was it an angel? Even now I can't say. I can't even say if it was male or female. But I sensed that it was a being of some sort, and that it conveyed authority and strength that was almost physical. It felt as solid, as cool, as serene as a marble altar. Something, or someone, was *there*.

I did not hear a word with my ears, but in the half a minute this experience lasted, words formed in my mind. I cannot remember them precisely, but the presence communicated to me that Ruthie would not survive this cancer, but that I should not fear, that all would be well, because this must happen.

And that was all. The presence departed, leaving me with a sense of calm resignation. *If it must be, it must be.* But I could not tell anybody but Julie about this, I resolved, because I didn't want them to lose hope. Then I fell asleep.

At lunchtime the next day Mike's buddies took him out to eat. Mam and Paw were in the hospital cafeteria, and Ruthie was in her bathroom, taking a shower. I sat in a chair in her hospital room, fingering my prayer rope. Suddenly, the phone rang. It was the nurse's station, saying that Ruthie or Mike needed to come down at once to talk to Dr. Miletello on the phone. Mike was gone, I said, and Ruthie is in the shower. There's no one but me. I'll be right there.

Dr. Miletello told me the results from Ruthie's PET scan were back, and the news was bad. Her brain was covered with cancerous lesions. And there was cancer on her hip bone. They would have to start radiation therapy at once.

When Ruthie came out of the shower in her new hospital gown, I gave her the news. She looked down at the floor, but showed no emotion. A few minutes later Mike came back from lunch. He sat in a chair in the room. Ruthie rested on her hospital bed, her legs dangling off the side.

"Tell Mike what Dr. Miletello said," she directed softly. Her vocal cords had been damaged by the surgery. Though they would heal somewhat, Ruthie's old voice was gone forever.

As he absorbed the news Mike shuddered. Ruthie looked at him, her face a portrait of heartbreak and guilt. "I'm sorry," she rasped. "I was hoping for better news."

Abby turned up shortly before the nurses came to take Ruthie to radiation therapy. "Come with me," Ruthie asked Abby, and she agreed. On the journey Abby pummeled the medical personnel with questions. Ruthie asked nothing. My sister was completely, bizarrely, at peace—even when technicians were immobilizing her head with a rigid metal frame.

"It was like a horrible mask," Abby says. "They had to keep her head completely still so they could hit the right points in the brain with the radiation. I was totally freaked out just looking at it. But Ruthie— you should have seen how calm she was. If it bothered her, she didn't let on. From the very beginning she made her mind up that she was going to do whatever it took to get better, and that was that. She had this plain, unemotional determination to endure whatever they threw at her."

On the way to radiation therapy Ruthie and Abby had run into a young man they knew from back home who was on the hospital staff. While Ruthie was receiving radiation, Abby found the man and asked him what he could tell her about Ruthie's condition.

"I've seen her stuff, and it's not my place to tell her this, but it's pretty bad," he said.

"How long does this give her?" Abby asked.

"In cases like this? Three months."

———

Ruthie never asked how much time she had, or for any details about the severity of her cancer. From the moment she awoke on her hospital bed from the surgery, she told her doctors she did not want to know. Ruthie was a numbers person and knew herself well enough to be certain that facts and figures would destroy her will to fight the cancer.

"Ruthie was a researcher, but I'm telling you, from that first day forward, she didn't read any literature, she didn't look anything up," says Abby. "She just trusted the doctors."

Tim reached the hospital while Ruthie was in radiation, and spoke by phone with Dr. Miletello, who was preparing to meet with Ruthie and Mike after she finished her session. Dr. Miletello had convened a meeting of his oncology team to study Ruthie's case and devise a treatment strategy.

"Bad illness, Tim," he said. "But I have fallen in love with this family, and I am going to do everything in my power to fight this thing."

Later that day Dr. Miletello saw Ruthie for the first time since the morning of her surgery. Mike was with her. The doctor knew Ruthie didn't want to talk prognosis. If she had, he would have told her this cancer was incurable, and in her case it was so far advanced that she could be dead in six weeks to two months. But he couldn't say that to her. Rather Dr. Miletello told her as much as he could within the bounds of the rules she set that first morning. Ruthie learned in detail that she had stage IV non-small-cell cancer—the worst—that had spread throughout her lungs, her brain, and to her hip bone. Worse, Ruthie would have to complete a course of radiation to stop the brain lesions from growing before it was safe to begin chemotherapy.

Dr. Miletello was struck by the solidarity between Ruthie and Mike, and how calm they were as he gave them the grim news.

"She was very accepting, she was not angry. She never cried. She was almost unemotional," he says. "You go into some people's rooms and you walk out, and before you can tell them much of anything, they have fifty questions they want to ask. And it's everything you just got through telling them, but they hadn't listened. It was not like that with Ruthie and Mike. It wasn't because they were naive. It was that they were more focused on each other."

"Ruthie just turned this over to her doctors, and to God," he says.

When I kissed Ruthie goodnight at the end of my third day home, she told me how much she loved seeing me getting closer to her girls. I had never had the opportunity to spend much time with them, because my visits had always been so short. But now I was with the children a lot—and Ruthie wanted me to know how happy that made her.

Tim Lindsey walked me to the hospital's parking garage. We talked about all we had seen from and around Ruthie since the morning of her diagnosis. Tim and I agreed that there was something profound, even uncanny, about what Ruthie was revealing to us all. She was showing us how to suffer.

"However long she has to live," said Tim, "whether it's weeks or years or decades, her children will always remember the courage their mother showed."

God knows we would all rather have had this cup pass by Ruthie. But even as the darkness increased around her, the light increased that much more.

———

The next morning, Friday, the girls skipped school and came down to see their mother in the hospital. Ruthie sat in a chair in the sunlight next to the window, talking cheerfully to her visitors. Claire sat next to Ruthie, nestled her head on her mother's left shoulder, and gazed out the window as Ruthie spoke to the others.

The sunlight fell on Claire's eyes, making them appear illuminated from within. She stared dreamily into the distance, a woozy half smile on her face. A wisp of her chestnut-brown hair dangled over her forehead. Claire appeared utterly lost in time, softly swooning, like a religious mystic rapt in the ecstasy of adoration. Ruthie didn't notice Claire—she was busy conversing with her visitors—but it didn't matter. Indeed the most striking thing about the image was that neither mother nor daughter saw each other. Claire simply felt her calming presence, and it was enough to help the young girl see past the pain and the terror that now besieged her family.

It was one of the most arresting icons of the spiritual power of a mother's love that I have ever seen. I quickly captured the image with my iPhone.

Over the next year I would stare at the photo and contemplate the look on Claire's face. She was only ten years old, and had no real idea what her mother and her family were about to go through. This is tragic, I thought at first. She doesn't know what time will do to her family. This was the last moment of innocence before the disease began to disfigure her mother. But I came to regard the image more hopefully. There is a purity and a timelessness in that little girl's face that nothing, not even suffering unto death, can tarnish or destroy. That child, resting in the primal simplicity of her love for her mother, saw with the eyes of her heart into a deeper reality.

That afternoon Laura Lindsey came down with art supplies for Claire and Bekah to make posters to decorate their mother's hospital room. Sensing that Hannah might be too old for an art project, I asked her if she wanted to take a trip with me to New Orleans, to the tomb shrine of Francis X. Seelos, a nineteenth-century Roman Catholic priest thought by many to be a saint. She was desperate to get away from the scene at the hospital. "Let's go," she said tersely.

I didn't expect to have this time with Hannah, and was grateful for it. In a way we had become closer when she hit the midpoint of her teenage years and found herself bored and yearning for escape from St. Francisville. From afar I tried to give her comfort and understanding, or, failing that, at least suggestions for good things to read. But there was distance between us too. On our visits to Starhill Hannah always seemed to be out with her friends. It seemed that she was happy for me to play the cool uncle, but only at a certain remove.

As we drove down I-10, rolling across concrete bridges high above the cypress swamps, my Methodist niece told me she had no idea what a saint was, and why we were going to light candles at one's grave. I had been living inside the world of saints and relics for so long that I had lost touch with how strange and exotic all this must seem to a girl raised in our family's religious tradition. The earthshaking news of her mother's cancer jostled open the door to Hannah's mind, such that she found herself on a pilgrimage that would have been unimaginable only a week ago. As her guide I had to improvise a quick catechism.

Catholic and Orthodox Christians, I explained, believe that anyone who lives in heaven is a saint. Some saints are officially recognized by the church. The saints are alive and able to pray for us in a special way, because they are already in heaven. Some saints here on earth, or in heaven after their death, I explained, are thought to have worked miracles of healing, through the power of God.

"They say that's how it was with Father Seelos," I said.

Francis Xavier Seelos was a German missionary priest and mystic who volunteered to serve in 1860s New Orleans because the disease-ridden subtropical city was considered a hardship assignment. Not long after he arrived yet another yellow fever epidemic swept the city. Father Seelos ministered to its victims and succumbed to the illness himself in 1867. He was forty-eight. His congregation buried him in Our Lady of the Assumption Church on Constance Street, where he served.

"His big message was that whatever crosses God sends us, we have to try to embrace them with a joyful heart," I told Hannah. "I'm going to ask him to pray for our family to do this."

"Why don't you just ask God yourself?" she asked. "I mean, why do you have to pray to a saint? That's weird to me."

"Well, if I ask you to pray for me, is that weird?"

"No."

"It's the same deal with the saints. They're alive in heaven. Don't you believe that if we ask people in heaven to pray for us, they will, the same way all the people in St. Francisville have been praying for your mom?"

"I guess so," she said. "But why do you have to go to Father Seelos's grave to ask him to pray for us? If he's in heaven, couldn't he hear us from anywhere?"

"Yeah, sure," I said. "But there's just something about making the trip. It's like a pilgrimage. You go to a holy place, where people come to pray, and there's just something powerful about it. The thing about Father Seelos's grave, people have been going there for a long time to pray for cures. Some of them say they got them."

"How do we know that?" she said, skeptically. The edge in her voice was very Ruthie Leming.

"I'm not sure," I confessed. "But a while ago the Vatican started investigating Father Seelos's case, to see if these miracles were real. There was this one account of a New Orleans lady whose liver had been destroyed by cancer. She had two weeks to live, but her liver grew back after she prayed to Father Seelos. Doctors who studied her case said there was no way medical science could explain what happened to her. That's the case the church used to beatify Father Seelos ten years ago."

"What's 'beatify' mean?"

"That's the first step to becoming a saint."

"So you think Father Seelos will pray for Mama to be cured?"

"Yeah, I do," I said. Then, remembering my experience with the presence in Ruthie's room, I added, "If it's God's will. All we can do is hope and pray, and trust."

We parked on the street outside the Seelos shrine in the old Irish Channel neighborhood, between the Garden District and downtown. The crown of a lone palm tree loomed over the church garden, and beyond it the parish's nineteenth-century tower stood tall over the church's copper roof. We walked past the garden's magnolia trees and palmettos, and into the narthex, or church entrance, where the shrine is. We stood there before Father Seelos's remains, which are interred in a large wooden reliquary, gold-plated and bejeweled, shaped like a house with a steeply pitched, scallop-tiled roof. Some of the beatified priest's personal belongings line the walls, illuminated by flickering candles lit by pilgrims.

We too lit candles, and prayed for Ruthie's cure. Before we left I obtained some relics of Father Seelos for Ruthie to keep by her bedside.

"What's that for?" Hannah asked.

"These are things that belonged to Father Seelos," I said. "The idea is that in some mysterious way, they have some holiness in them, and they're good for your mom to keep near her."

Hannah politely said nothing. I knew that the theology of relics was too much for a Methodist girl to take. Over the next month, though, several of Ruthie's friends or acquaintances would give her Seelos relics. Ruthie treasured them all. "You never know," she told me.

Back in the car I found a message on my mobile from Mam, calling to say the doctors were releasing Ruthie to go home early that afternoon. I texted my cousin Melanie, my uncle Murphy's daughter, in St. Francisville and asked her to change Ruthie's bed linens. She not only did that, but she also rounded up other Dreher cousins for an impromptu cleanup session at the Leming place. Thanks to them, Ruthie came home to a tidy house.

Meanwhile at Ruthie's school, the administration called an afternoon meeting of teachers and staff. It had been a devastating week, and the school's leaders wanted to offer the opportunity for Ruthie's colleagues to say what was on their minds. The meeting was voluntary, but not a single soul—not one teacher, not one secretary, not one janitor, not one cafeteria worker—failed to show. They met in the library and stood in a large circle, holding hands. If you wanted to say something, you did. If not, not. When you were done, you squeezed the hand of the person next to you, who spoke, or passed the chance down the line.

Everyone offered a prayer. Just like Mike's firefighters, Ruthie's colleagues had her back too.

———

The sun came up on Saturday and I thought about how I was going to tell my sister good-bye, not knowing if I would ever see her alive again. I asked her for some time alone before I went to the airport.

"Sure," she said, "Come over."

We sat down in the sun on her front porch, just the two of us.

"Well," she began, "I was diagnosed on Tuesday, and the next day was Ash Wednesday. I guess this is my Lent." Ruthie meant that her cancer fight would be a period for her to reflect and draw closer to God.

The theologian Alexander Schmemann says Orthodox Christians consider Lent to be a time of "bright sadness," because the contemplation of loss and death, if seen in the right light, paradoxically reveals to us the more important things in life—"and we begin to feel free, light, and happy." I hoped this would be true for Ruthie. I hoped it would be true for all of us making this terrible pilgrimage with her.

That morning in Starhill the japonicas were in bloom, and a lone paperwhite peered at Ruthie from just beyond the porch rail. It was crazy to think that just one week ago, Ruthie was reveling at the Spanish Town parade. Now she knew her body was being consumed by cancer. She was so beautiful that morning, in the sunshine, and an awful thought crossed my mind: *I'm never going to see her like this again.* She was forty years old, in the prime of her life, glowing with health; the black ridge at the base of her neck where surgeons had gone in was the only sign that something was wrong with her.

But my little sister was in trouble. I knew this, even if she didn't. I had read the medical literature given to my parents to help them understand Ruthie's condition. I had been on the Internet. I knew that very, very few people survive this type of lung cancer. The overwhelming majority don't make it a year past diagnosis.

Your sister is dying. You have three hours before you have to leave for the airport to go home. You may never see her again. There she is, sitting on the porch next to you. What do you say?

If you're me, you don't say anything at first. You simply sit in the winter sunshine, and say *yes, Ruthie, you're right, it is a beautiful day.* But you know that time may be short, and this is not a time to hold back out of anxiety or embarrassment. You think: these conversations only happen in the movies. They don't happen—they don't *have* to happen—in our lives, because things this terrible only happen to other people, and to other families.

But here we are. And time is passing. So, with fear and trembling, you begin.

"Ruthie…" I said, then stopped. I was speechless, and began to cry. She met my tears with tears of her own. She saw I was struggling to get words out, and tried to tell me to be at peace. But I needed to say these things.

"I have to ask you to please forgive me for every bad thing I ever did to you," I said. "I'm so, so sorry. There are things I did. There are things I should have done but didn't. And I'm sorry."

"It's fine, it's—" She couldn't finish the sentence. She flicked her right hand as if dispelling a moth, then grabbed the nape of my neck, pulled me in tight and held me. We cried together, like little children. I do not know what was going through her mind. Me, I was thinking about all the times I had been mean to her, made her cry. The pointless sibling jackassery. I thought too about the invisible walls that had for years separated us. Had I helped build them? What had I done to her that I needed to apologize for? I wanted to talk about these things, to name them, to cast them out and start over.

But that wasn't Ruthie's way. She wouldn't have it. It was gone with a wave of her hand. After a moment we both felt silly, sobbing like that. We separated, and giggled at ourselves.

"I hope you live fifty more years," I said. "But when you do pass over, please pray for my boys to get along. The only heartbreak of my life with them is that they fight, and nothing works to change that. The problem is so bad with Matthew."

Ruthie told me that she and Hannah had a difficult relationship for a while, and that she used to yell at her daughter. "When Mike went to Iraq, I stopped that," she said.

We talked about our children for a bit more. Then we talked about anger, and about how some of us in the family were struggling not to be mad at the Zachary doctor who had been her family physician for many years. We thought that he had downplayed the severity of her symptoms early in this crisis, until she finally was compelled to go see Tim Lindsey for a second opinion.

"Don't be mad at the doctor, Rod," she said, gripping my forearm. "I don't want any of you to be. He couldn't have found this cancer. Not even the specialists saw it five weeks ago. But oh, I am being taken such good care of now."

She then spoke with astonishment and gratitude about the compassion shown her by Tim, by Dr. Miletello, by the Lady of the Lake nurses and staff. "They treat two hundred patients in that radiation unit every day," she said. "Two hundred! Can you believe? And they still find it in themselves to be so kind to me. It's amazing."

Ruthie and I talked about the parade of visitors who had flocked to her living room since her diagnosis. I felt protective of her, and eager to help her rest and to spend time with her children before the radiation and the chemo took over her life. But she insisted on seeing everyone, if not for her sake, then for theirs. No matter what I said to encourage her to take it easy, she would not budge on this.

Where did she find the patience? On the way back from New Orleans the day before, Hannah and I agreed that neither of us could be teachers because we both lack the patience her mother had. Ruthie's determination to see the good in everyone, and not to push back or get mad, had long been a source of befuddlement and annoyance to some of us who loved her. We thought at times she let people take advantage of her because she was unwilling to provoke conflict. Mam and Paw and I talked about this often, even before Ruthie got sick.

"Her class this year is really tough," Mam told me just that morning. "The other teachers said to her once, 'How do you put up with them?' She told them, 'I love those kids, and maybe they can change.'"

It was that simple with Ruthie. But for many of us, that's the hardest thing in the world. I find it hard to love anybody who's not lovable. Ruthie found everyone lovable, if not necessarily likable. I never thought about where this instinct came from in her until that awful week, when I saw this habit of Ruthie's heart in the light of mortality—hers, ours—and in the light of the generosity from all those she had touched over her lifetime. By the time I made it to Ruthie's front porch that Saturday morning, I saw my country-mouse sister in a new way. I thought, *What kind of person have we been living with all these years?*

Ruthie and I talked for a while longer about the outpouring of support for her, Mike, and the kids. She told me she expected to beat cancer, but it made her happy to hear about people choosing to change their lives because of her story.

"We just don't know what God's going to do with this," she said, matter-of-factly.

Mike drove home from the pharmacy and joined us on the porch. He said while he was in town, he'd run into a friend, who was upset over the news of Ruthie's cancer. "He said, 'I have never in my life prayed, but when I heard this news, I prayed twice, dammit.'"

Ruthie slapped me on the shoulder. "See?"

It was time for me to leave. On the front porch we held each other again and cried once more. Would this be the last time we would see each other? Would I have time to make it back before she died? Ruthie must have seen in my face the pain these thoughts caused me, because she said, "I hate that you're having to go through this."

Typical Ruthie: worried that her cancer is a burden on others.

Putting my hand on her shoulder, I fixed my eyes on my sister's and said, "You are not walking alone through this. We are all going together, and it's going to hurt, but we are going to be purified."

This would be our family's Lent. There is no Easter without Good Friday.

Driving to the airport I told my parents how all this with Ruthie had knocked me down. After all, in my personal mythology, I was the brave Ulysses, an intrepid adventurer and man of the world who had gone away to make my mark; Ruthie stayed at home and tended her garden. I was the seeker. She was the abider. I never faulted her for that, and had always respected the way she chose to live her life. When

I departed St. Francisville for good in 1994, after my failed attempt at homecoming, I left behind all guilt over choosing to build my life far away from this place. Yes, Ruthie worried about me being so far from home—they all did—but what did a simple country girl from Starhill know about my world?

But now Ruthie had just started a journey unlike any I had ever contemplated, and for which nothing in my wide and vivid experience would have prepared me. But she was ready. She had been preparing all her life.

Since we were children, I knew Ruthie and I were different, but until that week I had never thought about the *way* Ruthie was different. After what I had just seen, I told my parents, I wanted to change the way I was living. To repair broken relationships. To apologize to people I'd offended—even if I had been right. Grudge-holding, I told them, did not matter. What mattered was love, and mercy.

Mam and Paw dropped me off at the Baton Rouge airport. I checked in, went through security, and sat with my thoughts, waiting for my flight.

I resolved to go back to Philadelphia and write to people with whom I was at odds, and to seek reconciliation, because that's what Ruthie would want. That's how I was going to share her walk. I would be stuck hundreds of miles away, unable to help, but I could at least do that thing, and do my part to make sure the agonies that awaited her on this sorrowful path were not wasted, but turned to the good. I needed to do the hard work of forgiveness, of putting aside judgment. I needed to love people. They might change. And even if they didn't, I needed to love them all the same.

That's what Ruthie would want. And that's what I was determined to give her.

Before the plane boarded, I wrote on my laptop to Andrew Sullivan, a prominent blogger with whom I had had friendly relations in the past, but with whom I had lately been publicly fighting over cultural politics. In my e-mail I told him what was happening to my sister, and what an example she had been to me. I asked him to forgive me for my hard-heartedness toward him. He responded in kind. We are destined to disagree, I felt, but we are not destined to be nasty to each other. I e-mailed him the photo of Claire on Ruthie's shoulder. He posted it to his blog, with prayers for Ruthie.

On Sunday morning I woke up and checked the comments on my own blog before getting ready for church. This is what I found from a reader:

> Dear Ruthie and Mr. Mike,
>
> I was your nurse for only 12 hours. I had six other patients that night, but you were the only one who smiled through tears after having received the worst news. I googled your name in hopes of finding your address so that I could write you, and I happened upon this site. I can see now that it's not just my life that you have touched in just a few short hours.
>
> I have been a nurse for more than two years and I have to say I have seen some things. Good and bad. You and your story will be one that will not be forgotten. I will always keep you and your outlook close to my heart. I kept asking myself that night, why God? Why does the worst always have to happen to those who are truly good?
>
> I've always questioned God's intentions and my faith, especially in my line of work. And here you are asking your daughters not to be angry at Him. You're an amazing woman. You'll never know how deep you have struck the chords of my own heart. Ruthie, meeting you and seeing your heart was the miracle I needed to remember to trust God and live life instead of being bitter.
>
> You reminded me that God is like the wind. You cannot see it but you can feel it and you know He is there. I do not have the right words, I

do not know the best doctor or the right treatment. This is the part of my job that frustrates me. All options are exhausted and I feel my hands are tied. All I can do is pray and I will pray for you and family. I only pray that the Lord God will give you the miracle you need.

    —Crystal Renfroe

See?

CHAPTER EIGHT

Standing in the Spirit of God

That first cancer weekend at home, Ruthie retreated to Paw's pond with Mike, their children, and their fishing poles. Nestled in the embrace of a pine grove, the pond, no wider across than a strong man could throw a stone, had always been Ruthie's refuge. And now she had returned once more, to gather herself before undertaking the fight for her life.

John Bickham knew what chemotherapy would do to Ruthie's body. He understood that this afternoon would likely be the last time the Lemings would be together, looking like themselves. He asked Mike for permission to linger unobtrusively among the pines, taking photographs of their day together. He thought these pictures might mean something to them one day. Mike agreed. That day John took a shot of Ruthie in a black tracksuit, pole in hand, line in the water, inside a hazy golden ball. It was probably a trick of light on the lens, but it looks for all the world as if Ruthie at that moment was literally dwelling within light.

"I know I'm standing right in the middle of God's will, where he wants me to be," Ruthie told me by phone on Sunday night, after I'd returned home to Philly. Though her breathing was labored, she sounded so sure of herself.

For Ruthie, standing in the middle of God's will was as easy as casting for bass. For her tortured, unsettled brother, it was not so simple. Several years earlier I had broken camp and continued my religious sojourn, leaving the Roman Catholic church and settling among Orthodox Christians. Five years of thinking and writing about the Catholic child sex abuse crisis had eroded my ability to believe the claims of the Roman church.

At the beginning of my journalistic writing about the scandal, Father Tom Doyle, a heroic Catholic priest who destroyed his own brilliant clerical career to speak out on behalf of abuse victims, warned me to proceed with great caution.

"If you go down this path," he said, "it will take you to places darker than you ever imagined."

Maybe so, I reasoned, but what choice do I have? I can't turn away from this story, neither as a journalist nor as a Catholic layman and father. I had assumed that as long as I had the theological arguments straight in my head, my Catholic faith could withstand anything.

Had I taken Father Doyle's warning more seriously, I would have prepared myself better for the descent into the scandal's consuming blackness. I had too much faith in my own reason, and in my capacity to think on these grim facts and events without losing my spiritual equilibrium. Five years later, in 2006, the anger, fear, and loathing within me at the Catholic bishops who had allowed this corruption to flourish eventually overcame the intellectual foundations of my Catholic faith—and, I worried, threatened my ability to believe in Christianity at all. For my wife and me, from a theological point of view, Orthodoxy was the only place left to go.

Leaving Catholicism—or, to be more accurate, having my Catholicism torn out of me—was the most painful thing I've ever gone through. I don't know what my sister thought of this, but if she gave it any thought at all, she probably figured it was more of her flighty brother's churchy nonsense.

Becoming acquainted with the Orthodox way of approaching

God—a more mystical, less intellectual method—helped me understand how and why I had allowed the storm of scandal to leave me shipwrecked. And the image of Ruthie standing in the light called to mind a story I had learned about St. Seraphim of Sarov, a Russian Orthodox monk and mystic of the early nineteenth century. In the Bible figures who are dwelling within the will of God—Moses on Mount Sinai, Jesus on Mount Tabor—are seen by followers enveloped by dazzling light. The monk Seraphim is believed to have shown this to Nikolai Motovilov, a religious seeker who came to visit him at his forest hermitage near the rural town of Sarov.

Motovilov wrote that the elder explained to him that the purpose of living a Christian life is not to say prayers, fast, receive the sacraments, and go to church. Those things, rather, are good only if they help one "acquire the Holy Spirit." On that day in the snow outside of Sarov, Motovilov asked Seraphim to explain what he meant by this. Seraphim took his guest by the shoulders and said: "We are both in the Spirit of God now, my son. Why don't you look at me?"

Seraphim's face and clothing had become a luminous white, shining so bright it hurt the seeker's eyes to look at him. The saint told Motovilov that he too was in the shining. This, he explained, is what it means to be illuminated by grace. Seraphim told the young man to go into the world and tell what was revealed to him so that others might believe more deeply. Said the elder, "The Lord seeks a heart full to overflowing with love for God and our neighbor."

Whether John Bickham's camera captured something mystical about my sister, or more likely caught the sun's rays at an odd angle, there was no doubt in my mind that I was seeing the beginning of a transfiguration within Ruthie. The week before she was, to my eyes, just my sister. She was a kind, happy, loving country girl, certainly, and a friend to all—and that was more than enough. But now I began to suspect that something else was going on, that there was more to Ruthie than I had imagined—and that it was slowly being revealed.

Was I guilty of imposing a story I wanted to see and needed to hear on an ordinary cancer patient's experience? Maybe. Or maybe I was seeing grace. Whatever the truth, my skepticism was not strong enough to prevent me from reaching out to an estranged Louisiana cousin and asking his forgiveness for hurtful things I had said and done many years earlier when we were on opposite sides of a political fight. He graciously accepted my apology, and offered one of his own. We agreed that what we had seen these past few days in and around Ruthie had given us a new vision of life, and how we could live together as a family, in spite of our past.

It is an awesome thing to realize that forgiveness is always possible to offer, and to receive. Ruthie was no more special or kind or loving today than she was the week before, the month before, or the year before. The only difference was that we now knew that she was really sick. It took this catastrophe of cancer to make me see Ruthie as she truly was—and to see myself as having the opportunity to live within that purifying light.

I remember thinking at the time: *Why is it like that with us? Why do we turn away from the opportunities for grace and mercy, and withhold them from others, who need them as much as we do?* Like Motovilov we fallible creatures sometimes need to see something amazing to make us grasp that *life is a miracle*, and that hope and redemption are in all things, every day of our lives, if only we could be humble enough to accept them.

Perhaps God was bringing about harmony and healing of souls through the radical disharmony Ruthie's cancer was causing in her body. Her ultimate healing—that is, her final reconciliation with God, which might or might not include the healing of her body—would, I thought, depend on her being confident that God's hand is in whatever happens, and that He will bring good out of it.

Days later Julie flew down to Louisiana to visit Ruthie and do what she could to help the Lemings adjust to their new life. When she returned I mentioned to her that this cancer thing with Ruthie would probably be like 9/11 was for those of us who were living in New York in 2001.

"Remember how we thought nothing would ever be the same again, but everybody eventually got used to it, and got on with their lives?" I said.

"That's it," Julie said. "And let me tell you, they're already there. Ruthie's house is bubbling over with joy these days. She's *fine*. I mean, she's *not* fine, she's got cancer, but she and Mike are dealing with it amazingly well. They're laughing all the time, enjoying their friends, and even making cancer jokes. They hadn't gotten around to taking down the Christmas lights from the front porch, so Mike's calling them 'cancer awareness lights.' "

Julie went to Louisiana with a heavy heart, but returned strangely cheerful. Working at Ruthie's kitchen table, she collected the small mountain of cards and letters pouring in from family, friends, and people Ruthie barely even knew, and filled a scrapbook with them. She said it was breathtaking to watch Ruthie's joy, and to see the outpouring of love surrounding the Lemings. She talked about how the "family" from the Baton Rouge Fire Department, as well as the Lindseys, John Bickham, Big Show, and others, were all working together for Ruthie's sake.

"I kept looking at Ruthie thinking about how I would react if it were happening to me," she continued. "I told her something like, 'Okay, I can go organize this for you, and clean up that, and we can get this and that in order.' And she just looked at me and said, 'Well, we could. Or we could just sit here and make *queso* and talk.' I wanted to wrestle this to the ground, but she was happy just to be."

————

Back in Philadelphia I was not as accepting as my sister. I was struggling with Ruthie's admonition not to be angry at God and to accept

her cancer as somehow part of His plan. Ruthie's hair had begun falling out from the cancer treatment, my folks told me, inspiring Ruthie to
have her head shaved. My mother said that the beauty of Ruthie's face
surprised them. Her hair had always been so thick and lustrous, and
had given her face such an air of feminine softness, that the architec-
ture of her bones—especially the strength in her high cheekbones—
was a revelation.

———

Cancer may not have broken my sister's spirit, but it brought with it
logistical challenges. Daily life needed to be rearranged. Ruthie had
always taken the girls to school. That task fell to Mike, when he was
home from work, and otherwise to Mam, mostly. Abby managed the
meal-delivery schedule with the community volunteers. Someone had
to look after the girls when Mike and Ruthie had to be in Baton Rouge
at chemotherapy. Someone had to cut the grass when Mike couldn't get
to it. There always needed to be someone. In Starhill there always was.
In a time of great need the Leming family wanted for nothing.

In those early days of treatment, drugs made it difficult for Ruthie
to sleep regularly. She passed those lonely hours of the night sitting
in her bed, resting against a slope of pillows, praying. She expanded
her practice of writing down names of people who had asked for her
prayers, or whom she thought needed her prayers. Sometimes these
fragmentary lists would be on scraps of paper—whatever she had near
to hand when someone had first asked her to pray for them. Ruthie
took these requests seriously, and wrote them down so she wouldn't
forget. There she would be, in her sickbed, her chest and her brain rid-
dled with cancer, moving through the endless night with her prayer
lists before her, asking God to show mercy to others.

At breakfast one day she told Mike that it was a good morning.
He asked why. She said she had had a mysterious encounter the night
before.

She had been awake in the middle of the night, praying about her situation. As she was praying Ruthie felt a distinct presence in the room, by the door. She didn't know what it was, but she continued to pray. The presence lifted a weight from her—Ruthie felt this physically—and then it left. She never talked about who or what she thought it was. She saw no reason to question something that gave her so much comfort and relief. After that night she didn't worry so much.

———

Had she known just how critical her medical condition was, Ruthie might have been consumed by anxiety. Mike was curious, but felt bound to honor Ruthie's strategic decision to remain in the dark. It was hard for others to believe that Ruthie really didn't know how sick she was, and that she didn't want to know. Knowing that Ruthie had heavily researched her condition prior to the cancer diagnosis, Abby asked her once if she had gone onto the Internet to look up her form of lung cancer.

"No," Ruthie said.

"Don't!" Abby warned. That was all Ruthie needed to hear.

Still I found it difficult to accept that she refused this information. Speaking by phone with Ruthie a month into her chemotherapy, I asked her why doctors hadn't given her a prognosis. "Do you know all this and you're just not telling the rest of us?"

"No, not at all," she replied. "I told them from the start I didn't want to know those things. Remember, I'm a numbers person, and if I knew the numbers, I wouldn't be able to get them off my mind. And there's nothing I can do to change them anyway. I told the doctors to keep that information to themselves, unless they just have to tell me, and to just tell me what I need to do. I'm going to do everything they say to do, and stay positive, and live every day with hope."

This I never understood. If I had cancer, I'd demand to know everything at once, on the theory that information is power. And then, me being me, I would surely brood over it incessantly. Ruthie, on the other hand, figured that information would be disempowering. She understood that she was in some respects living an illusion, but if she was going to live at all, she had to be able to curtain off the terror of death. She was walking a tightrope stretched high over a chasm, and could not afford to look down, not for a single second.

Dr. Miletello, Ruthie's oncologist, saw wisdom in Ruthie's approach. He has had patients who didn't enjoy their lives at all, spending every waking moment second-guessing their doctors and seeking out second and third opinions at every turn. In the end these people end up getting worse care.

"They can never let go," he says. "And they spend what time they have looking for something else, some new secret, some new doctor who's supposedly going to help them beat this. Nothing can make them happy because they're looking for something that's not there."

To underscore his point Dr. Miletello told a story about two patients he'd had fifteen years ago, diagnosed on the same day with the same kind of tumor, at the same stage of development. One lived three months; the other lived three and a half years.

"It was all up here," he said, tapping his head. "One guy walked out of here and said, 'You said I have cancer, and if the treatment doesn't work, I'll be dead in a year.' The other guy said, 'I've got better things to do than to die from cancer.' He dedicated himself to living life to the fullest, right up to the very end. The first guy, he worried the whole time, and spent the three months before he died in bed. Comparing those two taught me right there: My God, this is what you can do with the right attitude."

———

In March, as word spread of Ruthie's cancer, the town continued to rally around the Leming family. One firefighter approached Mike and with tears in his eyes opened his wallet, turned it upside down, and shook every bill out of it. He told Mike that he was sick that he couldn't do anything more to help, and he hoped this would be enough.

Meanwhile at the middle school Ruthie's class—the one that had been the worst-behaved of her entire career—had undergone a change of heart. At a school assembly a girl named Lyric Haynes—a profoundly impoverished child whose mother was in prison, and who was one of Ruthie's most challenging students—stood and made a short speech. All the teachers knew how hard Lyric's life was, and how much courage it took for her to go before the entire school to make a presentation.

"This is about Mrs. Leming," Lyric said. "As you all heard, Mrs. Leming has lung cancer. She always wants us to do good for ourselves, and make the right decisions. Now that she isn't teaching here anymore, we are trying to make her proud.

"She used to go head over heels for us, and now we are going to do the same for her," Lyric continued. "Mrs. Leming, you are the best, and we love you very much. You will always be in our hearts."

Ruthie loved that. She told me once on the phone that her cancer opened the door to experiences of others, and of their goodness, that she wouldn't have otherwise had. "All this love," she mused. "It's unbelievable how blessed I am."

Good things kept happening. Mike's firefighter colleagues planned to host two chicken-dinner fund-raisers (in the end, that effort raised twelve thousand dollars). And some other friends were planning a fund-raising concert called Leming-Aid in April.

The Leming-Aid concert started when Starhill neighbor Mel Percy, Baton Rouge firefighter Robert Triche, and David Morgan, Ronnie's son, decided that they wanted to do something to ease Mike's and Ruthie's minds about their finances. Ruthie was a public school teacher, Mike a firefighter. They didn't have a lot of extra money coming in during the good times, and these were not good times.

Mel called Abby Temple to ask her to approach Ruthie with the idea. Abby thought it was a terrific plan, but Ruthie didn't like it. She thought she didn't deserve it. She didn't want to be a burden to anyone. When Abby told her the concert was a way for people to feel like they were doing something for her—in other words, that by allowing them to put on the show, she was doing them a favor—Ruthie reluctantly consented.

"Mike and Ruthie were so loved that this was easy," Mel remembers.

Nobody had ever asked the parish Parks and Recreation Department for permission to hold a concert in the sports park. When Mel approached the Parks and Rec director with the idea, he said, "Man, no problem."

Mel is a Freemason. When he reached out to his brother Masons, they said he could count on them. Then he called a pal who is a sheriff's deputy and asked if he would help with parking. The deputy told Mel he would help out if it was fine with Sheriff Austin Daniel. Mel called Sheriff Daniel, who told him not only was it okay, but that he would park cars himself if they needed him to. And so on.

Mel had a reputation for irascibility, but the things he saw began to soften his heart. "It was everybody saying 'whatever we need to do, you got it, you got it, you got it.' The brotherly love I saw throughout this process was so humbling, and amazing."

"Doors opened everywhere, all over town," Abby adds. "Anything you asked somebody about, they were there, and wanted to do it. You had tons of people offering to work, any way they could."

Abby, Mel, and the other concert organizers wanted Ruthie to use the money raised for something special for her and her family. If she needed it for medical expenses, fine. But if her medical insurance was sufficient (as indeed it turned out to be), then they wanted the Lemings to use that money for a vacation. Says Abby: "She was such a penny-pincher, and hated the idea of being extravagant."

Mike had to work an overnight shift at the fire station the night before the concert. Ruthie felt frail and exhausted, and asked Abby to spend the night with her, as she often did when Mike worked the overnight; she was coughing up blood and was frightened. Nearly two months into her cancer treatment, radiation and chemotherapy had wrecked her trim, athletic body. She was so badly swollen that her breasts were leaking, her face was disfigured, she had near constant diarrhea, and she had to use an oxygen tank from time to time.

I arrived early that Saturday afternoon on a plane from Philadelphia and went straight to Ruthie's place. I found her sitting in her chair in the living room. She looked like crap.

"You look like crap," I said.

"Yep, it's the look of cancer!" she snickered in a tiny, crackly voice, and smiled.

I hugged and kissed my sister and silently thanked God that I had gotten to see her again.

Late that afternoon I drove Mam and Paw to the large covered barn at the far end of the sports park. We arrived early to get a good parking spot and were surprised by how many people were already there. Volunteers set up the beer, soda, and food stands on either side of the stage. There was a big area down front for dancing, and scores of folding chairs stretching to the back of the barn. At the rear sat a travel trailer, its air conditioner humming. A friend of Ruthie's brought it to town for the evening so Ruthie could have a cool place to rest and receive oxygen if she needed it.

By the time the sun went down a crowd of five hundred people milled around under the barn. Suddenly a few people at the far side began to cheer. Everyone turned to see Ruthie and Mike slowly making their way into the arena. Then an enormous whoop broke over the crowd like a thunderclap. Everyone stood, yelled, applauded. Ruthie, her bald head hidden under a baseball cap, brought her hands to her swollen face and stopped, overcome by emotion. Mike, beaming, steadied her and walked toward the front row of chairs. Ruthie sat with her head down for a few minutes, crying and gathering herself before beginning to receive a long line of well-wishers.

Our folksinger cousin Emily Branton opened the show. After several numbers Emily struck some familiar chords, then sang:

Hey where did we go,
Days when the rains came . . .

Mike helped Ruthie to her feet, and led his girl to the dance floor. They couldn't do much, given her shortness of breath, but they held each other close, Ruthie staring up at her husband with her chestnut eyes, smiling broadly through her pain.

"We love you, Brown Eyed Girl!" Emily called from the stage. Ruthie grinned and waved with both hands.

David Morgan and his band took the stage after dark and the crowds kept coming. Many people passing through the gates gave far more than the admission price, telling the ticket takers to keep the change. Amanda McKinney, Abby's sister, had designed a special T-shirt for the event, and organizers had bought so many they despaired of selling them all. As it turned out they ran out early; Abby figured they could have sold four times as many. It never occurred to my sister how many people loved her.

It was a revelation to me too. I ran into many old friends that night, some of whom I hadn't seen in twenty years. The three Wilson sisters, who grew up next door to us, came in together. Angela and Susan had driven in from north Louisiana for the show; Teresa, the youngest, came in from Memphis. I hadn't seen Angela or Teresa for decades.

"I can't believe you're here!" I said.

"No way we were missing this," said Angela, now the mother of grown children. The last time I laid eyes on her was as a high school senior dancing in her living room to *American Bandstand*.

I met a woman who traveled from Houston, six hours away, for this concert. Ruthie had taught her children when they lived in town, and had meant the world to them.

"We love her so much," the woman said. "She has given so much to our family. We couldn't *not* be here."

I kept hearing this over and over that night: *We had to be here.* The most touching stories came from people whom Ruthie had taught, or whose kids she had taught. Ruthie disappeared at one point to go rest and get oxygen, attended by Tim Lindsey. David Fournet, an old classmate of hers, stopped me, upset that she might have left before he was able to say hello. "You see her, you tell her I love her. Because I do!" he said, fighting back tears.

I watched a man who barely knew our family paying for hot dogs with a hundred-dollar bill, and saying, "Keep the change." My mother observed one woman from a poor family at the show. "I know how little they have," Mam said, "and they still came to give to Ruthie." Members of the Baton Rouge Fire Department showed up en masse as a sign of respect for Mike.

It was an evening of beer drinking, country dancing, and merrymaking, the likes of which there had been far too little of since that awful day in February. For Ruthie this was an *It's a Wonderful Life* moment as the people of the parish took the opportunity to show her and tell her what a difference she had made in their lives. At the end of the evening, over a thousand people had come through the gates, and the people of our little country parish had raised forty-three thousand dollars for Ruthie Leming. "This is how it's supposed to be," an old friend said to me that night, looking out over the crowd. "This is what folks are supposed to do for each other."

CHAPTER NINE

Expecting a Miracle

After the initial harshness of chemotherapy and the catharsis of the concert, Ruthie and her family finally settled in to everyday life with cancer. Ruthie's brain lesions retreated, Dr. Miletello adjusted the chemo doses, and her swelling subsided. The main tumor, the one pressuring her superior vena cava, responded well to chemo, and shrank a bit. She looked more like herself again, absent a full head of hair. Inside, though, she was changing in subtle but important ways.

I was startled but pleased to learn that Ruthie asked Abby to take her down to pray at Father Seelos's shrine, where I'd taken Hannah right after her mother's diagnosis. Ruthie had always been prayerful, but not open to new religious experience or practice. She wouldn't have judged Catholics for their pious customs, but wouldn't have sought those customs out, either. Cancer changed that.

As word of Ruthie's cancer spread friends, neighbors, and even virtual strangers threw everything they had at her, spiritually speaking. Protestants sent Bible verses and prayers. Catholics passed along blessed objects, including Father Seelos's relics, and rosary prayers. In the journal she kept spottily, Ruthie wrote down Scripture passages ("From Uncle Butch: 2 Corinthians 1:3–7"), psalms ("Psalm 91: 'He who dwells in the shelter of the Most High will rest in the shadow of the Almighty ...' "), and specific prayers.

One day that spring Ruthie finally made it down to the Seelos shrine when Abby drove her to a healing mass.

Ruthie did not know what was expected of her at the shrine, but wasn't bothered by it. Before she got sick Ruthie never would have come to a place like this. Too exotic. Too strange. But now she was happy to be here. She made sure to venerate all the relics, to light a candle, and to pray before Father Seelos's tomb. She spent so much time in preliminary prayer that there were no more seats left in the church for the mass. As she and Abby made their way through the crowd of sick pilgrims to the balcony seating, a woman Ruthie had never seen before walked straight over, looked her in the eyes, and said, "Expect a miracle."

"I tell you what, that made me feel so good," Ruthie told me on the phone that night. "I really got a lot of hope out of that."

I was worried that she would read too much into this happenstance.

"You need to be careful," I said. "If you get a miracle, it might not be a healing. It might be something else. We don't know for sure what God's doing here."

"I know," she said. "But it was still neat to hear."

We talked about how cancer was changing her spirituality, and how it was opening her mind and her heart. I mentioned that a Turkish Muslim reader of my blog posted a comment saying he would pray for her. She was so touched by this, and asked me to thank him. "Honey, I'll take prayers from anybody who'll give them, because I sure need them."

The humility imposed by cancer created an opening for Ruthie, giving her a fresh willingness to accept God's graces through unfamiliar channels. There was Father Seelos. There was also Sister Dulce.

If you live in southeast Louisiana and have cancer, sooner or later you are going to hear about Sister Dulce Maria Flores, a Roman

Catholic nun living in Baton Rouge, who is said to have a mystical healing gift. The Texas-born nun, a member of the Mercedarian Sisters of the Blessed Sacrament order, believes that the voice of God saved her as a child when she nearly drowned in the Gulf of Mexico while vacationing with her family at the Texas coast. The five-year-old girl had strayed too far from shore, and slipped beneath the waves. Under water and about to lose consciousness, she heard a voice telling her to put one foot in front of the other, and keep walking. She did, and made it to safety.

Years later Sister Dulce was working in a California mission when she claimed to have had a vision while in prayer. During the mystical experience God imparted a healing gift through her hands—something she said she discovered only after laying them on a woman dying of pancreatic cancer, and finding that she could absorb some of the woman's pain into her hands.

In 2000 Sister Dulce found her way to Baton Rouge in response to what she described as a command from "Papa," the name she used for God. She began visiting with the sick and praying with them. Word spread fast around town that the chubby little Latina nun with the cheerful personality was a vessel of God's healing mercies. Within a decade she and her supporters opened the Cypress Springs Mercedarian Prayer Center, a chapel, convent, and retreat house in a wooded south Baton Rouge enclave.

The nun believes that God sometimes heals through her touch. Often the healing is not physical, but a spiritual and emotional closure that allows the terminally ill to reconcile themselves to their condition and die in peace.

Why would my Methodist sister seek out a Catholic faith healer if she had accepted her fate? The answer is that Ruthie was of two minds about her cancer: if God meant for her to die, then she would accept that. But she was not convinced that this was God's will. Perhaps this was a test of faith, and He would restore her, if she prayed, and if she believed. That was her hope, anyway—a hope that led her to Sister Dulce's prayer center early in her cancer fight. In the nun's office that spring day Sister Dulce and Ruthie had a general conversation about her medical condition. Then Sister asked Ruthie to step closer.

She put her hands on Ruthie's torso, on top of her clothes. The nun almost gasped. "Oh, child," she said, "You are so sick." Ruthie stood expressionless, blinking. Sister Dulce held Ruthie's hands, and said she was going to talk to Papa. She added that she would walk this road by Ruthie's side, if it took her through to healing, or if it ended in death.

Tears spilled over Ruthie's cheekbones as the little nun spoke, but she left the prayer center feeling more confident about the road ahead.

This vulnerable Ruthie—the cancer sufferer who wept, who feared, who anguished—was not the Ruthie nearly everyone else saw. Only Mike and Abby saw her in these moments of doubt and pain. To her children, her parents, her friends, and her community, Ruthie was a tower of faith and a beacon of hope.

After Ruthie's treatment started Tim Lindsey moved into a medical support role in Ruthie's life. He didn't see her as often in his office, but he did see her around town. At birthday parties, ball games, parades, school events, and anything her girls were involved in, Ruthie was there with a smile on her face. The townspeople were amazed by the fight she had in her. "Her cancer is really bad, right, doc?" a patient asked Tim. "But she came to my kid's birthday party anyway."

"I saw her at the football game the other night," another one said. "It was raining and everything, but she didn't miss it."

At one point in her struggle, Tim could see how much pain she was in, and confronted her with some difficult questions.

"Have you thought about whether or not there's a time when we need to call hospice, when you're done with this treatment?" he asked. "You have to let me know, because I'll support you a hundred percent. How are you dealing with this? Do you need anything for your emotions? How are you doing all this?"

She had not thought about hospice care. She had not seriously considered that she might not survive.

"Tim, if I think about truly how sick I am, it will overwhelm me," she said. "I have to focus on what I have, what I've been given. Otherwise, I'm not going to be able to make it."

The way Ruthie was, if she believed she was fine, and acted like she was fine, then she would be fine.

Tim's wife, Laura, heard the same thing from Ruthie. In the summer of 2011 Laura was picking up her daughter at cheerleader camp when she saw Mam, who told her that Ruthie was at the hospital having X-rays. She had fallen the night before and hurt her ribs. Ruthie eventually showed up at the camp and told Laura nothing was broken, but she was in a lot of pain.

After the program ended Laura's friend Betsy approached them and asked Ruthie how she was doing.

"I'm fine, I'm good," Ruthie said. You could believe that, too, because she didn't say these assuring things in a nervous, defensive voice, but rather in her customary calming cadence.

Laura wasn't fooled. She looked at Betsy and said jokingly, "Ruthie's lying to you. She hurts a lot."

"No, I *am* okay," Ruthie insisted. "This is the deal: if I tell myself I'm okay, I'm okay. But if I tell myself I'm not okay, I'll crawl in a hole and I'll never come out of it."

That same summer Ruthie and Abby went for a drive into Mississippi to shop for antiques. On the way home they stopped at a café for lunch. Abby had been grappling with anger at God for what had happened to Ruthie, and trying to understand Ruthie's peacefulness in the face of her pain and suffering.

"Ruthie, do you think about tomorrow?" Abby asked. "Do you think about the future? Do you plan?"

"I don't think past today," Ruthie replied.

"Do you make yourself not do that? Because if I were in your shoes, I would have to force myself to stop thinking about tomorrow. Don't you?"

"No, I just don't."

As crazy as it sounded Abby respected Ruthie's denial as a commonsense strategy to help her endure the seemingly unendurable. Ruthie had told Dr. Miletello to do whatever he thought best and placed her trust, and her life, in his hands, and in God's. Besides Abby knew, if Ruthie did not, that her best friend faced very long odds with this cancer. If choosing not to look at the monster under the bed helped Ruthie sleep better on the nights she had left on this earth, well, who was Abby to question that?

Though I didn't dare say so, there were times when I wondered whether what looked like bravery was in fact a form of cowardice in the face of the awful truth about her condition. It didn't make sense to me. Everybody could see how serene, how happy, and how joyful Ruthie was, despite suffering terribly. But did this count as courage if she achieved that state of equilibrium by refusing to know the truth?

I was scared to ask her, afraid that I would plant doubt in her mind, doubt that would act as a gust of wind that would topple her from the high wire she was walking. And for what? Nothing I could say to Ruthie would prolong her life, or make her better able to enjoy whatever time she had left. Her doctors were throwing everything medical science had at her. All the extra information could only sap her will to resist. The truth—the whole truth, that is—would not set her free, but would make her captive to anxiety, and tempt her to despair. This was not a classroom exercise in faith versus doubt. This was not an argument at a college cafeteria table between philosophy students who had the leisure to speculate on ultimate questions. This was reality. This was a woman who was waging a desperate guerrilla war for her life. What good would it do her to hear me say that the forces of death arrayed against her were overwhelming?

And yet there was no getting around Ruthie's cognitive

dissonance—that is, the difficulty in squaring her confident faith in God's providence with her white-knuckled refusal to admit any facts that stood to undermine her hope. I finally reconciled it, at least in my mind, by considering two things. First, while my nature was con-templative, Ruthie's was active. Second, that nature served her moral commitment to duty, even to the point of self-sacrifice—the bedrock of Ruthie's character.

Survival for the sake of Mike and the kids became the absolute focus of her life. It had always been hard to convince Ruthie to do things for herself, but if she came to believe it was for the sake of others, there was nothing she wouldn't attempt. Ruthie found the thought that she wouldn't be around to care for her family intolerable. By force of will she pushed aside anything that she reckoned would compromise her commitment to them. Contemplating the philosophical aspects of her situation was an indulgence she could not afford.

There was no real contradiction between believing that her fate was ultimately in God's hands, but also doing all that she could to cooper-ate with His will—which she believed could and indeed would include a complete physical healing. Miracles, after all, do happen. If there was a miracle in store for her, Ruthie believed she had to be open to receiving it, or it might pass her by.

Still I worried about the effect of Ruthie's strategy on her children. She never leveled with them about her condition, never convened a family discussion to talk about the possibility that she might not sur-vive. "I'll never lie to you," she told the girls, and she made good on that promise. But she didn't tell them that there was a chance cancer could win, and that they should prepare for that possibility.

Here too, Ruthie understood her children well. She grasped that if the girls admitted to themselves that their mother might die, they would fall apart. Whatever time Ruthie had left would be spent not living with joy and light, but rather trying to hold her frightened, shat-tered children together as they waited for the end. So she told her girls when the news from the doctor was good, and she told them when it was bad, but she kept the discussion vague and general. "Girls, I'll answer any questions you have," she said. They never had any questions. They didn't really want to know.

It was easy for Claire and Rebekah, who were still young, to accept on faith that there would be a happy ending to their mother's story. As old as they were at the time—Claire was eleven, Rebekah, eight—they still possessed a remarkable capacity for childlike belief. Besides their mother had raised them to be reticent about asking questions. It was much more difficult for Hannah, who was not only temperamentally more inquisitive than her sisters, but also had turned seventeen only three months after her mother's diagnosis.

Hannah had always played the part of the Golden Girl. Straight A's. Involved in every club, academic and social. Cheerleader. Churchgoer. Obedient. And then, after doing everything right, she woke up to find that her mother had lung cancer. She rebelled. She stayed out of the house as much as she could, because that's where the cancer was. When nobody was around Hannah threw things, and tore her clothes. Sometimes she would climb aboard the four-wheeler, motor to Paw's pond, and, far from anyone's ears, scream as loud as she could. She wanted to yell at her mother, too. In her heart she screamed, "Stop having cancer! Be our mama again!"

Some of this was no doubt standard teenage rebellion. Even before Ruthie got sick, she and Hannah fought. Hannah was tired of living in that boring old town, and couldn't understand why her mother was so happy there. Nothing ever happened, nothing ever changed, and nobody ever talked about anything other than what other people were up to. As Hannah saw it, her mother had settled; that was something she had no intention of doing. She didn't know what she wanted out of life, but Hannah was certain she wasn't going to find it in St. Francisville—and she thought less of her mother for her contentment with such a dull way of life.

Ruthie was not prepared for this, and came down hard on her daughter. In fairness to Ruthie, Hannah *was* behaving selfishly, and had been since before the cancer. And she had resolved that her mother would never understand her, so she had stopped trying to explain herself, leaving Ruthie in a difficult position. Nevertheless Mam and Paw warned Ruthie to be patient, not to make the same mistakes as Paw had done with me. Ruthie was immune to their advice, or so it seemed to them. Nobody knew. Ruthie kept these things within her own family.

I'm not sure when it happened, but at some point well before Ruthie got sick, I began to sense a yearning in Hannah for something she couldn't define, but that was beyond her experience in West Feliciana. I knew that she was going to face a personal crisis over this issue before she did; I had been there myself, and knew how it would be for a teenager like her in a family like ours. Over the years my bond with Hannah thickened as I saw her sensibilities and eccentricities resemble my own as a child. Now, having noticed that she was a dedicated reader, I thought about what escapist literature appealed to me at her age, when I was bored, sullen, and eager to leave. That's why I sent Hannah a copy of *A Moveable Feast*, Ernest Hemingway's memoir of his years in 1920s Paris.

It was just the thing. After reading the book, and rereading it, Hannah, at fifteen and sixteen, would lie in bed at night, imagining herself in Paris, sitting in a café all day, talking to strangers, adoring beauty, cultivating passion, being cosmopolitan. This is how my niece became a nascent Francophile, something she revealed to me that first cancer summer, as she planned to fly to Philadelphia to visit us. Julie and I offered to take her anywhere she wanted to have a big dinner.

She chose Parc, an upscale French brasserie on Rittenhouse Square in downtown Philadelphia. Reading about it online Parc struck her as the Frenchiest place in town, the kind of restaurant that would provide a real Boulevard Saint-Germain thrill. As soon as the three of us stepped inside the restaurant that warm Philly evening, I knew she was right. The gleaming zinc bar, the leather banquettes, the tile work, the sepia walls, waiters in white aprons striding by bearing trays laden with crocks of onion soup smothered in gooey Gruyère. Hannah had chosen well: this was as close to Paris as you were going to get this side of the Atlantic. In a giddy fugue she had that night her first taste of champagne, her first raw oysters, her first boeuf bourguignon. Hannah's conversation bubbled with enthusiasm about why beauty is so important in life, and how she wanted to fall in love with a man who could appreciate a restaurant like this one.

"Just make sure he's a man who will be just as comfortable at Mam and Paw's table in Starhill as he is at this one," Julie cautioned. Exactly right, I thought.

Late in the evening Hannah swooned, "Aaaaah, this is like a movie. This is how I want to live my life."

She was coming to the conclusion, she confided, that happiness matters more than being dutiful. "Why not be happy?" she said. "Why be satisfied with the same old thing? I know life can't always be about pleasure, but what is wrong with looking for pleasure?"

I knew those thoughts and feelings well. They had been mine when I was her age, rebelling against Paw's rigid, small-town expectations for me. I had felt guilty enough about my rebellion then, knowing that there was nothing wrong with my contrarian thoughts, but also ashamed that I was disappointing my father, and in turn ashamed for being ashamed. What would it have been like for me if my father, the man against whose granitelike, immovable character the teenage Rod was sharpening himself, had been stricken with terminal cancer? Chances are I would have been as fraught with self-doubt and anxiety as Hannah was.

On that visit to Philadelphia I tried to talk with her about her mom's disease, to find out what she knew, and what she thought about it. Very little, as it happened. She made it bluntly clear that she neither wanted to think about it nor talk about it. That's how Hannah and her sisters wanted it. That's how Ruthie wanted it. That's how it was going to be, Uncle Rod.

The girls were sheltered, but Mam and Paw were not. They knew the odds. They had to watch their only daughter waste away, knowing that she didn't grasp the full measure of the danger she was in. They were not children. They believed in miracles too, but they also knew, in a way Ruthie, Mike, and their children did not, how badly their daughter needed one.

————

Cancer is a family disease, and after the diagnosis the pain spread beyond the Leming household. Night after night Paw sat in his armchair praying for the child who, as a little girl, would fix fences with him in the morning and sit in his lap and snuggle with him before her bedtime. He tried to bargain with God for Ruthie's life. One night Mam heard him in the living room crying, "Just take me, make me sick, make me go, not my little girl." He never quit trying to strike this deal.

My parents needed help; John Bickham and his wife, Sandy, stepped up. John took over more caretaking duties around the Dreher place. Sandy, appreciating the magnitude of Mam's and Paw's need, accepted with a generous heart that she was going to see a lot less of her husband for the duration of Ruthie's health crisis. John mostly served by being present, and listening patiently to Mam and Paw talk about Ruthie. He focused on Paw, working to keep the old man from sitting in his armchair, brooding. John had lost his brother to cancer. He knew from experience what it felt like to be powerless to help your loved one. Over and over he'd tell Paw, "Look, we can't fix this, all we can do is keep putting one foot in front of another."

John spent countless hours simply being there, hearing the same things, and saying the same things. It was a kind of ritual. This meant the world to Mam and Paw.

Ruthie Dreher Leming, days after her cancer diagnosis; February 2010.
Courtesy of Jeannie Frey Rhodes

Ruthie at age five.

Mam, Rod, Ruthie, and Paw, on the day Rod left for Washington, DC; 1992.

Mike Leming
and Ruthie
Dreher;
December 30,
1989.

Mike arriving
home in Starhill
from his tour
of duty in Iraq;
July 14, 2008.

Aunt Hilda *(left)* and
Aunt Lois *(right)*
holding baby Rod;
1968.

Ray "Paw"
Dreher and
Dorothy "Mam"
Dreher, on their
back porch.

John Bickham, a surrogate
son for Paw.

Ronnie Morgan.

Abby Temple
Cochran and
Ruthie.

Dr. Tim Lindsey,
at Ruthie's kitchen
table.

The Leming family: *(left to right)* Claire, Mike, Rebecca, Ruthie, and Hannah. This photo was taken days after Ruthie's diagnosis. The family wanted to have a portrait taken before Ruthie's appearance changed because of chemotherapy and radiation. *Courtesy of Jeannie Frey Rhodes*

Three generations of West Feliciana homecoming queens: Mam, Ruthie, and Hannah.

Ruthie and daughter Claire in the hospital after her diagnostic surgery; February 2010.

The author and his sister, Ruthie.

Mike on the day Ruthie's tombstone was delivered to Starhill Cemetery; May 15, 2012.

It meant a lot to me too. There was very little I could do for my family from so far away, but I did telephone Mam and Paw every morning and every evening, to check on them. They hurt, and they hurt bad. It seemed that every time I called, John Bickham was there with them, or John Bickham had just left, or John Bickham had just called to say he was coming by. In short John was the son they needed at that excruciating time in their lives, but didn't have.

The way John figures it, all the Starhill people who came by to see Mam and Paw, and sit with them on the front porch, were a big part of what kept them going. For the most part, though, Ruthie kept them calm, focused, and hopeful. She wouldn't tolerate their depression, and did everything she could to put on a brave face to lift their spirits.

Big Show often drove up from Zachary to do chores for Paw around the place. He never came to Starhill without stopping in to check on Ruthie. As her cancer progressed Ruthie had fewer visitors. Many people were afraid to stop by. With her muscles wasting away, she began to appear more skeletal. This frightened people. They didn't know if she was too sick to see them. Some didn't trust themselves not to cry in front of her. (Even Paw couldn't stand to see his child in this condition without crying, which made Ruthie feel bad for causing him sorrow.) Others, perhaps, were afraid seeing their friend like this would remind them of their own mortality.

Yet Ruthie was lonely. Big Show saw that side of her suffering, and did his best to take it away.

"She just wanted somebody to talk to," he says. "We'd talk about our kids, how hardheaded our kids were. I'd try to keep her spirits up, joke around with her. But I'd feel bad because if she'd laugh too much, she'd start coughing. I just wanted to spend time with her, because I knew how much she was hurting for company."

In one visit Show confessed that he was furious with God for allowing her cancer.

"You can't be!" she said. "I'm not giving up hope. He has a plan for me."

Big Show would listen politely, and he'd try to believe. He really would. Yet he invariably drove away from Starhill mad, and stayed mad all the way home to Zachary.

If her old friends had trouble keeping faith, Ruthie drew closer to two new confidantes in the chemo room, fellow cancer patients who knew exactly what she was going through. She became especially close to Stephanie Lemoine, a Baton Rouge mom. An elderly woman they knew as Miss Joyce completed their trio.

"We called our times together a chemo party," Stephanie remembers. "Miss Joyce was so cute, in her little wig. We laughed and talked, and had a good time together. Whenever we had chemo we would always hold seats for each other, so we all three could sit together. We just loved being together."

Stephanie began going to the chemo room after her diagnosis of Hodgkin's lymphoma. She saw Ruthie walking around the room, and because Ruthie was so young Stephanie figured her for a breast cancer patient. One Wednesday they sat next to each other as they waited for blood work.

Stephanie smiled at her. "I guess you're a Wednesday girl too, huh?" she said.

"Sure am!" said Ruthie, grinning. And off they went, into their friendship.

When Ruthie came home from the hospital that afternoon, she told Hannah it had been a great day. "I'm so happy," she said. "I made the best friend at chemo today. She's just like me."

They really did have a lot in common, Ruthie and Stephanie. They were both in their early forties. Both married their high school sweethearts. Both had three kids. And both were fighting for their lives.

Stephanie was struck by Ruthie's simplicity and purity of heart. "Ruthie and I knew that we had it all," she remembers. "All we ever really wanted was our families. We talked about everyday things a lot, because that's all we wanted: everyday life with our husbands and our kids."

It was hard not to be friends with Ruthie. People who had just met her often recall having felt like they'd known her for all their lives. She was warm, open, and empathetic. I credit our mother teaching her children empathy by example. With Ruthie the lesson sank in. Mam's tough rural childhood had given her a soft heart, especially for children who didn't have much. She was that way with all underdogs and outcasts like Miss Clophine, the mom of James, one of my summer baseball league teammates.

Miss Clophine, as we knew her, was very poor and rough-hewn. She had been born into a Cajun farm family, and married to James's father, Mr. Huey, at an early age. Hard fieldwork was all she knew. She worked their family's melon and tomato patch in the hot Louisiana sun while Mr. Huey—"Salty," as his family called him—was at his day job on the river ferry. She was skinny as a sugarcane stalk, her skin as brown and leathery as a battered saddlebag. Miss Clophine, who never learned how to read, gathered her wiry hair in crazily jutting pigtails. She spoke English with a muddy Cajun accent, peppered with profanity. A lot of better-off folks looked down on her, but to be fair it was hard to know how to take Miss Clo.

One night we were late getting to the ballpark. Mam arrived at the bleachers to find that the other women seated in the stands had formed a large circle around Miss Clophine, clearly not wanting to converse with her. When Miss Clo spotted my mother, she stood and announced, "Hey you bitches, here comes Miss Dorothy. She'll sit wit' me. She's my friend."

Mam was, and Mam did. That was her way. As she explained to us kids at the time, "You have to understand how much it hurts to be left out, and looked down on."

Every Christmas we would exchange family presents with Miss

Clo. The Toneys had so little, and their need was so great. Miss Clo was our neighbor, though, not a charity case; she had dignity. She gave us kids presents too: one year, a pair of tube socks for me, and a comb for Ruthie. Miss Clo picked up pecans on her hands and knees throughout the fall to make enough money to buy Christmas gifts for those she loved. One autumn she called Mam and told her the pecan crop had been sparse that year; she worried that she wouldn't have enough to buy Ruthie and me anything.

In the summer Miss Clophine and Mr. Huey would load watermelons from their field into the back of their old Chevy Nova, and deliver them to us. Mr. Huey would unpack them and lay them in the shade of the tallow tree in our yard. Sometimes Miss Clophine got out of the car, but other times she wouldn't. Though they were invited inside, Mr. Huey felt they had no right to come into our house. Poor country people are like that sometimes.

In the summer of 2010 Julie and I flew with the kids to St. Francisville to see Ruthie and the family. Ruthie told me that my old teammate James Toney had been coming by to see her. After graduating high school James went to work at the war veterans' home in a nearby town, had a religious conversion, and took up preaching to small country Pentecostal congregations. When he heard about Ruthie's cancer he started driving over from time to time to pray with her and for her. He even raised three hundred dollars from his tiny rural congregation for Ruthie. Those folks didn't have much, but they shared from their measure.

On Father's Day I stood in Mam's kitchen making deep-dish pies out of tomatoes, sliced onions, and pepper jack cheese. Through the back door of the kitchen came James. I hadn't seen him in thirty years or longer. He looked and sounded great. Mr. Huey had died a few years back, and he had driven his mother out to visit the grave. Miss Clophine, as was her custom, remained outside in the car. While James and I sat in the kitchen getting caught up, Mam went out to talk to Miss Clo.

After James and his mother left Mam sat with Julie and me at the kitchen table and cried. She explained that Miss Clophine was in a bad way. It hurt her to see her old friend so sick and broken from age, weariness, and dementia.

Mam said that out in the driveway Miss Clo was struggling through her sickness to talk. She kept patting the tops of her thighs, saying, "Christmas! Christmas!" Mam realized that she had given Miss Clophine those pants for Christmas one year. The poor woman was trying to let Mam know that she remembered.

"I kissed my fingers, then leaned into the car window and touched them to her forehead," Mam told me. "I told her that I loved her. She kissed her fingers, reached through the window and touched my forehead, and said, 'I love you, Miss Dorothy.'"

Mam broke up, and excused herself. I sat there with Julie, and told my wife, "That lady, Miss Clophine, has had an unbelievably hard life, and my mother is one of the only people in this world who treated her with dignity and compassion. That's my Mama."

I was so proud of her. Mam wouldn't know how to be any other way. I shared that story with Ruthie the next morning. She told me that she learned from our mother the wisdom of refusing to return cruelty with meanness. "Don't you remember, Rod, the stories about how Aunt Rita and Mullay"—Paw's mother—"would be so nasty to Mama, trying to put her down and make her feel like dirt?" said Ruthie. "She never fought back, and she kept doing nice things for them when they needed it."

———

That summer vacation in Louisiana was the first time our kids visited their aunt since her diagnosis. It was hard on them to see her without

hair. Her cancer was abstract to them until then. Though I was grateful
for the week we spent with Ruthie, I worried about Lucas, my middle
child. He was only six, and was by far the closest of my children to
Aunt Ruthie.

Lucas, always an early riser, appointed himself to run out to the road,
pick up Aunt Ruthie's newspaper, and deliver it to her. Blond head bob-
bing, he would dash across the grass, wet with morning dew, let himself
in to Ruthie's house, and, newspaper in hand, climb into bed with her.
Every night in Starhill—every single night—Julie and I would have to
answer Lucas's questions about cancer, almost always the same ones, and
then listen to his ideas about how to save Aunt Ruthie from this disease.

"Could Aunt Ruthie swallow some tiny thing that could go through
her body and zap all the cancer?" he said one night.

"What if, like, Aunt Ruthie's doctor got some lasers and blasted
through her skin and destroyed the tumors?" he said on another.

There was always in Lucas's mind some potential *Star Wars*–style
solution to Ruthie's illness. He was sure that if only the doctors would
think hard enough, they could figure out a way to fix his aunt. And
they would, sooner or later, because she couldn't die. That sort of thing
did not happen, not in this world.

Lucas wasn't the only one struggling on this trip. On our final
night at Mam and Paw's, I stepped into our bedroom and found our
four-year-old daughter Nora lying on a mattress, staring at the ceiling,
scowling.

"What's wrong, baby?" I said.

"Nothing."

"No, something is wrong. Are you upset?"

"No."

"Are you sad?"

"No!"

I stretched out on the floor next to her mattress and put my head
next to hers.

"Is this because you love your family down here?"

"Yes!" she cried. She threw her right arm around my neck, buried her head in my shoulder, and wept.

The next morning, as Julie and I packed the suitcases, Lucas asked if he could take Aunt Ruthie her paper one more time. Fine with us, we told him, but take care, because Aunt Ruthie might be sleeping.

To our great lack of surprise, the kid didn't come home for an hour. Ruthie told me later that he had padded softly down the hall to her darkened bedroom, newspaper tucked under his arm, and poked his head in. "He told me that he listens to hear if I'm coughing, and if he does, he knows I'm awake," she said. "He brings me my paper, asks if I want a Popsicle, anything I want. My little buddy takes care of me."

That last morning he climbed into bed with her again, and stayed close for as long as he could. He was thinking that if he could be there to guard Aunt Ruthie, nothing bad would happen to her.

Back home in Philadelphia that night, I carried that sobbing, keening little boy to bed. "Why did we have to leave?" he wailed. "I want to stay there. I love them so much."

————

A week after our return, we had some news from Ruthie. She saw Dr. Miletello for results from a new CT scan. She texted me:

> Tumor got smaller! Fluid in lung almost gone. Dr. Miletello was very excited. Your prayers are working. Please keep it up. Love, Ruthie

Tumor got smaller! The only three words I could think of at that moment that would have sounded sweeter were "I am cured." But when you're dealing with stage IV cancer, you take what you can get.

Truth to tell Ruthie really *was* doing a lot better. So I allowed myself to hope that maybe Ruthie would be one of the tiny number of non-small-cell lung cancer patients—one percent—who make it five years or longer. Only two percent of lung cancer cases occur in people forty-five years old or younger; might Ruthie not be as lucky now as she was unlucky before? Perhaps she would achieve her goal of surviving until Hannah's high school graduation in 2011.

Her old schoolmate Stephanie Toney Simpson ran into Ruthie at a football game during Hannah's senior year.

"I have been feeling so bad, and I know things have been progressing, and I know things are happening, and I won't be here as long as I want to be," she told Stephanie. "I'm asking you to pray for me to stay alive long enough to see Hannah graduate."

"I will pray that for you, Ruthie," Stephanie said. "But I will also pray that God will let you live to see all your girls graduate."

"I guess I'm selling myself short, huh?" Ruthie said.

Every time Stephanie spoke to Ruthie after that, Ruthie would assure her, "I'm going to make it!" Ruthie was still going strong that fall when her family reached an emotional milestone: Hannah was elected homecoming queen of West Feliciana High—just as her mother had been. Mam had been on the school's homecoming court in her senior year, nearly fifty years earlier. At halftime in the homecoming game, three generations of West Feliciana homecoming royalty stood on the football field together and received honors.

"It's quite an exciting thing for an old lady," Mam joked to a reporter for the Baton Rouge *Advocate*. "I'm very proud. I'm very humbled."

———

When Christmas came Ruthie wanted everything to be the same as it always had been with her family. She was thin and worn-out, but worked hard to make it a happy time. For many years Ruthie and Mam had had a tradition of lighting candles on every grave in the Starhill cemetery at dusk on Christmas Eve. That year Hannah recruited a few of her high school friends to help her, her mother, and Mam illuminate the darkness of the graveyard. It was for many folks a glorious thing to come home to Starhill after church on Christmas Eve and see hundreds of tiny flames hovering like winter fireflies over the graves of the dead.

At home the next morning Christmas was, reassuringly, the same as ever. Mike and Ruthie set the girls' presents out under the tree and phoned Mam and Paw to come over, as usual. And as it had happened every Christmas morning since Hannah was old enough to walk, Mam, Paw, Mike, and Ruthie sat by the tree watching the children run up the hall and see what Santa had left.

Two weeks into 2011 Ruthie had a new CT scan. Dr. Miletello noted a "marked worsening in the chest." This was the first time in nearly a year of treatment that Ruthie had not improved. The tumors had grown accustomed to the medicine. It was time for a fresh approach in che- motherapy. The new medicine worked, for a while.

That May we flew down from Philly for Hannah's high school grad- uation. She was the class co-valedictorian. The bleachers overlooking the football field filled with hundreds of parents and family members. We sang the alma mater ("Feliciana sons and daughters / Long have gathered there"), and settled in for the long graduation ritual. I sat next to Ruthie in the bleachers, watching her intently as they called Han- nah's name. I did not see my niece walk across the platform to receive her diploma; I was instead intently studying Ruthie's face, silently thanking God that she had lived to see this night. As hot and humid as it was that mid-May evening, Ruthie wore a herringbone woolen cap to hide her head, and a heavy purple shawl; in her cancer days even the warmest weather could not banish Ruthie's enduring chill.

"Hannah. Ruth. Leming," the announcer called over the PA. A broad smile bloomed on Ruthie's withered face. I could only guess what that moment meant to her. By that time, fifteen months after her diagnosis, over eighty percent of lung cancer patients are dead. That night was a stellar triumph for Ruthie. Stephanie Simpson ran into her at the ceremony and said, "You made it!"

"I did!" Ruthie said. "I did!"

We celebrated Ruthie's forty-second birthday that Sunday at Magnolia Café, St. Francisville's main hangout. The Mag is a rambling old wooden house that sprawls under a shady live oak grove. We all sat at our table in the Mag's spacious back room—which is to say, on St. Francisville's screened porch—our iced teas sweating in front of us, trying to forget our fear of the future, and simply to be grateful that Ruthie had lived to see another birthday. Julie and I gave her a triple bouquet of pink, orange, yellow, and purple tulips and a chantilly cream cake topped with berries. Looking today at the photos of that party, the thing you notice is how pinched Ruthie's face was, especially her eyes. Ruthie was so good at putting everyone at ease that none of us grasped how much physical pain she was in.

When Dr. Miletello saw her only two weeks later he was seriously troubled by her condition. The tumors had grown a great deal. Once again he would have to try something new. She was so sick by that time that the oncologist had to withhold another round of chemo long enough to give her frail body time to recover.

"Though I didn't tell her, that was when I started praying for her to make it to Christmas," Dr. Miletello says.

"We weren't expecting that news," Mike says. "It was very tough on Ruthie. She thought she was getting better. She was so upset by the shock of it. When the nurse came in to give her a shot, Ruthie broke down in tears.

Meanwhile Stephanie Lemoine received PET scan news the same day—and hers was upbeat. Her tumors were fading. "I knew she would be happy for me," Stephanie recalls, "but having gotten a text from her earlier that day with bad news, I couldn't bring myself to tell her."

Stephanie sent Ruthie flowers, then broke the news to her. Ruthie's response: "Thank you so much for telling me. Your news uplifts me so."

Stephanie was cancer-free and had no need to return to the chemo room. But she kept going every week—for Ruthie's appointments. She refused to leave her friend's side.

————

In that fateful June visit Dr. Miletello urged Ruthie and Mike to go on a family vacation before she began a new round of chemotherapy. What he didn't say was that if and when this next chemo regimen failed, there would be nothing left for Ruthie but hospice care. Ruthie and Mike gathered their girls around the kitchen table in Starhill and brainstormed. What about the East Coast? Ruthie had always wanted to go to the East Coast. True, she had visited us in New York City when Claire was a baby, but that didn't really count. She wanted to feel the Atlantic on her bare feet. In late July they picked Charleston, South Carolina, pointed their big black Ford eastward, and drove.

Hannah remembers the drive as difficult, and not just because smoke from Florida marsh fires that summer made breathing especially hard for Ruthie.

In the car Hannah felt the tension between her mother and herself. It was the same old things: the rebelliousness, the anxiety, the fear, the anger, the boyfriend with a bad attitude. Even if Hannah could have articulated her problems, she couldn't have spoken them aloud.

"Mom, why can't we just be happy?" Hannah would say.

"I don't know," Ruthie would reply, "Why *can't* we just be happy?"

They went on like this, all the way to South Carolina.

The Lemings arrived in Charleston, checked into a hotel, and set out to explore the harbor and the historic downtown. One afternoon Ruthie stayed in the upstairs bedroom of their suite, too tired to sightsee. Mike, Claire, and Rebekah went for a walk. Hannah sat alone in the courtyard, overwhelmed by sadness.

There was her mother, upstairs in the hotel suite. There she was, downstairs, alone, isolated. They were on vacation together and couldn't stand to be in the same room. Why? A fresh wave of anger welled up in Hannah's heart, and broke across her face in tears.

Ruthie saw her role as fixer of her family's problems. Hannah wanted her mother to quit trying to fix things and simply to listen to her. Ruthie found this difficult. That afternoon in Charleston Hannah slipped back inside the hotel room and climbed into her bed to sob. Ruthie heard her come in, let herself into her daughter's room, and sat on the edge of the bed.

Ruthie said nothing, only rubbed her oldest child's back, just like she had done throughout Hannah's childhood whenever Hannah was inconsolable. She didn't try to fix anything. She just caressed the distraught young woman, her firstborn. What must Ruthie have thought, drawing her thin, cold, dry hands across her daughter's supple back? Did she remember that she too had been in South Carolina in her seventeenth summer, in a hotel room near Fort Jackson, there to see Mike graduate from basic training? How different her life was from Hannah's at seventeen. Back then Ruthie felt at home in the world as she found it, had met the man she knew she would marry, and had her life set out before her. Ruthie possessed a confidence—rare in a seventeen-year-old—that comes from knowing who she was and what she wanted from life. And now Ruthie and her family could barely see the road in front of them.

Finally, in the cool of her hotel bedroom, Hannah opened her heart to her mother.

She confessed that she had been lying to Ruthie and Mike about where she had been going when she left the house. She had been secretly meeting the boyfriend she had been forbidden to see, and felt guilty about it.

"Mama, I've been so ungrateful for you," she cried. "I know how much you love me, and I'm so ashamed of the way I've been acting. Mama, I can't—I just love you so much. I love you so, so much, Mama." Hannah also disclosed to Ruthie how much anxiety and self-loathing she lived with. How she would go to bed at night tormented by her sins and failings. Ruthie was shocked.

"I had no idea, I had no idea," Ruthie said to her daughter. "How do you live like that? I can't believe you had to go through this, and I didn't know."

Things were better after that. That night at dinner they held each other's hand. They were connected again. Was it perfect? No. But the healing had begun.

After four days in Charleston the family drove out to Hilton Head and hit the beach. Everyone agrees that the rest of the vacation was wonderful. Though Ruthie's stark physical decline was undeniable, Mike wouldn't allow himself to think that this might be the family's last vacation together. These thoughts usually came to him driving home from chemo treatments, when Ruthie would fall asleep in the truck. His mind would wander. *I could be left here by myself,* he would think. As a firefighter his vocation is to save lives. Watching the love of his life taken, bit by bit, by death left Mike, a strapping, six-foot-tall war hero, feeling humiliated by powerlessness.

He banished these thoughts at Hilton Head. All he allowed himself to see was the sun, the sand, his true love and their girls. All he allowed himself to see was the blessing of the present moment. That's what Ruthie wanted.

———

As summer ripened and faded toward fall my morning and evening calls to Mam and Paw took on a darker, more desperate tone. At Ruthie's house one afternoon, Mam rubbed her back to comfort her, and nearly withdrew her hand in shock; she could feel the sharp edge of Ruthie's bones through her shirt. Ruthie took such care to keep up appearances, and was often successful, through her genial spirit and clever sleight-of-wardrobe, in making everyone around her disbelieve their eyes. But she could not lie to her mother's hands.

The phone message to me from Starhill was the same, day after day: *We're losing her.*

One late summer afternoon after Sunday dinner, Ruthie and Mam sat on Mam's back porch, by themselves. Ruthie sat quietly, staring at the ground. Mam could tell she had something on her mind. Then a single tear rolled down Ruthie's right cheek.

"Mama," Ruthie said, "if things don't work out like we want them to, I need to know that you will help Mike raise our girls."

"Ruthie, you know I would. You don't even have to ask."

"No, I need to hear you say it."

Mam made that vow.

"Good. I just needed to hear you say it, Mama."

One early September afternoon Ruthie's feet hurt intensely, so Mam sat with her on the couch at Ruthie's place, massaging her daughter's feet. Suddenly, for no apparent reason, they both burst into tears. Not a word passed between them. Several minutes later mother and daughter gathered themselves, wiped their eyes, and resumed their conversation.

"Ruthie," Mam said resolutely, "this does not mean your mama is giving up hope."

"Me neither, Mama. We just needed to cry."

That August Hannah moved into the dorm at LSU to start her first year of college. Ruthie was thrilled that Hannah had settled on LSU, because it was so close to home. She wanted to be part of Hannah's big moving day. "I hope Hannah's not on the third floor," Ruthie told Mam that morning. "But if she is, Mike says he'll carry me up the stairs, and I'll help her get the room set up."

As it turned out Hannah's room was on the ground floor. But Ruthie was still so exhausted after walking from the parking lot that she could only sit quietly while Hannah and her father carried her things in.

By then Ruthie could no longer hide how much she was hurting. Tim Lindsey checked in to ask if she needed more pain medication. He had given her a prescription for Lortab, a strong, hydrocodone-based painkiller, months earlier. She barely used it.

"I'm so nervous about that stuff," Ruthie told her doctor. "I just don't want to get used to the Lortab."

"Ruthie!" said Tim, shocked that a cancer patient as advanced as she was would worry about addiction. "Ruthie! Are you hurting?"

"Yeah, I'm hurting."

"Do they help?"

"Oh yeah, they help. I just don't want to take more than one a day."

"What pharmacy do you use, because I'm calling it in."

Tim also phoned in a prescription for a medicine cancer patients call "magic mouthwash," which takes away pain from mouth ulcers. A few nights later Tim received a text from Ruthie:

> Magic mouthwash is wonderful! I've also been taking Lortab more, which helps. If only there were something for hand and foot syndrome, I would be set. ;) THANK YOU FOR ALWAYS CHECKING ON ME!

Around the same time I made my customary phone call to Mam and Paw on my way in to the office one morning. Mam was in an especially anxious mood.

"Ruthie told us she's been having dreams," Mam said. "Julia came to her, and Mullay, and Dede." These were, respectively, Mam's sister, who died of cancer at forty-two, and our paternal grandparents, both long dead.

"What did they say in the dreams?" I asked Mam.

"Nothing. Ruthie said they just smiled at her."

I thought, *They're coming to help her get ready to die.*

That night I called Ruthie to confirm the story.

"Yeah, they came," she said, as matter-of-factly as if the deceased kinfolks had dropped by for coffee.

"All at once?" I asked.

"No, I had three dreams."

"What did they say?"

"Nothing. They just smiled at me, and looked real peaceful."

"Do you think maybe they've come to, you know, prepare you for something?" I said, uneasily.

"Nope," she said. "I really don't think so."

I believed these dreams were real, but I did not believe they were meaningless. Back in 1990, when my mom's sister Julia was in the hospital being treated for cancer, my paternal grandmother Mullay, dead for fourteen years, came to me in a vivid dream. She told me to go to Julia and tell her death was nothing to fear. I did as I was told. Julia was gone within days.

This is why I took Ruthie's dreams seriously, even if she didn't. I believed she was going to die soon. But when? Would I have time to see her? I hoped so. I wanted to save my vacation time and my money for one last visit from our family. Maybe Christmas? Yes, Christmas.

On Monday, September 12, I called Ruthie to check on her. "I'm feeling pretty good," she told me, which I knew was a lie. As usual she didn't want me to worry.

We talked about Hannah. I told her I was worried that Hannah wasn't coming home often enough. Though she had been at college for only a few weeks, Hannah had spent most of the summer at camp and at the beach, away from her mother. Now, even though her mother was in steep physical decline, and her dorm at LSU was only half an hour away, Hannah never came.

Judging by my conversations with Mam and Paw, and the eerie dreams, I was concerned that Ruthie could die any day, leaving Hannah crushed with regret and self-recrimination. But I didn't dare speak that plainly to Ruthie.

"Oh, don't be worried," Ruthie said dismissively. "Hannah's doing what she needs to be doing. I want her to be at college, having fun."

I knew this wasn't true either. Mam and Paw had shared with me their worries over how much Ruthie missed seeing Hannah. But I also knew that Ruthie had intentionally made it easy on Hannah to run from the catastrophe at home. She didn't want Hannah to suffer. *But how much will Hannah suffer if you die and she didn't come home?* I thought.

I phoned Hannah the next night, determined to urge her to go home to see her mother. I knew it was a delicate matter, and if she told Ruthie I had intervened, Ruthie would fuss at me. After talking about her classes, and how she was adjusting to college life, I asked her how often she was able to go home to see her mom.

"I don't want to talk about it, Uncle Rod!" she shot back. "Just stop!"

I tried again, but she cut me off. The girl was plainly terrified. There was nothing left to say.

The next day Julie and I went with the kids out to the rolling hills of Bucks County, north of Philadelphia, to look at a Colonial-era farm-house we were thinking of renting. It seemed like a perfect place for us, and our family was excited about the prospect of moving out of the city. We loved the house and the grounds, and left it that afternoon assuming that signing the lease was a formality we could execute in a day or two.

Down in Louisiana Ruthie spent that day with Claire and Rebekah, who had the day off from school. Stephanie Lemoine, her chemo buddy, texted her that morning inviting her to come to Baton Rouge that night for a women's spirituality class and talk led by Sister Dulce at her retreat center chapel. Ruthie and Mike had been to see Sister once since their first visit. Sister had prayed that time with Ruthie, and asked that God's will be done. That day in September Ruthie thought it might do her good to be with Sister again. Sister always made her feel good.

Ruthie texted Abby to ask if she would be willing to drive. Abby was all in. The best friends had not seen much of each other in recent months. Abby had met a man, a lawyer named Doug Cochran, and fallen in love. Doug lived in Baton Rouge, which meant Abby was around St. Francisville less often. Ruthie was thrilled for Abby, but it was hard not to see Abby's smiling face and hear her sassy talk as often. When they spoke Ruthie confessed to Abby that she was tired and lonely. Nobody was coming around to see her much anymore. My sister was alone for long stretches of the day when Mike was at work and the girls were at school.

When Abby came by that evening, Mike showed her how to work Ruthie's oxygen tank. By that point, Ruthie could barely breathe on her own. And off they went to Baton Rouge.

"All the way down, we talked about how she was feeling, her chemo, and the chemo nurses," Abby recalls. "We talked about all her friends— the ones who came to see her, and the ones who couldn't make it."

Ruthie was exhausted, and feeling miserable. Abby dropped her and her oxygen tank off at the chapel door, and drove off to park the car. Stephanie had arrived earlier, and saved a seat for Ruthie in the back of the chapel so Ruthie could leave easily if she became too tired.

"All of a sudden, I felt a little light tap on my shoulder, and I turned around, and there was that angel's face," Stephanie remembers.

Ruthie, Abby, and Stephanie sat together, and listened to Sister Dulce's talk. Neither Abby nor Stephanie remembers what the nun said. When she finished Stephanie asked Ruthie if she would like Sister to pray over her. Ruthie said she would.

Sister ran her hands under Ruthie's shirt to feel her body. "We need to get you well," the nun said. "Honey, you can't worry about this cancer."

"No, ma'am," Ruthie said. "I'm not."

Sister prayed quietly over Ruthie, then said good-bye. After the service Abby brought the car around to pick up Ruthie, who was standing at the chapel door talking to Stephanie.

"Ruthie," Stephanie said, "I don't know why we met, but I know we met for a reason."

Ruthie smiled, and said, "It's God."

On the drive home Ruthie was animated, even excited.

"Wasn't it weird how Sister talked about all the things we talked about on the way down?" Ruthie asked.

Abby wasn't sure what Ruthie meant, or even if they had heard the same talk. To Abby it had been simply a general sermon about the spiritual life. Ruthie, though, believed Sister answered all the questions weighing on her mind that night, and that that had been an incredible grace.

That night in bed Ruthie and Mike stayed up late talking about Sister Dulce.

"She was feeling so bad. It wasn't an easy trip, but it was a good one for her," Mike says. "She told me that Sister is an amazing woman, and the things she talked about made her feel peaceful."

"Peace," Mike says. "That night Ruthie had peace."

CHAPTER TEN

"I'm Scared"

The next morning—September 15, 2011—Paw left before daylight with his friend Hershel Morris, headed to visit a sick pal in north Louisiana who had been their LSU classmate half a century ago. Paw's usual habit was to pick the morning paper up out by the road, deliver it to Mike and Ruthie, and drink a cup of coffee with them. Not this morning, though.

Ruthie woke up feeling out of sorts. She told Mike she wouldn't be able to ride with him to take Rebekah and Claire to school. That was unusual, Mike thought. Ruthie always pushed herself to take that ride. But on this morning she made the kids' lunches, and wrote her daily notes to the girls. Since she became ill Ruthie had been penning short, encouraging messages to her children, and leaving them in their lunch boxes. That way they would know that Mama was with them throughout the day.

The girls kissed their mother good-bye, climbed with their father into the Excursion, and left for school. Mam planned to go to Zachary that morning with her friend Kay Graves to get her hair done. Mam's hairdresser, Big Show's wife, Jan, customarily held a Friday morning slot for Mam, but this week Jan changed the appointment.

166

Mam rang Ruthie to see if she wanted anything from the store, besides cat food.

"No, ma'am, the cat food is all I need," Ruthie said.

"Do you need me to come over?" Mam asked, worried by how weak Ruthie sounded.

"No, I'm going to lie down for a few minutes and get some rest before we go down to get my blood work done."

"Okay, good. I'll see you later, then. Love you."

After dropping the girls off Mike figured that if Ruthie was sleeping in, he had time to stop by the fire station north of town to check out the new four-hundred-thousand-dollar rig that was both a rescue truck and a pumper. He wheeled in, said hello to the men, poured himself a cup of coffee, and gave the gleaming red truck an admiring once-over. After an hour or so Mike said good-bye and headed home to be with Ruthie.

When he arrived Mike walked to the back of the house and stuck his head in the bedroom. Ruthie was awake, but still in bed. She said she would join him up front shortly. Mike excused himself, went to the living room, sat on the sofa, and picked up the newspaper. Their routine was to sit together on the couch, read the paper, and talk about the day ahead. That morning Ruthie shuffled up the hall in her pajamas, sat down next to her husband, and did what she did every other morning.

After resting quietly on the couch for a while, Ruthie lunged forward and began coughing violently. Mike saw a startling amount of blood pouring from her mouth. She had coughed up blood before, but nothing like this.

"I'm having trouble breathing," she rasped. "Turn my oxygen up." Mike did, but the blood kept coming. Ruthie tried to wipe it away with tissues, but couldn't keep up with the flow. Mike retrieved the pulse oximeter to check the oxygen level in her blood.

"I can't breathe!" Ruthie gasped. "I can't breathe!"

The oximeter reading was eighty-four—far below the normal measure. Mike knew this was a real emergency and phoned Tim, who was with a patient. He left a tense voicemail.

"Hey, Tim, it's Mike," he said. "Ruthie's having a real tough time breathing. Bleeding a lot. Her oxygen is about eighty-four, eighty-five. Just wanted to . . . see what we needed to do. Thanks."

Ruthie choked out words conveying to Mike that she couldn't breathe at all. "Call nine-one-one!" she rasped. Mike was alarmed before, but now he was terrified. He ran to the kitchen, made the call, and before he could get off the phone heard the fire department dispatch notice go out on his police radio. Mike darted into the living room to look in once more on Ruthie, still on the couch. She was struggling to catch her breath, drowning in her own blood as the main tumor was most likely knifing through an artery in her lung.

Mike, panicked and feeling helpless, dashed back into the kitchen and phoned the fire station where he had just visited, to tell the rescuers that the call was for *his* wife, and to please, for God's sake, hurry. He hung up, shot back to the living room, and saw the love of his life, spattered with blood and terrified. For the first time since they had begun this journey, Mike saw fear in Ruthie's big brown eyes.

"I'm scared," she whispered. Then Ruthie fell forward, into her husband's arms, and died.

"Ruthie!" he screamed. "Don't leave me!"

Mike, a trained EMT, put Ruthie on the floor and began CPR, but he knew it was too late. The paramedics arrived, pulled him away from Ruthie's body, and began working on her.

Across the road from Ruthie and Mike's place, Ronnie Morgan was at home when he heard the emergency dispatch on the police radio. He knew this was the call he had been dreading for nineteen months. He followed the paramedics in through the front door. Seeing Ruthie's body on her living room floor, all Ronnie could think about was the child whose diapers he had changed. *She was like one of his own,* he thought. *And this is how it ends for that sweet little girl.*

Ronnie hustled Mike into the kitchen, away from the grim scene unfolding. Mike telephoned Mam, who was twenty minutes away in Zachary. Mam was loading Ruthie's cat food into the back of her SUV when the call came through. Mike was crying so hard Mam had trouble understanding him.

"Mam, Ruthie's in trouble," he choked out. "Come home quick."

Moments later the phone rang at the Leming house. It was Tim Lindsey returning Mike's earlier call.

"She's dead! She's gone! My Ruthie's gone!" Mike shrieked. "The ambulance is here. I've been doing CPR on her. She passed out. I put her on the floor. She's gone. She's gone..."

Mike was screaming so loud Tim had to hold the receiver away from his ear.

"I'm on my way," Tim said.

Tim jumped into his pickup and flew south to Starhill. Meanwhile in the Walmart parking lot Mam had pulled the SUV around to the entrance and waited on Kay Graves to come out of the store with her bags.

"Hurry, Katie!" she yelled through the open window. "Something's wrong with Ruthie!"

Kay swung the side door open and threw in her plastic bags so hard that they burst. She jumped into the passenger side and hit the button to turn on the flashers. They sped away. Within minutes Mam hit Highway 61, turned sharply north, and pushed her big Ford as hard as it would go. The speedometer, Kay noticed, read 120 miles per hour.

Mam's mobile phone rang. Because Kay and Mam have an understanding that neither will speak on the phone while driving, Mam told her friend that she would have to answer it. It was Ronnie. He asked to speak to Mam.

"She can't talk, Ronnie, she's driving."

"It's Ruthie," Ronnie said. "She's not here at the house. They took her to the hospital. Tim thought that was the best place for her."

"Ronnie, are you telling me that she's gone?"

"Yeah, she's gone."

Kay ended the call and asked Mam if she understood what had just been said.

"Yes," Mam said flatly.

"Dottie, do you need me to drive?"

"No," said Mam. "You drive like a grammaw. I need you to call Ray and tell him."

"But Dottie—"

"I'm driving! You call him."

Kay looked out her window at the sky, and said silently to God, *I'm about to tell a man that his daughter is dead, and You are going to have to help me do this.* She dialed Paw's number.

"Ray," she said, "this is Kay."

"Yeah, baby, what you need?"

"Ray, Ruthie is gone. She's gone, Ray. Do you understand what I'm telling you?"

There was silence.

"Ray, take a deep breath. Tell me, do you understand what I've just said?"

"Yeah," Paw whispered. "Yeah, I do."

"Do you have somebody with you?"

"Yes."

"Go to the West Feliciana Hospital. That's where she is."

Paw started to cry.

"Ray, I love you."

"I love you too, Katie."

Tim passed the ambulance on Highway 61, on its way to the hospital. When he got to Starhill there was Mike, sitting on the front porch in a rocking chair, with his head in his hands. Ronnie Morgan and his wife, Carolyn, were there with him. As Tim approached Mike broke down in tears.

"She's gone. She's died. My baby's gone."

Mam wheeled her white SUV into the gravel in front of Ruthie's house, slammed on the brakes, jumped out, and demanded, "Where's my baby?!" She did not remember—or more likely, could not accept—the telephone conversations that had just taken place in her presence. Maybe Ruthie would be there after all. Maybe her body wasn't really at the hospital.

Carolyn tried to embrace Mam, but Mam brushed past and stood before Mike, who sat on a chair, hunched forward.

"Mike, we need to go to the hospital to be with Ruthie," Mam said. "You want me to take you?"

Tim told Mam that Ruthie had passed away. For the first time Mam understood this nightmare was for real.

"I knew this day was coming," Mam wailed. "Oh, my baby, my baby. My Mike, my Mike. Come here, baby. We lost our Ruthie."

Mam took Mike into her arms.

"Where is my baby, Tim?" she asked. "I want to see her."

"Listen," Tim said, deflecting the question. "They're taking her to the hospital. They're doing CPR. They're doing everything they can do. Mike said it was really, really bad, Miss Dot, but she hasn't been pronounced. We're going to go to the hospital, and we're going to see. But I'm really distressed about this situation, and I don't think there's going to be a good outcome."

Kay turned to Mam and said, "Honey, she's in a better place now. She's not hurting. Let's go to town and tell her good-bye."

Mam and Kay helped Mike climb into Mam's Ford. The three of them drove on to the hospital in St. Francisville, with Tim following. Nobody said a word.

At some point Tim called Laura at home and told her Ruthie was dead. She jumped into her Suburban and headed out to Starhill. She passed Mam and Mike driving north, with Tim behind them, signaling for Laura to call him. On the phone Tim told her to head out to school to pick up Claire and Rebekah.

Laura phoned the office at Bains Elementary and asked to speak to Dot Temple, the principal, who is also Abby's mother.

"She's in a meeting."

"No, I need to speak to Mrs. Temple," Laura insisted.

"She's in a meeting."

"No, I have to talk to Mrs. Temple *right now*."

"Why?"

"I have to talk to her! Please go get her, it's an emergency."

Dot Temple came on the line. "Mrs. Temple," Laura said, "Ruthie is dead. We need to get Rebekah. I have to get Abby too, but she won't answer her cell phone."

As it happened Tim had already reached Abby by phone and had her secretary put the call through to her office at the high school.

"You know, Ruthie is very sick," Tim said.

"Yeah, is there something new?"

"She died this morning."

"What?! But I just saw her. Where is she? What happened?"

"Abby, her body was just so tired. I'm so, so sorry."

Abby's shock was genuine. She had been with Ruthie the night before. She knew Ruthie was on a steady decline, she had lost hope a long time ago that Ruthie was going to receive a miracle cure, but she was still poleaxed by the news. Because Ruthie didn't believe she was going to die anytime soon, Abby let herself believe it too.

And now her best friend was dead.

Tim said, "I need you to go get the girls."

"Do they know?"

"No."

"Do you want me to tell them?"

"No, just get them to the hospital and I'll tell them. Laura's coming to get you."

Abby went to Maria Peterson, the secretary for the principal, with tears in her eyes.

"I'm leaving, Maria. Ruthie's dead."

Maria broke down. The receptionist from the front office walked in, and was told the news. She too burst into tears.

When Abby walked out of her office, there was Laura, waiting and weeping. They embraced, then walked resolutely out to the car, and drove down the Bains Road to the elementary school to pick up Rebekah.

Everyone in the office at Rebekah's school knew. When Bek came out Abby told her that her mother was at the hospital, and that she and Miss Laura had come to pick her up. Abby could not contain her grief, so Laura took control, talking to Bek in an easygoing, motherly way that gave not the slightest hint of what awaited Ruthie's children. *Thank God Laura is here,* Abby thought.

Then it was off to the middle school. Laura and Bek stayed in the car while Abby went in to get Claire. Claire was at PE and had to change. Nobody at the middle school knew yet. Abby worried that the news would get onto Facebook immediately and that was how Hannah would learn.

When Claire emerged Abby told her Ruthie was at the hospital and they needed to get there. On the short drive into town the girls remained calm, quiet, and tearless. *They look like innocent puppies,* Laura thought.

Tim arrived at the hospital and met the physician on duty, who said, "Doc, she was a DOA. They're still performing CPR, but it's a moot point."

Tim said, "She's so sick. She's suffered. She's gone. Please call the code."

Ruthie Leming was now officially dead. Tim went into the room where they had her body. It was not a pretty sight, from the hemorrhaging, and the swelling from the violence of the rescue efforts. Tim and the hospital staff discussed cleaning Ruthie's body up and making her presentable for good-byes.

Standing outside the room where staffers worked on Ruthie's body, Mam demanded to see her daughter. They told her she couldn't, not yet.

"I'm telling you that I want to see my child," she insisted. Someone from the hospital led Mam and Mike to a waiting room and asked them to please be patient. Finally they were invited in. Mike went in first. And then Mam followed.

She was not prepared to see her daughter looking so beautiful, and so peaceful. Ruthie's struggle was over at last. Mam leaned in and pressed her cheek to Ruthie's. It was still warm.

"Ruthie," she spoke into her ear, "I'm going to keep my promise. I'm going to help Mike and the girls. I'm going to keep my promise." Then she sat down next to the man her daughter loved above all others, and they grieved together.

When Laura and Abby drove with the Leming girls into the hospital parking lot, Tim was outside waiting to receive them. Tim understood that Mike, still grieving at Ruthie's side, was in no state to break the news to his children, so he appointed himself to stand in.

The Suburban came to an abrupt stop next to where Tim stood, trying to summon the courage to speak the awful truth on the worst day of these children's lives. Claire and Rebekah climbed out of the Suburban. Tim took a knee. Claire stood in front of him. Bekah stood by Laura.

"Where's Mama?" Claire asked.

"I'm so, so sorry, my sweet girls," said Tim. "Mama has died."

The girls were in shock. They had not imagined, they could not have imagined, that this was coming. Ruthie had protected them from the thought, reckoning there would be time to make them ready. Bekah wept in Laura's arms. Claire collapsed into Abby.

"What am I going to do without a mama?" Claire said. "I can't be without a mama."

"I know," said Tim.

"Where's Daddy? Where's Daddy? *Where's Daddy?!*" Claire asked. Tim, Laura, and Abby led them down the gauntlet of sobbing friends and family, into the hospital room where their father abided with what remained of their mother.

Claire and Bekah wanted to embrace their mother's body, but they were frightened. *Is this really Mama?* Claire thought. Ruthie's face was visible, and a blanket covered her body. Their father, consumed by grief and fear, could not comfort them. All he could say was, "I'm alone. My baby's gone." Claire was scared. She had never seen her daddy like this. Her big, strong daddy looked small, weak, lost, and frightened. The world was turned upside down.

The sisters took in the full vision of their mother, her face pale, cold, dead on a hospital bed. Turning from it they threw themselves into their father's arms. "I'm going to be so alone," he cried. Rebekah turned away from her father, then stood at the foot of Ruthie's bed, saying, "Wake up, Mama. Wake up! Mama, don't go, please don't go."

As Paw began the three-hour drive home, he tried to call me in Philadelphia, but couldn't get through. Julie was at the weekly home-schooling co-op class with the kids when he reached her by phone.

"Ruthie's not doing well at all, and I can't get Rod," he said. She could tell from the tone in his voice that he was scared.

"Don't you worry about it. I'll get him," Julie said. "I love you."

At our apartment in Philadelphia I heard the text alert ding on my iPhone as I walked into the living room from the shower. It was from my wife.

"CALL ME STAT!" it read.

Seconds later Julie was on the phone. "Something's really wrong with Ruthie. You need to call your dad right this second. He's on his cell phone."

I hung up, then punched in Paw's number.

Paw's voice sounded dry and fragile. "Son," he said, "your sister is dead."

I told him I would catch the next plane home.

Julie was still at the co-op classes with the kids when I phoned her with the news. She said they would be right home. I took my icon of Christ from the mantel, knelt with it on the floor, and prayed for the peace of Ruthie's soul. I prayed for strength for our mother and father, suffering this morning what no parent should have to endure. I prayed the same for Mike and his children, and for their friends. So many mornings and so many evenings, I had prayed against this day. But also, from the time I lay in Ruthie's bed after her diagnosis and felt a divine presence tell me that she would not survive, but that all would be well, I prayed for the grace to accept the will of God. Once again I asked God for that grace. Then I booked a flight and packed a bag.

Julie and the children came home, wrecked. Lucas was especially bereft. "Y'all come down when you can," I said, then told them good-bye, and caught a train for the airport.

When the train rolled into Thirtieth Street Station in downtown Philly, I reached Tim by phone. He said Ruthie had passed quickly, that everyone was hard hit, but all was well. I knew all couldn't be well on this most terrible of mornings. But I also knew that wall of love surrounding my family in this crisis was rock solid, and would not be breached.

As the plane took off I stared out the window at the receding city of Philadelphia, fingering the knots on my prayer rope, quietly reciting, "Lord Jesus Christ, have mercy on me, a sinner."

For the first time in all my life I was going home and Ruthie would not be there. Ruthie, the anchor, the fastness, the tower and the ark that would carry our West Feliciana family into another generation. Long ago I accepted that I would never settle there, and I always felt ever more free to roam the world over, knowing that Ruthie would always be present on the ridge in Starhill. I would often think about the years to come, when both of us, grown gray-haired and plump, would gather for Thanksgiving with our children and grandchildren, playing where we had played, thinking as children do that it will all last forever. Ruthie, the matriarch and successor, the sustainer of the fields and the pond and the trees and the hollows of our father's land, the upholder of tradition and the guarantor that, however far away I or my children or my children's children strayed, they would always have a refuge in the Felicianas. Where Ruthie was, there was our home.

Not anymore. *She is gone, she is gone,* I thought. *What will become of us now? What is required of me? Lord Jesus Christ, son of God, have mercy on me, a sinner.*

At West Feliciana Middle School Principal Ben Necaise called the eighth-grade teachers together in Rae Lynne Thomas's classroom. He shut the door, looked at them all, and said in a calm, measured voice, "I just want to let y'all know Ruthie passed. Take as much time as you need to do what you have to do. We'll cover your classes for you." Ruthie's devastated friends and colleagues gathered their things and headed south to the hospital. Ben Necaise was true to his word; the school staff had the teachers' backs, freeing Ruthie's friends to be present for each other, and for Ruthie's family.

Ronnie Morgan thought it was a mercy that neither Paw nor Mam were at home in Starhill that morning and compelled to see what they could never unsee. It didn't feel that way to Paw, though, as he endured a three-hour car ride to his dead daughter's bedside. Hershel, who drove, had lost his adult daughter several years earlier, in a car accident.

"Chief, you know what it's like," Paw said. "You lost your daughter."

"Yeah, that's right," said Hershel.

He understood what Paw was going through. He also knew that a man sometimes just needs to be alone with his thoughts. Some hurt is beyond the reach of words. They drove on in silence.

Paw and Hershel crossed the river at Vidalia and headed south through Mississippi on Highway 61. Meanwhile Hannah was at LSU sitting in biology class with her mobile phone turned off. When class ended she started walking toward her French class and checked her messages on the way. She knew something was wrong when she saw so many calls stacked up in her voicemail. And there was a text from her father: "Mom's not good, come home."

She panicked. She called Michael Steele, an LSU friend from St. Francisville, and asked him to drive her home because something terrible had happened to her mother. Michael ran at once to Hannah's dorm, took her keys, loaded her into her Jeep, turned on the emergency flashers, and raced out of town.

Hannah was hysterical, screaming and sobbing.

"Hannah, calm down!" Michael said. "I can't drive if you're like this." He told her to lay the seat back and get hold of herself. Hannah's mind reeled. She thought about how much she wanted to tell Mama that she loved her. How sorry she was to have been so ungrateful. How much she had always wanted to be able to love others as unselfishly as she did. Would she have the chance to say these things to her mother now? She hoped so. *Please God, just let me tell her.*

In the haste to get to the hospital Michael pushed Hannah's rattle-trap Jeep so hard that its radiator blew halfway to St. Francisville. He piloted the Jeep to the shoulder, steam billowing from under its hood. At that very moment a middle-aged couple pulled over behind them in a pickup truck. They opened Hannah's passenger door and saw her lying prone and tearful.

"Are you sick? Are you sick? Where are you going?"

"To the hospital. My mom is dying."

"Come on, we'll take you."

Hannah and Michael climbed into the backseat of the truck. The man and the woman asked them if they were Christians. Yes, they said. The couple prayed for Hannah's mother as she rocked back and forth, crying and trying to calm herself for the scene at the hospital.

In the room with Ruthie's body Laura continued to keep watch over Claire and Rebekah. Claire couldn't stop crying. At one point she looked at Laura and asked, "Can I go get a sip of water?"

"Yeah, baby, come on," said Laura.

"I mean, is it okay for me to leave?"

That was Claire, thought Laura. Claire would never leave her mama. When Ruthie was so sick, and Mike would be working Saturday nights at the fire station, Claire turned down invitations to do fun things with friends. She chose instead to stay home with Mama and watch movies, or play games. Anything to keep Mama from feeling alone. Even now, in death, Claire was faithful.

"Miss Laura, this was such a normal day," Claire said. "Mama had my lunch box ready. She kissed me ten times on my hand. I walked out the door and she said, 'I can't wait to see you when you get home.' It was a normal day. She told me good luck on my test, and I left."

Panic crossed Claire's face.

"My note! Where is my lunch box? Every day she writes me a note and puts it in my lunch box. Omigod, omigod, I've got to go out to the car and get my lunch box!"

Claire and Laura ran down the hall, out the hospital door, and to the Suburban. Claire yanked open the passenger door, grabbed her lunch box, and opened it. There, on yellow Post-it paper, were her mother's final words to her:

Good luck on a super day of learning.
I can't wait until you get home so I can have a hug.
Love, Mom.

Claire wept. "She's not going to be there to hug me. I can't hug her again."

"Claire, listen to me," said Laura. "That just shows you that at seven thirty this morning, when your mama sent you out the door, she didn't know she was going to leave you. The first thing your mama said to y'all when she told you she had cancer was 'We're not going to be angry at God.' Baby, I don't believe you can be angry with God about this. You can't. The one thing that she is free of is her sickness and her cancer. The hardest thing for her to do in this world was to leave y'all. She would never choose to do that."

When Rebekah saw Claire had her note from Mama, she remembered that she had left her lunch box at school. Laura drove out to Bains Elementary, three miles north of town, fetched Bekah's lunch box, and delivered it to her in the hospital room. Ruthie's final words to Rebekah were:

Have a special day! Hugs and kisses. Love, Mom.

The Good Samaritans from the highway delivered Hannah and Michael to the hospital, and quietly drove away. Tim, Abby, and other friends and family stood at the front door to intercept her. As Hannah barreled toward the door, Abby grabbed her.

"I've got to get to my mom now!" Hannah shrieked.

"Hannah, your mom died," said Abby.

Hannah drew back. She banged her head and her fists into the pebble-studded hospital wall, then kicked a trash can. She wouldn't let anybody touch her. Hannah threw herself onto the ground and wailed.

When Kay Graves reached her, Hannah was sitting on the ground, her back against the hospital facade, refusing to go in.

"I can't do it!" she said. "I can't go in there!"

"Hannah," Kay said sternly, "You have to get it together. You are a grown woman now. You are the oldest sister. Your family needs you. Now you stand up, and pull it together, and go in there to your family."

Tim and Kay helped Hannah to her feet. Kay took one of Hannah's hands, and Abby took the other. They led her down the hall, past all her mother's friends. Mam met them by the nurses' station. Hannah screamed and threw herself into Mam's arms. Outside the door to the room stood Mike, sobbing so hard he could barely catch his breath. They embraced wordlessly. And then Hannah went in to be at her mother's side.

Mam met Paw in the hospital parking lot and together they went in to view for the first time together the body of their daughter. Abby sat with them, thinking that Mam and Paw were much stronger than she expected them to be. Mike and the girls, though—that sight, Abby felt, would break your heart. Mike was so shattered that when the eye bank called to confirm that Ruthie's wishes were to donate her eyes, Abby had to handle the arrangements.

After several hours at Ruthie's bedside, Mike had had enough. It was time to go home. Everyone stood around Ruthie's bed, holding hands, just like at Sunday dinner. Mike and Mam each had a free hand on Ruthie's body, completing the circle. They said the Lord's Prayer together. And then Mike and the girls left for Starhill. Mam refused to go until after doctors had harvested Ruthie's eyes.

Jan Curwick, the new Methodist pastor in town, said, "Miss Dot, you need to go home. You can't be here for this."

"Jan, I'm not leaving. I'm not leaving my child."

"Miss Dot, I promise you I will stay with her," Jan said. "I will never leave her side, and I will escort her to the hearse. I promise you that."

Mam meditated on it for a few minutes and agreed to trust Jan to stand in her place until the last. "She stood there for me," Mam later said. "That's love."

When Ruthie's family made it home, they found that their house had been cleaned and that the tables and counters sat piled high with food delivered by the townspeople, who streamed in and out the rest of the day. There, under the oak trees in the front yard, sat Hannah's Jeep. When the men at a Starhill garage heard about Ruthie's death, and Hannah's car trouble, they drove toward Baton Rouge, searching the shoulders until they found the broken-down Jeep. They towed it to their repair shop, installed a new radiator, and delivered it to the Leming place while everyone was still at the hospital.

John Bickham didn't get word of Ruthie's death until later in the day. It was a busy time for him at the Exxon refinery. He was in a control room, outside of mobile phone range, and missed Paw's call. When he finally heard the message he told his boss he needed to go. He wasn't sure how this would be received. According to the plant's strict regulations, an employee can't leave under those circumstances unless the dead person was an immediate family member.

"Look, I need to go. This is family to me," John told his supervisor. He was prepared to throw his badge down and quit on the spot if the answer was no. But John's boss told him to hit the road, that he would take care of John's work that day. John Bickham drove straight to Starhill, where he found Paw alone at home, grieving.

As the long afternoon dwindled down into evening, friends told Mike to take a break, but he refused. Hannah wanted to be alone, wanted everyone to get out of her mama's house. But she saw that her father needed their friends around him, that he drew strength from their presence. Abby would later reflect that she had never seen anything like this. People weren't coming by with grim faces to pay their dutiful respects. They were so strangely, unaccountably happy. And they didn't do the usual thing, which is stay for what seems like a decent interval before slouching home from the scene of heartbreak and grief. They stayed. They laughed. They told stories about Ruthie.

God, thought Abby, *would Ruthie love this.*

In late afternoon, when Tim finished with his schedule of patients, he drove out to Starhill to check on everybody.

Tim too was struck by merriment abounding. Yes, the Lemings' was a house in mourning, but everyone there—Ruthie's family and her circle of friends—were living in the bright sadness they had first seen around Ruthie when she met her cancer diagnosis with such hope and gratitude.

"It was just friends and family loving on one another, and rejoicing for Ruthie's life," Tim told Laura later that night. "It was like a celebration. They were laughing and crying, eating food, drinking beer. It was a celebration."

What had happened that day was too much for one person to bear alone, Tim thought. But they were all holding each other up.

Hannah did not realize until then how her mother had been the animating spirit of every party at their house. *She made everything so fun,* Hannah thought. *Why can't she be here with us, having fun now?*

When I made it to Starhill that night from the airport, I sat with my father at his house, trying to work up the courage to walk across the field and see Mike. Mam walked in from Mike's place, kissed me on the cheek, and said, "You can feel Ruthie's spirit strong over there." I took a deep breath, and headed out into the warm autumn evening.

Opening the door I found Abby and Mike sitting together at the kitchen table, mulling over the remains of the day. Strangely enough, in Ruthie's kitchen that night, it felt like every other night. There should have been no peace there, but there was peace, an overwhelming peace. There was pain and there was exhaustion, but above all, there was peace. Mam was right: Ruthie's spirit was there. The most terrible thing had happened, God knows, but somehow there was a sense of order, and purpose, and serenity. Just like Ruthie told us there would be.

CHAPTER ELEVEN

"The Choir Invisible"

The sun came up for the first time on Starhill without Ruthie in it. And there, knocking on Mam's back door that morning, was Jane Daniel.

Jane and her husband, Bobby, raised their family a mile up the road, just around the bend from the Starhill cemetery. Mam and Paw used to see their little boy Robert Edward—"Red" was his nickname—riding his bike on the blacktop road past our house. He was a sweet kid who became a good man. And then, in his twenties, five months after his wedding, Red died of leukemia.

Jane, who had been mourning her son for five years, knew what Mam was going through. That's why she came that morning.

"Everyone's heart was broken, but Jane knew exactly how my heart was broken," Mam recalls. "I don't remember what she said, but her presence was what really mattered. I knew what it took for her to come. I hope that if anybody else around here loses a child, that I will have the strength to do what Jane did for me that day."

Across the field at the Leming house, things weren't so somber. I dreaded walking back into the house where Ruthie had died not twenty-four hours before, to be around her shell-shocked widower and motherless children. It was startling, however, to find that Ruthie's spirit still ruled over her household. I walked in and found several of

Ruthie's friends in the kitchen with Mike, drinking coffee and sharing happy memories. After telling a tale of mischief at Thompson Creek, one of Ruthie's friends slapped me on the back and said, "Your sister loved her cold beer, and she loved having a good time."

That's the Ruthie everybody gathered at the Leming house talked about in those days after her death. Day and night friends crowded into Ruthie's kitchen, drinking beer, telling funny West Feliciana stories, and laughing hard. There was one account that featured the phrase, "You know his momma lost all her teeth, right?" There was a tale of Baton Rouge firefighters responding to a 911 call from an obese naked woman who had eaten jalapeño peppers and gotten aroused. An irate Mel Percy was wound up about how his blind dog got lost that morning and drowned in the pond out back. "You want to know which end of a dead dog floats?" groused Mel.

I suppose all this merrymaking the day after Ruthie died might have struck some as being in poor taste. In fact there could not have been a greater tribute to the woman Ruthie was, and the effect she had on those who loved her, than their gathering in her kitchen to eat, drink, and comfort each other.

Late in the evening, folks began to peel away and go home, leaving Mike and his children alone with the embers of the day. After saying goodnight and taking my leave, I walked back to Mam and Paw's across the field. I saw deer running in the moonlight and surprised a possum eating cat food outside Mam's workshop. *How beautiful it is here in the country,* I thought. For many years now, I have lived away from this place, and dined out telling stories of Southern Gothic lunacy. Never making fun of this place, but celebrating its strangeness, its particularity, and its peculiar joie de vivre.

But there is something more here, I thought. I had just spent the darkest day of the Dreher family's life in the house where my sister had just died, and yet I felt unburdened by grief and anxiety. Those people,

Ruthie's friends, had given that to me. All of us were in mourning, all of us worried about what the future would bring for Mike and the children. But everyone knew that they would go through it together, that they would carry each other.

Nobody had to say it; everyone could see it with their eyes and know it in their hearts. In a way all those afternoons down on the sandbar at Thompson Creek, late evenings of margaritas at Que Pasa, nights of pool parties and barn dances and Ronnie Morgan's campfires followed by pancakes and kitchen camaraderie, and church on Sunday morning—these things were like a levee the people of Starhill had spent a lifetime building together. Now, facing a catastrophe that felt like it had the power to wash them away, the levee was holding.

This, it occurred to me, was the deeper meaning in the mournful merriment I had been part of that day. I stood at Mam's sink before bedtime, filling an iced tea glass with water, and thinking that I had underestimated this place where I was born. I knew it was a good place to be from. I had no idea how great a place it was to be.

———

As word of Ruthie's passing spread beyond West Feliciana, the family began to hear from faraway people to whom Ruthie meant something. Shannon Nixon Morell, who credited Ruthie with setting her on a path out of poverty and to professional success, wrote from San Diego to say that Ruthie had been an "angel" of rescue. Another of Ruthie's former students, a woman who had become a teacher, wrote with a story of a moment in Ruthie's classroom, seventeen years earlier, when Ruthie, in celebrating the straight A's the student had made on her report card, made her, a girl who lacked confidence, feel her own worth and capability. That was the birth of her teaching vocation, the woman said, because that was her "first true moment of when I knew what I was supposed to do."

Kendrick Mitchell, the child who had been a bullied sixth-grade outcast, called Mam from Houston to say that Mrs. Leming had been such an encouragement to him back then.

"You don't know me, ma'am," Kendrick said to my mother, "but I feel like I need to tell you this about your daughter. If she had not been there for me to encourage me and to let me know that things were going to get better, I might not be where I am today.

"Everything I am today," he said, "I owe it all to Mrs. Leming."

After Kendrick's call Kay Graves took Mam out for a ride around town, to get away from the hubbub in Starhill. They stopped at the Sonic Drive-In for a Coke. The girl who brought their drinks to the car said, "Are you Mrs. Leming's mom?"—and then started talking about how Ruthie had been her teacher, and all the wonderful things Ruthie had done for her. A man sitting in the car next to theirs, eating his burger, overheard this and said, "You're Ruthie Leming's mother? She taught my children." And off he went, talking about what a difference Ruthie had made in his children's lives.

The day after Ruthie died Mike's cousins Josh and Karen Gott rolled in from north Texas and quietly took over running the house, freeing Mike to give his full attention to the task of burying his wife. Mam, Paw, Abby, and I accompanied Mike to Charlet Funeral Home to pick out the casket and make the arrangements. Jan Curwick, the Methodist pastor, met us there, and helped us through the process. Everyone in St. Francisville knew the Charlet family, which has for two generations buried the sons and daughters of West Feliciana. Just a day earlier Mike had been sitting with his wife drinking coffee. This morning he was choosing her casket.

Julie and our children arrived from Philadelphia on Saturday. That afternoon Tim and Laura Lindsey came out to Starhill to check on Mike and the girls. Tim took several of us aside and advised us about what we could do to help them deal with the reality of life without Ruthie. Later Julie and I watched Tim and Laura sitting in rocking chairs on Ruthie's front porch, flanking Hannah, talking to her about her grief, and helping her understand, both emotionally and theologically, what it meant to face death.

As I watched Hannah taking Tim's message in, it struck me that although my sister was dead, and Tim's service to her as a physician was over, he didn't see it that way. There was still healing to be done in Ruthie's family, the kind of healing that medicine, strictly speaking, could not effect. Because Tim approached his vocation as a work of love, he found the strength, the direction, and the inner resources to treat the Lemings in ways beyond the reach of standard medical practice. Here was a family doctor treating his patients like family.

Later that morning, I said to Julie, "You know, I'm sorry we live so far away. I wish we had Tim taking care of our family."

Julie said, "I was thinking the same thing."

My sister had died on a Thursday. On my first Sunday morning without her, I needed to be in church. I drove into Baton Rouge to the Orthodox liturgy at St. Matthew's, a mission parish in a south Baton Rouge strip mall. At the end of the service Father Mark Christian announced that Ruthie Leming, who had been on the parish prayer list for the last year and a half, had just reposed. They sang "Memory Eternal" for my sister, whom none of them had ever met, but for whom they had been praying for these nineteen months. I was not expecting that, and had to fight back tears.

Back home in the country I found my parents wrestling with a problem. The phone had been ringing with people asking if Mike had set up an education fund for his and Ruthie's children. They wanted a way to donate more than flowers. It hadn't occurred to any of us to do that sort of thing. I called Bess Kelley from the Bank of St. Francisville to ask her what information I would need on Monday morning to set the account up for the children.

"Why don't we do it today?" she said.

"Well, it's Sunday. The bank is closed."

"I'll meet you there in an hour." Bess gave an hour and a half of her Sunday afternoon to make sure people coming to Ruthie's wake that night at the Methodist church would have a place to donate for the children.

———

That evening, as a warm rain fell, the doors of the Methodist church opened onto Royal Street for mourners to pay their respects. For hours they came, standing in the rain and amid the mosquitoes swarming in the muggy interludes between showers; white and black, children and old folks, people who had known Ruthie since childhood, people who had known her only the year she had taught them, and even people who only knew my mother and father, but came because they loved and respected them and knew they were hurting.

The church's bell tower stretches into the limbs of the live oak trees shading the structure, built on this patch of ground in 1896, when the congregation at the Bayou Sara church under the bluff grew weary of routine Mississippi River flooding. Built of wood and painted a chaste white, the Methodist church is as modest as the brick neo-Gothic Episcopal church across the way is grand, but no less dignified. The church is small, its interior unadorned, the pale abstractions of the stained-glass windows its only ornamentation. There are dark wooden pews, a dark wooden communion rail, and dark wooden trim around the arched windows. It is a plain country church for plain country Christians. Five generations of my family have gathered there to pray, to sing, and to consecrate the milestones—births, marriages, deaths—of our lives.

This little church had not been enough to hold me as a teenager, nor to reclaim my loyalty as a young man stumbling back toward the Christian faith. Today, though, I felt gratitude for this place. No European cathedral would have done Ruthie's memory justice like this Methodist chapel under the live oak trees. This church was who my sister was, and if I could no longer share the form of faith proclaimed and taught from its pulpit, I could love it all the same, if only because Ruthie, like so many of our ancestors, did.

Paw was not strong enough to be on his feet and settled into the second pew on the left—the Dreher pew—to receive friends. The rest of us stood in the front of the church, next to Ruthie's body in the open casket, which sat on the same place where she and Mike stood all those years ago and promised to be together until death.

Mam and I flitted around the church, greeting people in line, checking on Paw, and returning occasionally to our perch in the front. Mike and the girls, though, stayed in place, receiving mourners for four hours. Late in the evening Claire and Rebekah took off their shoes. They did it because their feet hurt from standing, but then thought it would be a fitting tribute to their mother, who was famously a fan of going barefoot. Few of those filling the church that night knew that Mike was in intense physical pain. He had injured his back trying to save Ruthie.

The line unspooled down the street and far around the block. A police officer told me the only wake she had seen as big as this one was General Robert H. Barrow's. General Barrow was a scion of an old West Feliciana family, a World War II hero who went on to become commandant of the US Marine Corps. He had turned down President Ronald Reagan's invitation to become chairman of the Joint Chiefs of Staff on the grounds that the armed services were not ready for a Marine in that role. Before retiring to his farm in the Feliciana hills, General Barrow was one of the most powerful men in America. It impressed me that, to judge by the police officer's comment, folks here had the same degree of love and respect for a humble schoolteacher known to virtually no one beyond the parish's borders.

At one point in the evening I left Mike and the girls and slipped through the back door into the church hall for a cup of coffee. Julie, who was talking to folks on the sidewalk out front, sent me a text. "Check your e-mail," it read.

There was a letter to us from the owners of that beautiful eighteenth-century farmhouse in Bucks County we had toured the day before Ruthie died. In the confusion after her sudden passing, we had not had time to work out the details on the lease before leaving for Louisiana.

Now the landlords had written to say they really needed to get this house leased before they departed for California. They were sorry, but they had decided to rent it to another family.

I dashed to the front of the church, expecting to find Julie in tears. We had lost our dream house! But when I found her she looked strangely serene.

Feeling bold, I confessed, "I have to tell you that I'm actually kind of relieved."

Her eyes registered surprise. "Me, too!"

Something was going on with us.

Just past nine that night the church had emptied except for a handful of friends, most of them schoolteachers who had worked with Ruthie. They planned to hold an all-night vigil with her body. Nobody could recall the last time anybody had done something like this for the dead in West Feliciana. But for Ruthie? Her friends figured it wouldn't be right to leave her there all by herself.

It began informally, with a reading by Nora Marsh, who by now had retired from the classroom. She was working as a school librarian in New Orleans, but drove up to the country for the wake. She had not only taught me, but Ruthie too. Nora recited the George Eliot poem "The Choir Invisible." "It made me think of Ruthie," she said. I understood what Nora meant when her recitation concluded with these lines:

> . . . *May I reach*
> *That purest heaven,—be to other souls*
> *The cup of strength in some great agony,*
> *Enkindle generous ardour, feed pure love,*

Beget the smiles that have no cruelty,
Be the sweet presence of a good diffused,
And in diffusion ever more intense!
So shall I join the choir invisible
Whose music is the gladness of the world.

In the Orthodox Christian tradition, mourners keeping an all-night vigil read the entire Psalter over the body of the dead. I had planned to stay there until I had prayed aloud all 150 psalms over my sister, but her friends said they wanted to take part too. After Psalm 25, I handed my Psalter to someone else, and sat down. When I left at midnight, one of Ruthie's oldest friends, Sarah Marquette Fudge, held Ruthie's casket with one hand and the Psalter in the other, and prayed over the body of a woman with whom she had played dolls as a little girl.

Ruthie's colleagues, most of whom I was just getting to know, wanted me to appreciate what kind of teacher she was. That night was the first I had heard of Lyric Haynes, the child whose mother was in prison, and who had read the speech about Ruthie at the school assembly.

When Ruthie died the teachers worried that Lyric, now in high school, would lash out at others and find herself back in the principal's office for fighting. In fact she only asked that someone take her back to the middle school where Ruthie had taught her. She told them that she remembered the middle school as the place where teachers loved her. And she told them that she was going to do whatever she could to honor Mrs. Leming's memory.

"If you really want to honor Mrs. Leming," one teacher told her, "you will be good and study hard, and go to college to learn how to be a teacher. Then you can come back here to work, and help other kids the way Mrs. Leming helped you."

"I'll do it," Lyric said.

I had seen Lyric hours earlier at the wake, in the line passing by

Ruthie's coffin. I only figured her as one of the many former Ruthie students moving through the church that night. Until Ruthie's teacher friends told me, I had no idea, no idea at all, of the drama of this child's life, and the part my sister played in giving her love, and hope.

As I drove back to Starhill, worn out, I thought once again about how little I really knew about Ruthie's life, and how I understood even less. I had somehow come to think of her living in a small town as equivalent to her living a small life. That was fine by me, if it made her content, but there was about it the air of settling. Or so I thought. What I had seen and heard these last few days showed me how wrong I had been. When I got to my parents' house in Starhill I found Mam at the kitchen table, eyes puffy, drinking a Coke. I told her the Lyric story. She said Lyric must have been the little black girl who spoke to her in line at the wake. "She told me, 'Mrs. Leming is dead. Who is going to love me now?' I'll never forget that."

I said goodnight, brushed my teeth, and crawled into bed with Julie, who had picked the kids up at our cousin's house after the wake and gone back to Mam and Paw's to put them to bed. I told her all the things I had seen and heard since we last spoke.

"It's strange," I said. "I find myself crying not so much because of Ruthie, but because of all the goodness of these people. It's so ... *pure* that it hurts."

Back at the church the party was just getting started. Ruthie's teacher friends—Abby Temple, Rae Lynne Thomas, Jodi Knight, Karen Barron, Jennifer Bickham, Ashley Harvey, and others—gave her the send-off she deserved. Why? As Rae Lynne wisecracked, "Because we're the funnest people we know."

They set up lawn chairs in front of the open coffin, just like at Ruthie's beloved creek, and sprinkled creek sand onto Ruthie's body. Ashley loves sparkles, and brought glitter to scatter on Ruthie, as a blessing. She even rubbed some on Ronnie Morgan's bald head when he dropped by. They painted Ruthie's fingernails so she would look good for her funeral. Emily Branton came by with her guitar. They all sang hymns, and "Brown Eyed Girl." Karen danced for Ruthie.

"It's exactly the kind of thing Ruthie would have loved: laughing with her, crying with her, singing and dancing," Abby remembers. "That is what Ruthie loved most: being around her friends and family, in her kitchen, and in her church. You just knew she was there with us that night, and loving it."

———

On the day of Ruthie's funeral a man walked into the St. Francisville post office. "Sure are a lot of cars in town today," a woman said. The man told her they were going to bury Ruthie Leming this morning.

"Oh, that lady died?" the woman said. "I saw her in here just last week. I said to her, 'Baby, you don't look like you feel too good.' She said, 'No, ma'am, I don't. But I'm gonna be good real soon.'"

The line of mourners passing by Ruthie's coffin for final good-byes started at ten. By early afternoon all the pews were filled, all the room to stand was taken, the church had folding chairs in the aisles, and still mourners massed on the lawn and the sidewalk out front.

As the time for the services drew closer Abby felt numb. She had seen this day coming for a long time, and thought about what she would say to eulogize her best friend. But she didn't put her thoughts together until a couple of hours before the funeral started.

Five minutes before the opening prayer she told Karen Barron she didn't think she could do it. She worried about what she would say. She worried about Mike and the girls. She worried how all this was going to play out for that family.

She worried.

"No, you can," Karen said. "Just look at me when you speak, Abby. It's going to be okay."

Mike, his children, and Mam and Paw sat on the front row. Ashley Jones, who had driven seventeen hours straight from Nebraska to get to her former teacher's funeral, squeezed into a space along the wall. Stephanie Lemoine came up from Baton Rouge, hoping to claim a seat in the back. She had arrived early, to have a word with Mike as he stood once again by Ruthie's coffin. Because her cancer was in remission, Stephanie, with her survivor's guilt, worried about how she would be received, but as soon as Mike saw her, he broke into a fresh round of tears, looked directly into her eyes, and said the only word he could muster in the moment: "You."

Stephanie wept.

"Ruthie loved you so much," Mike said. "She talked about you all the time. You have no way of knowing what a blessing you were to her."

"I'm so honored to be here with her today, and with you," Stephanie said. "I want you to know that I got a message from Sister Dulce on the day Ruthie died. Sister said that Ruthie's body was worn out, but she was finally at peace. She is with Jesus, Mike."

That got to Mike. He tucked his head briefly. He looked at Stephanie again, and smiled. He told her he had saved a place on one of the front pews, where family was sitting.

"I don't belong there!" Stephanie protested.

"Come on. You are like family," Mike said with a finality that made Stephanie believe it was true.

Jennifer Bickham played the piano that morning and didn't think she could make it through. But she thought about Ruthie, and doing right by her, and held her ground. Making beautiful music for Ruthie's funeral would be Jennifer's final thank you.

To the left of the altar sat the six pallbearers. Mel Percy, Big Show, and John Bickham were among them. These were big men who had avoided the pain of my sister's passing by keeping busy and doing things for Mike and my parents. Now there was nothing to be done to distract themselves, nobody to care for, nowhere to go. They had to sit facing Ruthie's coffin and deal with their grief. By this time I was used to seeing people cry over Ruthie, but watching tears roll down the cheeks of these strong men, impotent in the face of death, felt almost indecent. Men this tough aren't supposed to break. These guys were broken.

Pastor Jan began the service with a hymn, and prayers, and Scripture readings. Then Abby rose, strode to the pulpit, swallowed hard, and told the congregation that she had been missing Ruthie for a long, long time.

"She was my sidekick, my partner in crime. And anytime I came up with some idea about something I wanted to do, ideas that most of the time would be categorized as stupid or crazy by most, she was right there with me," Abby said. "I don't remember ever asking her to join me, I just remember her being there by my side. And it's been a while since she was physically able to do these things."

Shortly after Ruthie received her cancer diagnosis, Mike Clark, a church friend and ordained Methodist pastor, asked Abby to ride with him out to Starhill to visit Ruthie. Abby told the congregation she wanted to share with them the passage from the forty-third chapter of Isaiah that Mike had read to Ruthie and her that long-ago day. It had meant a lot to the three of them back then, and set the tone for Ruthie's fearless, faithful endurance through the trial ahead. Abby recited:

> But now, this is what the LORD says—
> "Do not fear, for I have redeemed you;
> I have summoned you by name; you are mine.
> When you pass through the waters,
> I will be with you;
> and when you pass through the rivers,
> they will not sweep over you.
> When you walk through the fire,
> you will not be burned;
> the flames will not set you ablaze.

For I am the LORD your God,
the Holy One of Israel, your Savior."

Out in the congregation Lyric Haynes snuggled close to Ashley Harvey, who had brought her to the funeral. Ashley was so glad she had Lyric to care for that day. It kept her from falling apart.

After Abby's Old Testament reading, Josh Gott, Mike's Texas cousin, took the pulpit and read from the New Testament. Then it was my turn to stand and say something about my sister. I rose from the folding chair in the aisle, quietly asked God to give me the strength to say what I needed to say, then walked to the pulpit.

Though I knew nearly every soul in the church that morning, I could not look them in the eye. Not if I was going to deliver this eulogy. *Ruthie,* I thought, *pray for me. Help me do this.* I fixed my gaze on the white wall at the back of the church, and began.

I told the story about the time little Ruthie, five years old, confronted our father and demanded to take the spanking I deserved for having been mean to her. That, I said, was the kind of person she was. This memory overwhelmed me, and I lost my composure.

Ruthie, help me. Please, help me.

I wiped my eyes, cleared my throat, and continued.

Ruthie's death, I said, makes no more sense to me than it does to anybody in this church today. It was a cruel and unjust thing. Yet the history of God's people is filled with cruelty and injustice. Cain slew Abel. Herod killed all the firstborn Jewish children. The crowds in Jerusalem demanded the murder of Jesus. And out of that pain, God brought forth salvation, and He would have us know today that there is meaning in suffering—in the suffering of Ruthie, now ended, and in the suffering of we who mourn her passing. It is a mystery that can only be grasped by faith.

"On a day like today," I said, "we may all feel so tired and sad that we can't see the goodness in these events. But our faith assures us that, in the words of the poet W. H. Auden, 'Life remains a blessing, although you cannot bless.'"

All of you saw how Ruthie accepted the cup of suffering life passed to her, I told them. She did not despair of God's love and care for her, nor did she doubt that His hand was in everything that happened. She remained steadfast in her love for Him and for others, and in her gratitude for the good life she had been given. The more her body declined, the more her spirit increased. We saw, here in our town, in the life and death of Ruthie Leming, a foreshadowing of the redemption of the world.

"She showed us how to live," I said, "and she showed us how to die.

"You may not know this," I continued, "but Ruthie was an organ donor. She gave her eyes so that some blind soul unknown to her could see. It seems to me that in a spiritual sense, Ruthie has given us all eyes to see. I want to see the world as Ruthie did, even just a little bit: as a place illuminated by love. I want to see every day as Ruthie did: as an opportunity to make other people happier. I once was blind, but through Christ, now I see. And through His amazing grace in the life of my sister, our beloved brown-eyed girl, I see more clearly. We all do."

I returned on my wobbly legs to my chair in the aisle. And then, to my surprise (because I had not read the program), the congregation rose to sing Ruthie's favorite hymn: "Amazing Grace."

The procession to the Starhill cemetery, six miles south of town, was seventy-five cars long. To honor Mike and his family, fire trucks and ambulances sat in the median along the last mile, lights flashing, firefighters and EMTs standing at attention. Some people who lived along the route down Highway 61 stood in their driveways to pay their respects. Evelyn Dedon, the mama of baseball phenom Roy Dale Craven, sat on the hillside near where her little boy was killed all those years ago, waving in salute as another lost child of Starhill passed on by.

As we pulled up behind the hearse in Mam's SUV, we noticed the six pallbearers standing there in bare feet, the cuffs of their pants rolled high over their ankles. What was this? Inspired by the sight of Claire and Rebekah standing in church barefoot the night before, Mel Percy thought it would be a proper final tribute to Ruthie, who loved being barefoot, to cast aside their dress shoes and carry her to her grave with the wet green grass of Starhill between their toes.

So those good men, the barefoot pallbearers, did, and it was a thing of beauty. Hannah, Claire, and Rebekah, seeing their mother's friends standing in the road shoeless by her casket, took off their shoes as well. They stepped out of their black Ford SUV and Hannah, taking hold of her sisters' hands, led them barefoot down the hill and through the grass to the graveside.

Mike, the girls, and Mam and Paw sat on chairs next to the grave. Julie and I stood with our children behind them. My cousin Drew, whom I didn't know well because I had been away for so many years, stood at my right shoulder with his wife, Jilliann. Before Pastor Jan began the brief service, Drew—burly old Drew, who looks like a pair of linebackers—leaned over and said in my ear, "Hey man, I love you."

That threw me. This family of mine—the cousins and their children—had been so terrific to us that week. Most of them live in or around St. Francisville. *If I lived here,* I thought, *I could get to know them, and really love them. Drew has little idea who I am, in truth, but he loves me because I am family, and there we all were, we Drehers, in the Starhill cemetery once again, where all our dead are gathered, burying another of our own.* Drew is not a tender man, but his words were sweet and true, and stayed with me the rest of the day.

The barefoot pallbearers bore Ruthie down the hill and set her casket on the platform over the grave. Fighting back tears John Bickham thought about what a privilege it was to carry Ruthie Leming that day.

After Jan and her assistant finished the final prayers, Mike rose, stood at the coffin, put his big, rough right hand on the foot of the casket, let it linger for a moment, then turned and walked away. The rest of us followed. There was nothing more to say, nothing more to do, but to let Ruthie go at last into the Feliciana earth, and rest a while.

We all motored a minute away down Audubon Lane to Mel and Tori Percy's big house for a much-needed drink. The Percys live on a generous, rolling spread that backs up to Paw's place. It wasn't long before their patio filled with family and friends who wanted to be together one more time in Ruthie's memory. Nobody wanted the funeral or the somber graveside prayers to be the last word that day. If Ruthie were here, she would damn sure want a cold beer.

There were hillocks of food there, much of it courtesy of the Methodist church women, and, this being south Louisiana, lots of beer, wine, and whiskey. About a hundred people were there, doing the same thing they had done every day since Ruthie died. During the party Abby pulled me aside and said she had never seen anything like what had happened in our town after Ruthie's passing.

"Rod, you haven't lived here in a while, so maybe you don't understand," she said. "Somebody dies, you go over and take food and pay your respects, but you don't see big groups of people coming over every night and staying, and drinking beer, and laughing. Everybody wants to be around each other. It's so Ruthie! And look at this, here at Mel's. It's all a celebration of her life. Everybody's having a great time. God, she would have loved it."

It has indeed been an incredible thing to see, I told Abby, and a tribute to Ruthie's gift for friendship. Everybody on Mel's patio, in his living room, and under his carport that afternoon had at one time or another been a guest in Ruthie's kitchen.

"How did she do it?" I asked Abby. "How did she inspire all this?"

"No matter who you were, Ruthie made you feel like you were *it*," Abby said. "You were her family, you were always comfortable—'Come in, sit down, let me fix you something to eat.' Everybody was welcome in her house. You knew you were at home there, and everything was good."

At Mel's that long afternoon we were all at home, and it was good, because Ruthie was there with us. Even in her absence, she was still the happy genius of the Starhill party.

Back at Mam and Paw's that evening, I thought about Mel, and John Bickham, and Big Show, and Abby, and Tim and Laura Lindsey, and all the men and women of this community who rallied to the Lemings and the Drehers from the beginning of our long cancer journey. I told my wife again that the purity of love these people showed to our family was so intensely beautiful that it was hard to look upon for long without feeling that it would destroy you. "Every angel is terrible," the poet Rilke wrote, meaning that God's messengers come to us with a beauty that inspires fear. To look upon beauty that powerful is to receive a calling and a command to change your life—and that can make you afraid.

It can always be refused, but grace like that doesn't come often in a lifetime. After we returned to Mam and Paw's that afternoon, Julie and I talked again about the possibility of moving there. It sounded crazy, but after what we had seen these past few days, the foundation of our settled life had been cracked and was crumbling.

We were scared, in a good way, because it felt like God was dealing with our hearts. My wife and I resolved to keep open minds, and to pray for guidance. We had a few more days in Starhill. Maybe things would become clearer.

We did not know it at the time, but Ashley Jones was way ahead of us. Having seen Ruthie's funeral, and having heard about the wake Ruthie's friends held for her, Ashley had an epiphany. *I have never heard of anything so beautiful in all my life,* she thought. *If I die, the only people who know me and love me well enough to do that for me are my friends back home.* She drove back to Nebraska, gave two weeks' notice at her firm, then promptly packed up and moved home to Louisiana. It took her a while but she landed a sales job in Baton Rouge. "It's not the most glamorous job," she told me later, "but it's a job, and it's close to home, and that's all that matters."

The Lemings had at that time a large teepee in their backyard, a gift from Mike's brother on the West Coast. Late that evening Julie joked to Mike that our family was loving it so much in Starhill that we might just move from Philadelphia right into that teepee, and never leave.

"Sometimes," Mike said, "you just have to follow the buffalo."

CHAPTER TWELVE

Lean on Me

Three days after we buried Ruthie, Mike set out for Baton Rouge to return her oxygen tank and breathing equipment. He also wanted to stop by the chemo unit at Baton Rouge General to thank Dr. Miletello and his nursing staff for all they had done for Ruthie. I asked Mike if I could go with him.

When we walked into the oncology unit, Buffy, one of the nurses at the front desk, embraced Mike and gave him a poem she had written in Ruthie's memory. Buffy had a habit of bursting into song whenever Ruthie walked in for her treatments. That sweet, silly gesture meant a lot to my sister. While Mike received condolences from the other ladies on staff, Buffy fetched Dr. Miletello from his office.

I watched as Dr. Miletello strode down the hall and embraced my brother-in-law. "She loved you," Mike told him.

"It's a good thing that we don't treat more people like Ruthie," he said. "It would be too hard. She was so humble. That's what you noticed about her. She never, ever complained about being sick. Never."

"She was an angel," he added.

We spent a few more minutes talking with the oncologist, then shook hands and headed back to the parking lot.

As we were pulling away, someone called Mike's cell phone to check on him. "We're leaning," he said, "but we're leaning on each other."

That line stayed with me all day. I thought about it when John Bickham, standing in Mam and Paw's yard, said to me, "What you've seen
here is because of who your sister was, but it's also because of who
your mama and daddy are."

He was right. The love that had sustained Ruthie through her cancer,
and that now surrounded and upheld her family, came from somewhere.
Like Ruthie, my mother and father had cultivated it, in this little patch
of ground, all their lives. They had no grand gestures of philanthropy
or goodness to their name, but rather they were always faithful in small
things. When Paw was the parish sanitarian, he helped impoverished
people, mostly poor black folks, bring running water and sewerage into
their houses. These people didn't have the money to pay for the job
themselves, so he showed them how to do it right, and never asked for
a penny in compensation. He did it because he was their neighbor. You
live in one place long enough, and live that way, the interest on your
good deeds will add up.

I did not live that way. I never stayed in one place long enough to
develop that kind of relationship with my community. Nobody ever
told me in New York, in Dallas, in Philly, or anywhere else that I was
not allowed to serve others in the community, or work to root myself,
a transplant, in new ground. It was so easy, though, to live inside one's
bubble, and not see your neighbors in the way West Feliciana people saw
their neighbors. Bowling alone, so to speak, was the way so many in my
circles rolled.

Not long after Ruthie's passing, I received a letter from Christian
Daniel Tregle, a woman who grew up down the road from me. Her
brother was Robert Edward Daniel, who died from leukemia (their
mother Jane was Mam's first visitor the morning after Ruthie died).
Christian was much younger than I, which meant that I didn't know
her in our childhood. Christian said that as a teenager she was just like
me in that she wanted to escape the boredom and the claustrophobia of
our small town. At LSU her mother would pass on news from home,

including good deeds and acts of kindness, but they didn't mean much to the undergraduate.

But as she grew older it dawned on her that the everyday goodness of the people back home was a lot more significant than she realized. There was a poor, hard-working family from Starhill who lived down the road from both our families. Christian's father, a game warden, knew that family hardly had a pot to pee in. Whenever the wardens confiscated game from poachers, Christian's dad would take it by this family's house so they would have meat on the table.

One day the daddy and sole breadwinner in that family was diagnosed with Hodgkin's lymphoma. Though he would be treated in the state's public hospital system, he was nevertheless so poor that he couldn't afford to quit his job during his treatments. So Christian's mother took the sick man's family groceries every week during his treatment. The man survived, and his family stayed together.

Christian learned that this kind of thing happens in our hometown all the time. You're going through a divorce, and things are hard for you, and you'll come home to find your overgrown yard, which you hadn't had time to mow, has been cut by a stranger. A hurricane will blow through town and the power won't come back on for a week or longer—but you don't lose all the food in your freezer because your neighbor down the street ran an extension cord across three yards to share his generator power with you. You are pregnant and on emergency bed rest, and a professional maid shows up at your door, having been hired by an anonymous person, who knew that you couldn't clean your house in your condition.

That sort of thing. All the time.

———

Julie and I had some long, emotional talks that week in Starhill. How do you live through a week like that—indeed, how do you live through the previous nineteen months with Ruthie—and remain unaffected? Ruthie and I were so very much unalike; as much as I admired her, it never occurred to me to shape my own life after her example. In the days following her death, it was easier, I found, to think of how I could be more like the people she inspired to works of love. Which is to say, I found in my heart an emerging desire to be like my brother-in-law Mike, to be like Big Show, to be like Mel Percy. I wanted to be more like Abby Temple, and John Bickham, and all the people in our town and less like the kid who sat inside watching MTV while his dad waited for the grass to be mowed.

Was God calling me to a new life? Maybe. Ruthie and I were both practicing Christians, yet we were utterly different in our approaches to God. Ruthie didn't have much of a theology. That's not how her mind worked. She believed that God existed and that He loved her. She believed Jesus Christ was His son and died for humanity's sins. She believed the Bible and, that whatever happened to her, that God was in it, and that He would never abandon her. That was the sum total of Ruthie Leming's theology.

And yet Ruthie, in her simplicity, was an extraordinarily accomplished theologian—if, that is, a theologian is not one who knows *about* God, but one who knows God. The ordinary Christianity she lived out among her family, her neighbors, her students, and all who came into her life, made her a Christian soldier and me an armchair Christian theoretician. As anyone who has sat through a bridesmaid reading Paul's First Letter to the Corinthians knows, "If I have the gift of prophecy and can fathom all mysteries and all knowledge, and if I have a faith that can move mountains, but do not have love, I am nothing."

For most of my life as a believing Christian, I read I Corinthians, and I thought I understood it. I did not understand it, not until Ruthie became ill. For many years I had lived in a fairly specialized world of elite journalism and traveled among groups of people who shared my intellectual interests, advancing my career, enjoying my life, and collecting experiences. But what, in the end, did it amount to? What did I have to show for it?

"If I woke up one day and found out I had terminal cancer, what would happen to me?" I said to Julie. "What would happen to you and the kids?"

"We have good friends in Philly," she said.

"I know," I said. "But we don't have a deep bench."

"What do you mean?"

"I mean we haven't been there long enough. We don't know enough people. If you think about it, we haven't lived anywhere long enough to put down the kind of roots that Ruthie and Mike have."

Nearly everybody in West Feliciana knew Mike and Ruthie, or at least knew Mam and Paw, I explained to Julie, who grew up in a Dallas suburb and knew no neighbors other than the people on either side of her house. Some relationships between families in West Feliciana go back for generations. My folks have a good name in the parish, and that means something there. People in West Feliciana remember these things, and the mutual obligation these communal memories impose.

I once asked Paw why, given that he was feeling sick that day, he was planning to go to the funeral of an old woman he didn't know well.

"Respect," he said to me, slightly annoyed that he had to explain the obvious. "That family has lived around here for a long time."

It's hard to know these things, much less find the wherewithal to behave this way, if you haven't lived in a place for years and come to make its stories part of yourself. Absence has consequences.

"When a community loses its memory, its members no longer know one another," writes the agrarian essayist Wendell Berry. "How can they know one another if they have forgotten or have never learned one another's stories? If they do not know one another's stories, how can they know whether or not to trust one another? People who do not trust one another do not help one another, and moreover they fear one another. And this is our predicament now."

Those of us who have moved away are not necessarily callow and ungrateful people. We live in a time and place in which we are conditioned to leave our hometowns. Our schools tell our young people to follow their professional bliss, wherever it takes them. Our economy rewards companies and people who have no loyalty to place. The stories that shape the moral imagination of our young, chiefly by film and television, are told by outsiders who were dissatisfied and lit out for elsewhere to find happiness and good fortune.

During the decade leading up to Ruthie's death, I had spent my professional life writing newspaper columns, blog posts, and even a book, lamenting the loss of community and traditions in American life. I had a reputation as a pop theoretician of cultural decline, but in truth I was long on words, short on deeds. I did not like the fact that I saw my Louisiana family only three times a year, for a week at a time, if we were lucky. But that was the way of the world, right? Almost everyone I knew was in the same position. My friends and I talked a lot about the fragmentation of the modern family, about the deracinating effects of late capitalism, about mass media and the erosion of localist consciousness, about the consumerization of religion and the leviathan state and every other thing under the sun that undermines our sense of home and permanence.

The one thing none of us did was what Ruthie did: Stay.

Contemporary culture encourages us to make islands of ourselves for the sake of self-fulfillment, of career advancement, of entertainment, of diversion, and all the demands of the sovereign self. When suffering and death come for you—and it will—you want to be in a place where you know, and are known. You want—no, you *need*—to be able to say, as Mike did, "We're leaning, but we're leaning on each other."

I deeply believed then, and believe today, that one day I will be asked to give an account of my life to my Maker. That fateful week in Louisiana I wondered: When I meet the Lord, will I be able to say that my life had been about giving, not just taking? Would being able to discern the difference between a Bordeaux and a Burgundy bring me any closer to tasting the cup of salvation?

In short: Did I have love?

Ruthie did, and she brought it out and passed it on to everyone who knew her. Me, it was hard to escape the unsettling conclusion that I was awfully close to being what St. Paul called a resounding gong. To be sure, I was a nice enough guy, in the way that most people are nice enough. But when you see in a life like Ruthie's what loving people beyond the ordinary can do for others, and for yourself, it makes you aware of your own lack—and, if your heart is in the right place, determined to do something about it.

I had to change my life. But how? Should I once again try the geographical cure for my restlessness, and hope this time that it worked?

That week, in the midst of marveling about the goodness of the townspeople, Julie and I wondered if we were romanticizing St. Francisville. After all this was at the end of one of the most emotional weeks of our lives. A local friend had said to me, "You have seen the town at its very best. You know, it's not always like this."

I knew St. Francisville's shortcomings. There is poverty. There is brokenness. There is drunkenness, and there are drugs. There is meanness, and conformity, and lack of professional opportunity. Of all the things that made me run from this place nearly three decades ago, most of them remain.

But Ruthie transfigured this town in my eyes. Her suffering and death made me see the good that I couldn't see before. The same communal bonds that appeared to me as chains all those years ago had become my Louisiana family's lifelines. What I once saw through the melodramatic eyes of a teenager as prison bars were in fact the pillars that held my family up when it had no strength left to stand.

We're leaning, but we're leaning on each other.

Over the years I had leaned on Ruthie in ways I hadn't grasped. Truth was I had always been a free rider on Ruthie's faithfulness and rootedness. Without realizing what I was doing, I had given myself permission to live a life of restlessness and liberty because Ruthie chose to live within the limits imposed by life in a small town. I had just witnessed the harvest Ruthie and her family reaped as a consequence of the limits she embraced. She pruned her vines, but I let mine grow wild and scattered. Now the fruits her children would enjoy were sweeter and more intense than what I was growing for my own.

What did this mean for my kids and me, so far from our family, our people, and the South?

There are so many opportunities for them in the North said the voice in my head. And that is true. What I could see now was the deeper, unquantifiable cost of these opportunities to my children and myself. Thanks to Ruthie, I now saw that I had the opportunity to be a part of something extraordinary. I had the opportunity to raise my children around their extended family and among the people who loved Aunt Ruthie and Uncle Mike, and Mam and Paw. I had the opportunity to serve my family, and to serve the people who served my family in their time of need. I had the chance to help Hannah with her French, and could give my Lucas the opportunity to take to the woods with Uncle Mike. ("Daddy, if we ever lived here, I would want to go deer hunting with Uncle Mike," Lucas had said that week. "I think he would like that because he likes me.") Two weeks before Ruthie died I left the Templeton Foundation to sign on as a senior editor with *The American Conservative* magazine. I could work from wherever there was high-speed Internet access and a nearby airport.

A new life opened itself up before Julie and me. But we had to choose.

Julie and I had been talking around this topic all week, and when we had a moment alone at Mam's kitchen table, I said it out loud to her: "Are we really thinking of moving to St. Francisville?"

"We really are," she said, and grinned nervously.

"Do you think we should?" I asked.

"Yeah, I do," she said. "I can't believe I'm saying this, but I do. Mike and those girls need us."

"Mam and Paw need us," I said.

"They do. It just doesn't seem right, honey, for us to go back up there and leave all these people hurting."

"That's what I'm thinking."

I told Julie I couldn't imagine the kind of life in which I called Mam and Paw to see how everybody was doing, and being so far away and unable to help. It was hard enough to do when Ruthie was sick, but I had no choice then. My job was in Philly. Thanks to the magazine, I had a choice now.

"But what about you and the homeschool co-op?" I added.

"Well, it won't be easy," she said. "I love teaching, and I've gotten pretty good at it. I'm never going to be able to find friends like those women in the co-op. I feel like I've helped build something up, and now we're going to pull out again. And the kids are going to miss their friends."

My face fell. Here I go again. The guy who uproots his wife and kids for the second time in two years.

"But think of what we would be moving to," Julie said. "Our kids would get to know their grandparents. We don't know how long Mam and Paw have. Any time with them is a gift for our kids, and a gift to them, too. We can be there to help Mike, and to get to know Claire and Rebekah. Besides I love these people here. They've been so good to us."

"I know," I said. "They make me want to be better. We've never lived anywhere but a big city, though. Do you think we can make it here?"

"I think we've had a chance to see what matters in life," Julie said. "I don't know about you, but the way I'm thinking right now, the question is not, 'Should we move to St. Francisville?' but 'Why shouldn't we move to St. Francisville?' "

I looked at my wife with wide eyes, and a "you're-so-crazy" smile. Little more than a week earlier, when we were swanning around the grounds of that gorgeous Bucks County farmhouse, this idea would have struck us as ridiculous. But now it was the sanest thing in the world.

We talked about it a bit more, and were both struck that this potential move felt not like a burden we would take up in noble self-sacrifice, but as a blessing, even a privilege. It wasn't our duty to move South; it was an opportunity.

"It's like this," Julie said. "We have the chance to do something really good and meaningful. How often does this happen in life? I don't think we should pass it up."

"Me neither," I said. "Let's do it."

"Let's. And let's not wait around, either."

———

On our last morning in St. Francisville Julie had to go by the school board office in town with paperwork for Ruthie's estate. I rode with her. While Julie was in a back office taking care of business, I caught up with Al Lemoine, a former teacher of mine. He's now a West Feliciana schools official.

"When are y'all heading back to Philly?" Al asked.

"Tomorrow morning," I said. "But you never know. We might move back. Julie and I were looking online last night for rental housing here, but there's such a bad housing shortage I don't know what we'd do."

"You know, that Bankston house just down the street came on the market a couple of days ago," Al said. "You ought to go look at it."

What?!

"When Julie comes out, tell her where I've gone," I said, and shot out the door.

Two blocks away, at the other end of Fidelity Street, stood a stately old house with a deep front porch and a big, shady beech tree in the front yard. It was magnificent. I called the number on the "For Rent" sign and talked to Kathy Bankston, who managed the house with her husband, Davis. They raised their kids there, but had recently moved out to another family house in Starhill.

"Give me ten minutes and I'll be there," she said.

By the time Kathy arrived Julie had made her way down Fidelity. Kathy showed us the house and disclosed the rental terms. The house belonged to her father-in-law and mother-in-law, Walter and Puddin Bankston, who live on the same block. Walter and Puddin are old friends of my father's.

While Kathy waited outside Julie and I stood in the kitchen and talked. This house, smack in the middle of the historic district, was perfect—just the right size for our family. And it had a front porch where I could imagine myself sipping bourbon and putting the world to rights.

"I think we should do this," I said.

"I think we should too," Julie replied.

We both felt the grace around us, pushing us forward.

We stepped back out onto the front porch and told Kathy we would like to start a conversation about renting the house. She said she was going to have to talk to Walter, and we said we had to see about tying up some loose ends in Philadelphia before we could commit. But things looked promising. She would be in touch.

On the drive back to Starhill Julie and I, dazed but giddy, kept asking ourselves, *How did that happen?*

A week later we talked to Walter, settled the terms, and officially rented the house on Fidelity Street. Walter was incredibly gracious, saying it was good to know the house would have people in it from a good family.

"Your daddy and my wife, Puddin, were classmates all through school," he told me. "He raised her 4-H Club hog for her when they were children, and she won first place."

I had interviewed Puddin for a newspaper article years earlier about the time she spent as a child in The Myrtles, a plantation house in town said to be one of America's most haunted houses. Puddin, whose given name is Alice, is the daughter of the late Davis Folkes, a Louisiana state senator and dear friend of my late grandfather Murphy Dreher Sr., whom he called "Mercy" because he couldn't quite say the name right. The old gents spent their last years sitting together every day on a bench outside a real estate office downtown, talking, listening, watching, and being with each other in the town they had shared all their long lives.

———

When we returned to Philadelphia we broke the news to our friends that we were moving to Louisiana. We made sure to explain that we weren't moving away from something bad—we loved them, and we loved our Philly life—but toward something good. We expected a lot of *Green Acres* jokes and bourgeois-bohemian ribbing about how hard it would be to live in a town without a Thai restaurant and an organic market, but the reactions were not at all what I expected. Our decision occasioned a number of e-mails and personal conversations, some of which were startlingly intimate, even painful.

Some told me stories about how isolated they felt, even in the city, and how lonely they are for community. Others talked about how much they envy me having a place like St. Francisville to go back home to; their families moved around so much that there's no anchorage in which they can find safe harbor. Still others expressed sorrow at how much they want what the people in St. Francisville have, but how very far they are from being able to get it. One friend living in Washington, DC, said that despite his broad social network, he couldn't think of a single person he'd trust enough to authorize to pick his kid up from day care in the event of an emergency. Another friend spoke to me with disarming bluntness about the loneliness and helplessness he and his wife are going through.

"Everything I've done has been for career advancement. Go for the money, the good jobs. And we have done well. But we are alone in the world," he said. "Almost everybody we know is like that. My family is all over the country. My kids only call if they want something. People like us, when we get old, our kids can't move back to care for us if they wanted to because we all go off to some golf resort to retire. This is the world we have made for ourselves. I envy you that you get to escape it."

Our friend Edie Varnado, who lives in the country outside of McComb, Mississippi, and makes soap for a living, wrote to encourage Julie and me. She told us that she and her husband stayed in Mississippi in part to be close to her folks. Her brother moved to New York City. One night, over dinner, Edie's father said to her, "Even with everything you have, or will have, to deal with, you have the better part."

She laughed gently at that, but her father looked at her seriously and said, "You really have." As the years went by she saw her father was right. Her brother carries with him his own mythology of all the hurts he experienced as a child. Edie had the time and the luxury to become reacquainted with her parents as adults, as real people, for better and for worse. Edie was able to be with both her mother and father when they died, holding their hands and reading the Psalms.

"It's hard, big, real, and dirty," Edie wrote of what lay before Julie and me.

And by Christmas it would be ours.

When we told the children that we were moving to Louisiana in December, that they would have Christmas with Mam and Paw, and Uncle Mike, and the cousins, Lucas pumped his fist in the air and yelled, "Boo-yah!" There would be Mam and Paw in my children's future, and Uncle Mike, and cousins. There would be crawfish, and jambalaya, and deer hunting, and LSU football, and all the good things that I had growing up (and, I hoped, fewer of the bad things).

Late one night this e-mail landed in my in-box:

> I just wanted to tell you how happy your mother and I are to know that you and your family are coming home.
>
> I have prayed for this to happen for years. Now it is finally happening. I realize that it could not happen before, but now my prayers are being answered. We love you and your family, son, and welcome home.
>
> Love, Daddy.

CHAPTER THIRTEEN

The Narrow Path

There are better ways to see America than from the cab of a twenty-six-foot Penske rig, but that's how I rolled home the week before Christmas. Julie and the kids corkscrewed themselves into her jam-packed minivan, while our dog Roscoe and I commandeered the big truck. The last time I'd driven a truck between the Atlantic seaboard and St. Francisville I was twenty years younger. By the time we crossed the Maryland state line, my back could tell the difference.

I hadn't been sleeping well in the nights leading up to the move. One night, just before dawn, I dreamed that I was standing in the living room of our Philadelphia apartment, surrounded by boxes, wrapping paper, and all the accoutrements of our impending move. I heard the door open downstairs and someone walking up the stairs. It was Ruthie. She was wearing a white sweater with a collar gathered close around her neck, and carrying a tin of muffins.

"I thought you were dead!" I said.

"Oh, I am," she said sweetly. "I just wanted to tell you that everything is going to be all right."

"Thank you for saying that. Will you stay for a while?"

"No, I need to get on back."

Then I woke up. The dream had been unusually vivid, far more

218

intense than usual. When I woke up I wasn't sure if I was still inside the dream or not.

At breakfast I told Julie about the dream. "Of course she brought muffins," Julie said. "That's just like Ruthie."

"Maybe it really was her," I said. "But I know how much I need to believe everything is going to be okay down there. I might have imagined it. I probably imagined it."

Matthew stumbled out of his room and trudged to the kitchen for breakfast in his groggy morning manner. When he heard us talking about a dream, he said, "The weirdest thing happened in my room last night. I woke up and felt someone in the room with me, sitting in the chair next to my bed."

"Who was it?" I asked.

"I don't know. I was facing the wall, and was too scared to turn over and see."

"Did the presence feel threatening?" I asked.

"No," he said. "It was just watching me."

"I think that was Aunt Ruthie, checking on you," I said, and told him what had happened to me during the night.

I kept the dream front to mind as we completed packing. Ruthie's consoling message remained with me as I bucketed southward, through Chattanooga, Birmingham, and Meridian. I was excited about the new adventure, but also anxious about the challenges. Would we be able to give Mike and the girls what they needed? Would Mam and Paw, reeling from the loss of their daughter, expect more from their son than he could give? Would my children become the collateral damage from my putting romantic notions about community to the test?

Matthew, our eldest, was about to become a teenager, and though he and I are so much alike, our relationship wasn't what it needed to be. Though I had struggled through my early teen years with my father's impatience and disapproval, I was on track to repeat some of his mistakes with my son. Matthew is very bright and generally cheerful, but has a slight case of Asperger's syndrome, a neurological disorder at the mildest end of the autism spectrum. Though he strikes most people who meet him as an intelligent, polite boy, Matt's Asperger's tends to make him rigid and inflexible—a quality that can at times come across as headstrong, petulant, and defiant. Though I was far more tolerant of his eccentricities than Paw was of mine, I still found myself quick to lose patience with him.

"Ruthie always thought you were too hard on Matthew," Julie had reminded me as we were packing boxes one day. "I need you to be careful about that. This move is going to be especially hard on him."

"I know," I said. "I ask her all the time to pray for me, to help me be patient with him."

What Julie had in mind was how Matt's condition makes him especially dependent on stability and continuity to maintain emotional balance. Plus Aspies typically lack a sense of emotional subtlety, which means they struggle with social interaction. Matt had finally found a good friend in our Philly neighborhood and now had to tell him good-bye. Moreover he was moving to a town where his father, who was geeky but far more socially adept than he, had left as a teenager because he couldn't stand the conformity, the intolerance, and the bullying.

Lucas? He would be fine. At seven it was hard on him to leave his Philly friends, but he was keen to live in West Feliciana, around family and the outdoors. Nora was more difficult to read. She turned five a month after Ruthie died. She didn't seem to understand what leaving Philadelphia for St. Francisville would mean. All she could think about was how she would get to see her grandparents all the time, and now, finally, she would have girl cousins to play with whenever she liked.

Julie's was a harder case. She agreed to marry me for better or worse, and my career peregrinations had usually been a winning proposition for her. Leaving Dallas, our church community, and her backyard garden had been punishing, but she landed on her feet in Philly, and threw herself into working with and teaching in the classical homeschool co-op. Julie discovered that she had a real gift, indeed a passion, for teaching grammar. She was so good at it, in fact, that the national classical homeschooling organization with which our co-op was affiliated asked her to travel around Pennsylvania conducting workshops for homeschool teachers. This gratified Julie immensely, and gave her a sense of self-confidence that she had never had.

Now I was asking her to put all that aside and move to my home-town, where all my difficult emotional baggage was stored. Visiting St. Francisville over the years, whenever something about the place would bother either of us, we could always count on the fact that we would be leaving shortly (and truth to tell, our relatives there counted on that too when we got on their nerves). There would be no place to run away to now if things got hard. What's more Julie had no idea how Claire and Rebekah, who were dealing with the loss of their mother, were going to take the presence of their aunt. Tim Lindsey had warned us, "Lots of times people in grief need to be angry at somebody, and you need to be ready for that somebody to be you."

What if it was us? Julie was scared of hurting them, and being hurt by them. And yet she wanted to move to Louisiana as much as I did. She loved my family and wanted to serve. She reminded me several times that autumn, as we packed our things, that no matter how hard we feared it would be for us in St. Francisville, it would be harder to stay away from our family when they needed us most.

On the third day of the thirteen-hundred-mile drive we stopped for gas just south of Jackson, Mississippi. I had a Moon Pie for breakfast. It seemed like the thing to do now that we were well and truly back in the South. The big truck lumbered toward Starhill, minivan bringing up the rear, until finally, at half past noon, I juddered to a stop in Mam and Paw's yard. Lucas made Julie stop the minivan at the end of the driveway so he could run the final hundred yards and leap into the arms of Mam and Paw, who stood outside waiting. I let the dog out, then walked over to embrace my father, who was crying.

"I'm so glad you're back, baby," he said and squeezed me tight. I could hear him softly sobbing on my shoulder. We were standing on exactly the spot where, twenty years ago, he told me good-bye before I drove the moving truck away to Washington, DC.

We spent that night at Mam and Paw's. The next morning we had our coffee and drove the final six miles into St. Francisville, to the house on Fidelity Street. Big Show turned up with a work crew to unload our stuff. John Bickham turned up too. Show's crew was getting paid to work, but on his day off John gave his time and labor for free. He floated around the house, a benevolent caretaking presence making sure everything went well. By the afternoon we were all moved in. I returned the truck to the Home Depot in Zachary. Julie picked me up and we drove back to our new home.

Christmas was coming in six days and we still had some presents to buy for the kids. To make matters more challenging Mam had said earlier in the month that she was too sad to make Christmas dinner this year, so Julie and I offered to host it at our place—this, even though we would be living out of boxes. We knew this first Christmas without Ruthie would be hard on her, especially given that Mam's birthday is on Christmas Eve. We were eager to do whatever we could to ease her burden.

This year Mam and Ruthie's Christmas Eve tradition of lighting candles in the Starhill cemetery would, sadly, be broken. Neither Mam nor Hannah had it within herself to continue. Mam told me she and Paw were planning to go to services at the Methodist church, and home to bed early. They didn't feel up to coming by the Dreher family Christmas gathering at my cousin Andy's place. They wanted to be alone, and quiet, with their grief.

Just after sunset, while Mam and Paw were at church, I drove out to their house to pick up some presents I had stored in Paw's barn.

Passing the Starhill cemetery I saw hundreds of pinpricks flickering in the darkness, like stardust sprinkled on the thick blanket of night. I guessed that Mam found the strength to uphold the tradition after all.

Half an hour later I was having a drink in Andy's living room when my mobile phone rang. It was Mam. She sounded distraught.

"Rod, did you see the cemetery?" she said.

"Yes, it was beautiful," I said. "You did a wonderful job."

"It wasn't me, baby," she said, choking through her tears. "I don't know who did it. Some kind soul lit the candles tonight. Oh, baby, whoever that was, they'll never know what they did for me tonight. They'll never, ever know."

"My God, Mama, I don't know what to say."

"Honey, find out who did that, would you? I have to thank them."

I told her I would do my best.

A few minutes later Mam called back.

"It was Susan Harvey," she said. "You remember her? Mr. Buddy Harvey's daughter? She's Susan Wymore now. She was the one who did it. Susan. Susan Harvey, God bless her. She will never, ever know what a gift she gave me tonight."

In the years I had been away Susan would call Mam to ask if she would like some help with the candles, but Mam always declined, telling Susan that she and Ruthie, and Ruthie's girls, had everything covered. This year when Susan called to offer her help, Paw told her that Mam was too down to do it this year.

"I thought it was important to keep it going," Susan told me when I called to thank her. Growing up Susan and her sisters lived two fields over from Paw's parents, who would welcome the Harvey girls into their little white wooden cottage. My grandmother gave them cookies and seeds to feed the birds. The Harvey girls' older kinfolks, Willis, Fletcher, and Romy, had helped my grandfather build that house by hand after the original cottage burned to the ground when Paw was a boy.

"My twins are buried in that cemetery," Susan said. "The first year your Mom and Ruthie did this, they also put out little crosses made of antique nails. They put two crosses there for the twins, one for each one of them, even though they share a grave. The twins were stillborn, and a lot of people don't know how to act around that. But your Mama and Ruthie, they put two crosses there. To me that acknowledged that the twins were people. I never forgot what your mom did for me."

"They've been dead twenty-one years," Susan continued. "But you never know when you're going to wake up one morning and it'll feel like just yesterday."

———

On Christmas Day the Starhill crew arrived at our house on Fidelity Street just after noon. After only six days somehow my tireless Julie had the house looking festive, warm, and welcoming. As Mam, Paw, Mike and his three girls sat down with us to feast on the turkey and ham, I popped the cork on a bottle of ice-cold Prosecco, and poured a glass for all the grown-ups. We lifted our glasses of bubbly wine and drank a toast. "To Ruthie Leming," I said, and we clinked our glasses.

After dinner everyone migrated to the living room, where Matthew had warmed up the Beatles Rock Band game on the Wii. Our cousins Melanie and Bob Bare came over, along with our musician cousin Emily Branton and her little girl, Ava. The wine flowed generously. Even Mike, who had been so solemn throughout dinner, began to brighten, smile, and sing along with the kids. At one point I went to the kitchen to fetch another bottle of wine, and came back to see a room full of family, all singing the Beatles together.

" 'Here comes the sun,' " my family sang in unison. " 'It's all ri-i-ight.' "

———

Coming home to the place where I grew up would not be easy, but if I was going to live more like Ruthie, I was obliged to stick it out, come what may. In this my patron saint, Benedict of Nursia, came to my aid. St. Benedict was a fifth-century Italian monk who more or less founded monasticism in the West. In his famous rule Benedict required his monks take a vow of what he called "stability." That means that the monastery in which Benedictine monks profess their vows will in most cases be their home for the rest of their lives. St. Benedict considered the kinds of monks who moved from place to place all the time to be the worst of all. They refused the discipline of place and community, and because of that, they could never know humility. Without humility they could never be happy.

The implication for me was clear: if I wanted to know the inner peace and happiness in community that Ruthie had, I needed to practice a rule of stability. Accept the limitations of a place, in humility, and the joys that can also be found there may open themselves.

I'm not sure what St. Benedict would have made of the Blue Horse Saloon, a downtown alehouse that was—until it burned down in 2012—one of a handful of places in town where nightly revels commenced. On Christmas week, one of the bar's more vigorous diversions had attracted the eye of my mother.

"I think," she told me, "that I'm going to ride that bull."

"You what?"

"The mechanical bull at the Blue Horse. I think I'm going to ride it on Friday night."

"Mama, are you out of your mind? You're sixty-eight years old. When was the last time you were in a barroom?"

"Hannah said that I should ride that bull. She was just messing with me, but I don't know, it sounds like a fun thing to do. I feel like I've turned a corner. I think it was the candles. I told Hannah that sounded like a good idea, and she put it on Facebook. Now she's got about forty people saying they'll come out and watch me do it. You want to come?"

On Friday night there was a rowdy scrum of Mam fans crowded

into the back end of the Blue Horse, a laidback but respectable honky-tonk with a handsome bar, a pool table, and an air of good cheer. When the bright blue inflatable pallet surrounding the bull began to rise, Mam's moment in the neon spotlight of the beer signs arrived.

"Go Mammy! Go Mammy!" the crowd chanted. Grinning broadly enough to swallow her ears, Mam, wearing a baggy red sweater and a pair of tight jeans, donned a straw cowboy hat and climbed onto the spongy pallet. But the years had not been kind to the six-time grandmother. She couldn't figure out how to mount the metallic beast.

Big Show came to the rescue. He gallantly offered his cupped hands as a stair step. This didn't work. Then Show seized Mam by the thigh and, with a mighty shove, hoisted her atop the bull. He gave her bottom a robust slap and wished her luck.

"Merry Christmas!" she cracked.

With a big smile we hadn't seen in ages beaming from her face, Mam lifted her cowboy hat high above her head as a signal for the bar owner to start the bucking.

The bull rocked back and forth gently, like an aged Holstein trundling out to pasture. Mam rolled with it, pitching and yawing and, incredibly, failing to fall off. She lasted almost thirty seconds before tumbling onto the pallet below, roaring with laughter. The crowd whooped and hollered, helped Mam to her feet, sweeping her up with a flood of hugs, backslapping, and words of encouragement.

She stayed till one in the morning, singing karaoke with Hannah, and for the first time in a very long time, having a blast.

Even though Mam's state of mind improved after the holidays, she still struggled to maintain her balance. She steadied herself by taking as much care of Ruthie and Mike's girls as she was able to—but that, at times, was too much for Claire and Rebekah. They sometimes felt she was hovering too close. For Mam, though, as long as she could feel that she had the chance to fulfill her vow to Ruthie, she had a reason to carry on. She had trouble finding a middle ground with Ruthie's children, and she struggled with her sorrow. Every evening at dusk Mam drove a mile up the road to visit the cemetery, to make sure the candle in the lantern she had set atop Ruthie's grave was burning. Paw worried that this prolonged her mourning; she promised him she would stop after the first year without Ruthie.

Paw was in rough shape too. Watching his daughter die broke his spirit. At seventy-seven, with his back and hip pain, he was too weak and infirm to be active. This was hard on a man who had always defined himself by what he could do. He spent too much time at home in his armchair, watching TV, drinking brandy, and despairing.

Right after we returned Paw said to me, "Not too long before he died, I took my daddy to a burial at the Starhill cemetery. When I was walking him out he said to me, 'I've had about enough of this place. I've come in and out of here too many times. Next time I come here, they just as well ought to leave me.' I feel the same way."

What consolation he found in the wake of Ruthie's death came from the company of others. He especially loved spending time with Lucas, who exudes ebullience and sunshine and was turning into an enthusiastic athlete and BB gun marksman. He was a city kid whose instincts were all country boy. That's why he and his aunt Ruthie were so close. It wasn't hard to figure why Paw felt so drawn to him these days.

One morning, on my way into Baton Rouge, I dropped Lucas off in Starhill to spend the morning with his grandfather.

"I'm glad we homeschool," Lucas told me. "That way I can go do things with Paw when he has time."

It seemed to his mother and me that this time with Paw added a priceless dimension to Lucas's education. Paw told me later that day how much he enjoyed his time with Lucas. They saw construction workers building a driveway. They went fishing on the pond. They learned about compasses. Lucas stacked Mam and Paw's firewood, and beamed telling us about how he'd helped them.

"He's Johnny-on-the-Spot, let me tell you," Paw gushed. "Lucas is ready for anything."

Though I was back in town John Bickham and Big Show remained Paw's main supports. They loved and respected him like their own father, and they could give him things—understanding, and practical help maintaining the land—beyond my power to provide. They were both aware of his faults, but they loved him—and he loved them in return—with a purity and simplicity that wasn't possible between the two of us.

I had no illusions about what my relationship with my father would be like when I returned. I had made that mistake once before. Besides I didn't need his approval as much as when I had returned nearly twenty years earlier. I had become my own man. I built a good career as a writer and journalist, had a wife and three children, and had been a success on my own. I was doing meaningful work, and was happy. I had nothing left to prove to him or to myself. I could therefore afford, emotionally and psychologically, to live close to my dad because my sense of self-worth no longer depended on his favor. He never has understood me, and may never, but I knew that he loved me, and that he needed me to be with him during these last years of his life. That was enough; I had no right to expect more.

Still, in my heart, I wanted a sign from him, however small, that he blessed, in retrospect, the journey I had taken through life—that even though I did not do it his way, the way I had done it was worthy in his eyes. Ruthie's contempt for things she did not understand—especially anything she considered artificial or snobbish—came from some- where. I may have decided to walk a path more like the one my sister had chosen, but that did not mean I believed my former path had been a mistake. Nevertheless I could not shake the dread that as Ray Dreher's only son and male heir—a big deal in Southern families—having turned my back on my birthright would always mark me as a man of suspect character.

If he were able to give me his benediction, it would be a matchless grace. The time for that, though, had surely passed. My task was to offer him as much grace as I could muster, to bless him with acts of love, and to forgive and forget the rejection and alienation from him that I had felt as a young man.

But I didn't like it when he was drinking brandy, and hated to be around him when he'd had too much. I understood why he was doing it; his child was dead, his body was breaking down, and even though he was tired of life, life wasn't tired of him. Blood may be thicker than liquor, but nothing was as thin as my patience. Big Show and John Bickham weren't like that. They knew how to abide. I had a lot to learn from them.

I had a lot to learn as well about how to make the transition back to a town where ancient history—my ancient history—still lives. One afternoon, not long after our return, I saw the girl who had been the chief instigator of my high school misery jog by.

She was now, of course, a middle-aged woman, but she looked great. She had mellowed over the years; you could see in her face that she was a much happier person now than she had been in high school. She stopped to talk to Julie and me, and was wonderful. It was awkward for me, though. Should I tell her that everything ugly that happened between us back in the day is gone and forgotten? For me it really was, and had been for a long time; the epiphanies after Ruthie's passing confirmed that. Would it be presumptuous to tell her I forgive her? After all she did not ask to be forgiven, and maybe she cannot even remember what she did. Maybe it's better to leave things in peace. I discovered years after her hazing of me that she herself was struggling with some serious personal problems during her teenage years; her torment of others and me was the result of her private pain.

Besides she had phoned me in Philadelphia days after Ruthie's diagnosis to tell me how sorry she was to hear the news, and that she was praying for our family, and for me. Maybe I should take her aside and tell her that things were fine between us, and that if she in any way labored under a burden of guilt, that she should not carry it on my account, because I held nothing against her. In fact if she and her friends hadn't made my life so unbearable back then, it is entirely possible that all the good things that followed for me, from the Louisiana School onward, might never have happened. What they intended for evil when we were kids, God, in the years that followed, turned into good.

This is what it meant to move home. Communitarian romanticism is fine, but what do you do when the past isn't even past, but is in fact jogging down your street, and stepping onto your front porch to say hello?

———

The people of the town had been terrifically welcoming to us. The real challenges to reentry were almost entirely within my family, and inside my head. For me to follow Benedict's rule of stability, I would need to work at achieving some kind of closure with my father and to get to the bottom of the root cause of an underlying tension that existed between me, a decent person, and my sister, a beatific one. Mam's anxiety and Paw's despair were tough cases, but I was on familiar ground with them. With Ruthie's children it was a different story.

One afternoon before she returned to college for the spring semester, Hannah and I borrowed Paw's truck and drove to Baton Rouge, stopping off at furniture stores, looking for chairs for our new house. She was anxious and confused about her mother's death, and what it meant for her.

"Why does anything mean anything, Uncle Rod?" she asked as we motored into the city. "I mean, we're here, and then we die. What's the point of any of it? Why don't we just do whatever we want to do while we're alive? We're going to end up dead anyway."

I had to remind myself that I too had once been a teenager who dwelled on these kinds of philosophical questions. I did it out of curiosity, but in Hannah's case fate had taken her hard by the hair and rubbed her nose in them.

Hannah knew her mother was a good woman who did everything right, and still she died young and in pain. I quickly discerned that Hannah didn't really wonder how she should be living. What she was really asking was how to reconcile what happened to her mother with the belief that God is all good and all powerful.

"I don't know why this happened to your mom," I said. "And I can't tell you why anybody has to die the way they do. There *are* answers, but it's not for us to know them now."

"But I want to know!" Hannah said. "I want to know why this happened."

"But you can't. Nobody can. What if you could know? What if God gave you a piece of paper with all the answers written on it? Would that make it any easier to live without your mama?"

She didn't answer me.

"Hannah, your mom never questioned why this had happened to her. It's why she had so much peace. If I had terminal lung cancer, I would read every theological book I could get my hands on, and at the end, after all my searching for answers, the best I could hope for would be to have the peace that your mom did from the very beginning.

"She didn't try to understand the mystery. She just tried to live it. We have to try too. There's no other way."

Hannah said nothing. I was out of things to say. We drove on.

Ruthie's younger children, Claire and Rebekah, posed a different kind of challenge. Claire was twelve when we moved back; Rebekah, nine. They remained shy, polite, deferential, and distant. How could it have been otherwise? We were the uncle and aunt they saw only a few times each year, and we spent all that time talking with the grown-ups, and Hannah, who was older, while they played with our kids. For all they knew of us, we were strangers who moved in and out of their lives, and never stayed.

One late winter night Claire and Rebekah spent the night with us. After dinner while Bekah played the Wii with Lucas and Nora, Claire and I sat in the room off the kitchen and talked. She was quiet and poised, but spoke tartly about her ongoing arguments with Hannah. I told her I worried about that she and Hannah were laying down battle lines that would define their relationship for the rest of their lives.

"Your mom and I did that," I said. "Mam and Paw tried to warn us, but it happened anyway. We were both at fault, but as time went by, something hardened. After a while, there was nothing I could do to cross the line between us. We couldn't even talk about it. And now she's gone. I so don't want that to happen to you and Hannah."

Claire sat in the leather armchair across from me, a tendril of hair falling out of her ponytail and over her forehead, watching me with wide eyes, listening intently.

"Hannah has not been doing right by you, and she needs to change," I said. "But you need to try to understand what the past few years have been like for Hannah. She told me that she felt like an outsider and a misfit in the family sometimes. The things that come easy for you— feeling at ease with yourself and like you belong in this place—are hard for her."

"Your mom and I weren't as close as I wish we had been," I said. "I was a jerk to her when we were young, and when we got older, she thought I was weird. We loved each other, but I'm not sure how much we liked each other. It's too bad, because we can't fix that now."

Claire looked at me, blinking calmly.

"Your mom never knew that what she had, was what I wanted so much," I said. "Your Mama knew who she was and where she was supposed to be. I've struggled all my life with that. I admired what she had and wanted to be like her. I really did. And I never told her that."

Claire's eyes widened.

"You wanted to be like Mama?" she said.

"Yes."

"You *wanted* to be like Mama?!"

"Yes, I absolutely did."

Relief flooded her face. I thought, *Maybe I've gotten somewhere tonight.*

———

Reconciliation with my folks, my nieces, my town, and my past would not come quickly or without difficulty, but with patience it might. Though Ruthie's death had the unanticipated effect of making this broader reconciliation possible, she and I would never be able to reach an understanding. She was gone, but I still strongly felt her presence, and not in a peaceable way.

We may have informally put aside our differences on her front porch that warm February morning in her first cancer week, but that did not explain why things were always so difficult between Ruthie and me. God knows I held no grudge against her, but I could not grasp why I was perhaps the only person on earth whom she didn't treat with patience and understanding. As I had explained to Claire, at some point after our childhood, an invisible wall came up between her mother and me. We could talk over that wall, but could not breach it. I would have loved to have spoken intimately with Ruthie before the end, to have cleared things up between us, to make sure we were solid with each other. Ruthie wouldn't have it. She wouldn't talk about matters she found unpleasant, and after she fell ill, resisted having "serious" conversations, because that was the kind of thing a dying person would do. What's more, Ruthie had always been the sort who, having made up her mind about something, found it very difficult to question her own judgment.

So she died and I was left to wonder why I was such a bone in my sister's throat. Now that I was home I was able to explore what wrong I might have done her, and why things went so wrong between us.

On a Sunday afternoon in early March Abby Temple sat in a leather armchair in my den. I poured her a glass of wine and we talked about her upcoming wedding to Doug Cochran. At a party in Abby's honor a few weeks before, she had toasted Ruthie's memory and gotten choked up talking about how much she would miss having at her wedding the best friend who had prayed so faithfully for her to meet someone. When she walked down the aisle later that month in the Methodist church to become Doug's wife, she would carry in her wedding bouquet the photo of Ruthie and her dancing on the bar at Angelle's Whiskey River Landing.

I took the chance to ask Abby why Ruthie had such a hard heart toward me. Abby took a deep swallow of her wine, set her glass down on the table between us, folded her hands in her lap, and said that yes, she was quite familiar with the tension between my sister and me. And yes, she said, I was the only person in the world Ruthie had no patience for.

"Remember how you said to me that you believed your dad saw your being so different as a rejection of him?" Abby said. "I think that's how she felt. She never said that, but if you'd hear her talk, that's the feeling you'd get."

Because Ruthie took things so personally she never tried to understand things Julie and I would do that did not make sense to her, Abby explained. When Hannah came to visit us in Philly and we took her to the fancy French restaurant on Rittenhouse Square, Ruthie sniffed to Abby that our gesture to Hannah had been "extravagant."

"It *was* extravagant!" I protested. "It was one of the most expensive

meals of my life, and the only time in two years in Philly that we went
to a really nice restaurant. But we love Hannah and wanted to give her
something she'd dreamed of. It was worth the money. I can't for the life
of me understand why Ruthie was against that."

Abby moved to the edge of her chair and leaned forward.

"Rod, here's something you probably don't know about your sister,"
Abby said. "Ruthie was the kindest, most accepting person, but she
had something against wealth, and people with wealth. Anything having to do with wealth turned her off."

Ah. That was news to me, and strange, too, because I have never
been wealthy. True, I've always made more money than Ruthie, but
I've also lived in far more expensive cities. I traveled for pleasure in
Europe a fair bit, but I always did so cheaply, adding a leg onto a business trip, or traveling in the off-season and staying with friends. For
Ruthie going to Europe was something rich people did. I could have
spent twice as much to vacation in Florida, one of Ruthie's favorite
spots, and she wouldn't have noticed.

"Ruthie couldn't see how things could be different," Abby said.
"In her mind there was absolutely a right way and a wrong way. She
couldn't accept that the things you loved and wanted were different but
also valid. There was right, and there was wrong. She was a lot like
your daddy in that way."

I had to agree with that. Because Ruthie was a public school teacher
she took our decision to homeschool our children as a rejection. I can't
blame her for being naturally skeptical. Over the years, however, I
explained to her on several occasions why we chose to do this, given
Matthew's Asperger's and his intense emotional struggles. She listened politely, but refused to take me seriously, or engage beyond a
level I found patronizing. I didn't expect her to agree with me, necessarily, but I hoped to help her see that our decision was reasonable. She
could not, or would not, do it—and judged us harshly.

A few days later I was having a cup of coffee with Mike in his kitchen, and shared Abby's take with Mike. Did he agree with Abby? He nodded his head yes.

"It hurt Ruthie that you left," he said. "She just had the sense that family was everything, and we all stay here on the ridge together. Nobody ever leaves. And she never could understand how you could make a living as a writer." My sister was a math person who hardly ever looked at the newspaper; she had no idea how hard I worked, or why my work was valuable. And she never asked. The fact that I could make a living by writing looked to her like a continuation of a pattern she had seen back in college when I wouldn't go to class but still did well on a test.

It was frustrating to hear all this, and to think about how much closer Ruthie and I could have been if she had only been able to approach me, her brother, with the same empathy she relied on to help her understand and embrace the children in her classroom. Mike and Ruthie's friends wanted me to know, though, that despite this sibling tension, Ruthie loved me fiercely and was proud of me, even though she wouldn't admit it.

That she loved me I could accept—but that didn't prove much. Ruthie would not have shirked what she would have seen as her familial duty to love her brother. My concern had to do with whether or not Ruthie thought I was sound; that is, if she believed that beneath all my cosmopolitan vices, I was a man of integrity. Despite her all-too-human flaws, I really believed my sister was a saint, and it kind of broke my heart that I could not share in the uncomplicated love and adoration the whole town felt for her. "It's a sibling thing," Abby said, trying to console me. Maybe so, but it stinks being the only guy in town who could tick off a saint.

All I wanted was a sign that even though she didn't understand me or accept my ways, she at least thought I was good. If I could not be at peace with Ruthie's memory, could I ever really be reconciled to my home? Ruthie, Paw, and the Land: the years had tangled them thickly

together in my imagination, like the ropy old vines that cling insepa-
rably to the trunks of old oak trees deep in the swamp. Again I turned
to Benedict, who had encouraged his monks to "not be daunted immediately by fear and run away from the road that leads to salvation. It is
bound to be narrow at the outset."

CHAPTER FOURTEEN

One's Destination Is
Never a Place

A few years back, feeling the generous uncle, I promised Hannah, "When you finish high school, I'll take you to Paris." It took a year past her graduation date, but I finally made good on my vow.

Hannah had never been overseas before. When I broke the news to her after dinner at our place one night that she would have a taste of April in Paris, she could hardly contain her excitement. I was pretty jazzed myself. After spending what should have been a joyous time in her life watching her mother die, Hannah deserved to have a fantastic trip, to have fun, and to be reminded that the world is a good and beautiful place, despite it all.

"One's destination is never a place, but rather a new way of looking at things," said Henry Miller, the expatriate American writer who lived in Paris. This is what Paris had long been for me, and what I hoped it would be for Hannah. Maybe I could pass down the love of France to the first generation of our family who never had the chance to know Aunt Lois and Aunt Hilda.

In my mind Paris stood for cosmopolitan beauty—art, the Gothic cathedral, the grand boulevards, the elegant food and wine—lightness, liberty, and imagination. To me Starhill always meant natural beauty—which left me, an avid indoorsman, largely unmoved—everydayness, obligation, and a closed-mindedness that scorned imagination as artifice and the assertion of personal freedom as an abdication of duty. To be sure, that was *my* interpretation, not Hannah's. Still I knew that her experience had been close enough to my own that she would gain a certain perspective from seeing Paris.

"Be careful," Julie warned me. "Remember, Hannah's Paris is not necessarily going to be your Paris. You don't want to make her feel like she has to see things your way." The message was clear: she's your niece, not your acolyte. True, and important to keep in mind. It would do my young niece no good to cast off the burden of her late mother's worldview, only to be shackled by her overbearing uncle's.

We landed at Charles de Gaulle airport on the Saturday morning of Easter weekend, and found our way into the city, and to our little hotel in Saint-Germain-des-Prés, on the Rue de Lille, one block off the River Seine. I had chosen this neighborhood because it had been in Hemingway's Paris, and I knew Hannah would recognize some of the place names. On the flight over she said that she wanted to go dancing, and to hear the music that Hemingway did. You really can't, I said; Cole Porter and Josephine Baker are long dead. She looked disappointed.

"I'm just hoping that I'm a different person in Paris," she said.

"You won't be, not at first," I said. "If you think you're going to get off the plane and all the things you don't like about yourself are gone, well, it's not going to happen. Paris will change you, if you let it, but you're not going to be able to tell how for a long time."

After storing our suitcases in our rooms, we ambled around the corner and up the street to Le Voltaire, a homey Parisian café directly across the Seine from the Louvre. It was lunchtime, and we took a booth near the door. The sound of tinkling glasses, clattering silverware, and lilting French voices sounded like a cantata for flute and wind chime. In my halting French I ordered two glasses of red wine, a bottle of water, and a *plat de fromage*. The server brought the cheese, and Hannah took a bite of raw-milk Camembert. Her face lit up.

"Oh my God, Uncle Rod, this is so good!" she said. "I can't believe it. I can't believe I'm finally in Paris!"

After lunch we crossed the Pont Royal and wandered past the Louvre. We walked to the Marais and met an old Parisian friend and her family for tea at Mariage Fréres. Then we walked over to the Place des Vosges, Henri IV's seventeenth-century garden, and standing under the linden trees, waited for my friends Philippe and Beatrice Delansay to drive by to pick us up.

My friendship with the Delansays is the happy fruit of my long loneliness as a teenager in St. Francisville. I wrote to a pen-pal agency, which matched me with Beatrice's sister Miriam, from Valkenswaard, a small town in the southern part of the Netherlands. We struck up a terrific epistolary friendship, and on my first trip to Europe, at seventeen, I visited Miriam and her family. In the years that followed I came to know the family and others in the Netherlands well, and visited many times. In 1996 I took Mam and Paw to Holland, and we all had a great time. When I became engaged to Julie it was important for the people I had come to think of as my Dutch family to meet her before we married, which occasioned another trip. In 1998 Beatrice and her fiancé, Philippe, a native Parisian, invited Julie and me to their wedding in the Loire Valley, which turned into one of the great adventures of our married life. I counted it a privilege to share these dear friends with Hannah.

Bea and Philippe gave us a car tour of the Champs-Élysées, which ended at a nearby restaurant that had been recommended to me by a maître d' in New Orleans. Hannah and I were so waylaid by jet lag that we could hardly pay attention to the meal. The Delansays dropped us at our hotel and promised to meet us in front of Notre Dame cathedral the next morning for Easter high mass.

Hannah and I met downstairs in time to get breakfast before mass. Walking along Boulevard Saint-Germain, the first open café we came to was none other than the Café de Flore, famed hangout of Parisian writers and intellectuals, including Hemingway, who is said to have written part of *A Moveable Feast* there. We took a table at one of the red leather banquettes and had croissants, butter, and café au lait, then hurried through the Latin Quarter and across the river to the cathedral.

As we stood with Philippe and Bea under the great arches of Notre Dame, listening to the Latin chants fill the vault, I wondered if the stones spoke to Hannah's soul as the stones of Chartres had spoken to mine. I asked her what she was thinking about, and she smiled nervously, but said nothing.

Oh look, you're doing just what you swore you wouldn't, I reproached myself. *You can't just leave the moment alone, can you? You have to pin the butterfly to the desk. Let it fly!*

After the mass we beavered through the throng in front of the cathedral, crossed the Petit Pont back to the Latin Quarter, and landed at Le Petit Pontoise, a tiny restaurant specializing in French country *cuisine de grand-mère*. We walked off the repast in the Luxembourg Gardens, where Bea and Hannah spoke privately, and Philippe and I talked about what it means to move home for the sake of family. A decade earlier Philippe helped found a software company in Silicon Valley and had been quite successful. But after years of living the fabled American dream, he and Beatrice had moved with their children to the Netherlands. Bea's mother had died, and her family needed them.

"When y'all moved back," I told my friend, "I was secretly happy. Even though it means we probably won't get to see y'all as often; for some reason I wanted Leon and Sophie to grow up knowing their European heritage, not as Californians."

"It was the right thing to do, no doubt about it," Philippe told me. "But it's hard. You know, we lived in Tokyo for a while before we married, and then we had all those years in California. It's tough when you go home, though, because if you've lived all those other places, and had all those different experiences, it's hard to relate to the people you grew up with. It's not your fault, and it's not their fault. But all our friends who have done what we've done have the same experience."

He was right, of course. You can't unsee what you have seen, unlearn what you have learned. The only way to live entirely at ease with one's hometown is never to have left, never to have seen how life is elsewhere, right? Or maybe not. Ruthie's nature was not my nature. For me the only reason I was able to return to St. Francisville in the middle of my life was because I left it so long ago and satisfied my curiosity about the world beyond. Had I chosen Ruthie's path when I was young, my way through life would likely have been bitter, filled with regret about the roads not taken.

Could the Simmons sisters be my role models? They had lived all over, but returned to Starhill, the place of their birth, to live out their last years in a tin-roofed cabin under a Chinese rain tree. Despite their poverty and great distance from the grand boulevards of the cultural capitals, Lois and Hilda created a salon for themselves. And Paris would always be within them—the city's mythic allure was still strong enough in them at the end of their lives to pass Paris onto a boy in diapers.

Later I tried to talk to my niece about her experience at Notre Dame, but she deflected my questions. As we walked around the city and I would ask her what she thought of a building, she would demur. On the evening of our last full day in Paris, I told Hannah I was going to take the train in the morning from Gare Montparnasse to Chartres, to pray in the cathedral.

"Uncle Rod, if it's okay with you, I'd like to stay in the city and go to the Musée d'Orsay instead," she said.

I was crestfallen. How could a teenager mourning her dead mother prefer to open herself to the lightness, color, and gaiety of the world of the French Impressionists when she could be tromping around a gray Gothic pile with her flying butthead of an uncle, contemplating God, medievalism, and the meaning of life?

The question is ridiculous, of course. *Remember, Hannah's Paris is not necessarily going to be your Paris. Maybe this is for the best,* I thought. *That girl has had a lot more religion in her life than I had at her age, and a lot less art.*

"That's fine," I said. "Just be careful."

"I will. Thank you, Uncle Rod."

The next morning I took a taxi to Gare Montparnasse and took a train to the southwest of Paris, to Chartres. Two hours later I found myself standing at the heart of the medieval labyrinth on the cathedral floor, gazing at the rose window on the west portal, trying to recapture the shock of awe that captivated my imagination at seventeen. It would not come. You can meet your true love for the first time only once.

But then, I, a believing pilgrim, did not need that awe now as I needed it then. It was enough to stand here, in the presence of God, and in this incomparable house built to His glory, and in honor of the Virgin Mary, and to be grateful. With the noonday sun streaming pale on my face through the image of Christ the Judge, I prayed for Ruthie's soul and for our family back home, and I grieved for how cracked and broken we all are. Love is the only thing that can fill in the cracks and make us whole and strong again.

There is a side altar in the cathedral where pilgrims can light candles and kneel in prayer. I said a rosary there for my family. As I walked away I saw a plaque on a pillar, honoring the poet Charles Péguy, who walked from Paris to Chartres in 1912 to pray for his sick child. Péguy, shot dead in the war two years later, revived the medieval custom of the Paris-to-Chartres pilgrimage. In *The Portal of the Mystery of Hope*, his book-length poem to the Virgin Mary, Péguy said there are two kinds of saints: those who come from the armies of the righteous, and those who come from the ranks of sinners: "Those who have never caused any worry, any serious dread, and those who have almost caused despair." Two paths diverging in the wood, but both leading home to heaven. Péguy continues:

Thus God did not want
It wouldn't have pleased him
To have only one voice in the concert.

I spoke to my sister in prayer, asking her to help me find my way home, and in so doing I felt again the distance between us. Then I asked her to pray for me, to help me be at peace with her memory.

And then I said good-bye to Chartres, where I first learned to delight in God.

Walking up Boulevard Saint-Germain to our last dinner in Paris, Hannah gushed about her day in the museum, and how she bought a bottle of wine, some cheese and some bread, and had a picnic on a quai by the river. Yes, it had been the right thing to let my niece have this day on her own, to guide herself by her own desires. As we waited in front of Les Deux Magots to cross the boulevard, she said something startling.

"I thought I would come here and never want to go home," Hannah said. "I found out, though, that I miss my family a lot more than I thought I would. I don't ever want to live too far from them. And I need to be closer to the country than I thought. Are you disappointed?"

"Hannah, that's great," I said. "No way am I disappointed. That surprises me too, but see, Paris showed you something important about yourself."

"I'm afraid I disappointed you," she said, as we crossed the street. "I think you wanted me to have this big intellectual experience. To me it was just a great vacation. I've been so sad since Mama died, and it was so much fun to leave all that behind, and just enjoy myself."

"I'm sorry if I made you feel that way. Paris gave you what you needed now. You can always come back for the rest, if you want. My Paris isn't your Paris, and that's okay."

We turned onto Rue Montfaucon and stepped into a petite oyster bar, clean, bright, and crisp as freshly starched tablecloths, and took a table at the far wall. Philippe had introduced me to raw French oysters on Sunday night, at a place in the Marais, and I had been knocked flat by their intense flavor. They were grenades of the sea, exploding with salt, iodine, and the taste of the ocean—and they had instantly made of me a traitor to my beloved Louisiana oysters. It turned out that Huitre-rie Regis, one of the best oyster bars in the entire city, was there in our neighborhood. This was my second visit there on this vacation.

We ordered our oysters—exquisite *fines de claires*—and two glasses of Sancerre. Soon the server returned with a platter of glistening oysters on the half shell, resting on a bed of crushed ice beribboned with seaweed. I plucked a shell out with my left hand, gently loosened the oyster from its shell with my fork, and slurped it down.

I sipped my wine, then began subjecting my poor niece to an achingly sincere and Sancerre-addled oration about how the deliciousness of oysters tells us something about the nature of God. Hannah listened to a few minutes of this pretentious codswallop. Finally she couldn't take a second more.

"Uncle Rod, you're too intense!" she spat. "Remember, Mama made fun of you and your friend in college, sitting there talking about philosophy? She was happier than you, and she had a good life. Why shouldn't I live that way?"

That stung. As we made our way through the oysters, I conceded that yes, my weakness was to overintellectualize everything, but that she had no way of knowing that her mother was happier than I. If happiness means the absence of internal conflict, then yes, Ruthie was happier.

"She kept that up by refusing to think about anything that upset her settled opinions," I said. "That's not going to work for you. You are too curious! If you decide you have to hide from the big questions to be happy, you are going to spend your whole life running faster and faster to stay ahead of them. You can't live that way. It's always better to live in the truth, as hard as it is, than to live a happy lie."

We paid our bill and stepped stiff-legged and nervous out into the cool night air. It began to rain softly. We walked back down the boulevard, toward Rue du Bac, looking for a place to have dinner after our oyster appetizer. The evening seemed to be listing beyond my control.

"Uncle Rod, I need to tell you something," Hannah said, her voice rising. "I really think you and Aunt Julie should stop trying so hard to get close to Claire and Rebekah. It's not going to work."

"Why not?"

"Because we were raised in a house where our Mama a lot of times had a bad opinion of you," she said. "She never talked bad about you to us, but we could tell that she didn't like the way you lived. We could hear the things she said, and Paw too. I had a bad opinion of you myself, until I started coming to visit y'all, and I saw how wrong they were.

"I was fifteen the first time I did that," she continued. "My sisters are still young. They don't know any different. All they know is how we were raised. It makes me sad to see you and Aunt Julie trying so hard, me knowing you're not going to get anywhere. I don't want y'all to be hurt."

I *was* hurt. And furious because Hannah told me that her mother's criticism carried on beyond that moment on Ruthie's front porch the week of her diagnosis, when I thought everything was made right between us. Things were fine, Ruthie had said, but in truth they weren't fine. With this sudden revelation, I felt trapped by my family's legacy—and unable to do anything about it. How could I compete with the lasting power of Ruthie's judgment—and, to a lesser extent, Paw's? I wanted to be a different man, a better man, but in that emotionally charged moment it looked like Ruthie had closed the minds of her children to the possibility that I had anything worthwhile to offer them.

In fact it felt like 1994 all over again: the same feeling I had the night Paw told me that he was glad I had come home because it meant I accepted that he had been right. That ghost found me all these

years later, on Boulevard Saint-Germain. Once again it frightened
and humiliated me, but this time it was even scarier. In ninety-four
I was the only victim of my bad judgment. Now I had uprooted my
wife and children because of what now looked like my foolish belief
that our family could change, and that we could live in peace and
mutual acceptance. As I stalked up the boulevard with Hannah, my
heart pounded less from our pace and more from a crushing feeling
of betrayal and self-loathing. I had been seduced by my own chronic
yearning to return to a sense of unity with my family and my home,
and, in the high emotion following Ruthie's death, had allowed myself
to be seduced.

My stomach knotted and my throat tightened.

"Let me tell you something," I growled. "Sometimes your mother
and your grandfather could be ignorant and mean. They had no idea
what they were talking about. They just judged. Why do you think I
had to get out of there? I couldn't take it! Do you understand that Julie
and I uprooted our family and moved to Louisiana, mostly for your
sisters? And now you're telling me that Ruthie poisoned the well for
them."

I regretted these words as soon as I said them. My temper had gotten the best of me, and I had spoken out of hurt and fear, piercing my
niece's heart with the sharpness of my words. She had no way to com-
prehend the long and difficult family history that provoked a reaction
in me that must have seemed wildly disproportionate. The kid did not
deserve this.

Hannah started to cry. "I wish I had never told you!"

"No," I said. "No. I'm glad you told me. Didn't I just tell you it's
always better to live in truth than to live a lie? You did the right thing.
Honest, you did."

"But now you're mad."

"Yeah, I am."

We walked on. I felt like an angry teenager again as we turned the corner and walked south down Rue du Bac. The initial rush of hot anger subsided, giving way to a sense of overwhelming sadness.

"It was such a waste," I said, fighting back tears. "Ruthie and I could have had so many good years together. She wouldn't let it happen."

"Mama wasn't a bad person!" Hannah said, defensively. "She loved you."

"I know!" I shot back. "I think she was a saint. It makes no sense. That's why this is driving me so crazy. I *know* she loved me. It would be a lot easier to figure out if I believed she didn't."

"What are you going to do now?" Hannah asked.

"I don't know," I said. "We signed a two-year lease on the house. I'll stay until that's up at least, and probably until Mam and Paw die. Then we'll see. What I'm not going to do is keep fighting this same stupid battle for another generation. I don't have it in me."

"Uncle Rod, you can't leave!"

"Yes, I can."

"No! I need you! Please, don't go." She grabbed my arm. I thought about how when she was just a baby, this girl, this Hannah, had the power to pull me from the press gallery in Congress to a barn in rural Louisiana, where I spent cold, wet winter days in Paw's barn, painting a high chair and a footstool for her in bright, festive colors. I poured my desire for this baby's happiness and aesthetic delight in the world into my work on those objects. I had come from the Starhill barn to the streets of Paris out of the same love for her, and the longing to give her my best.

And now I was giving her my sorrow. It was wrong. She had far too much to bear as it was.

That took the fight out of me. *I don't have any right to put all this on this kid,* I thought. Her mother is dead. Just let it go.

"We'll see, baby. It's just hard, you know? Family is so damn complicated."

"I know. Uncle Rod, can we please change the subject? It's our last night in Paris. Let's go to this place on Rue de Lille I found last night. I had a kir royale there. They were really nice."

"Sounds good. Lead the way."

Back in my hotel room that night I was too rattled by Hannah's revelation to sleep. I did not doubt that Ruthie loved me, and was a deeply good woman. But I could not easily reconcile that thought with the way she thought about me, and treated me.

Then I realized that like Ruthie's death, this wasn't a problem to be solved, but a mystery to be lived. Ruthie's tenacious simplicity caused her to make unfair judgments of those she considered privileged or sophisticated, but it also allowed her to empathize more than most with the poor. Her fierce unwillingness to consider ideas and information that challenged what she preferred to believe cloistered her fine mind from the complexity and beauty of the whole wide world, but it also confirmed her in her trust of God amid a terrible trial, and it also likely gave her a year or more of life that she wouldn't have otherwise had if she had chosen to know the full truth about her condition. And Ruthie loved her family with such self-sacrificial purity that anything less than utter commitment to it struck her as a very personal kind of treachery.

Which was the real Ruthie?

The question was absurd: it was the Ruthie who loved, however imperfectly. It was the Ruthie who threw herself across the bed and begged for the spanking I deserved for treating her so cruelly. That was the Ruthie I believed had now been completed in heaven and given perfect vision. This would be the Ruthie I would have to choose to see. This wasn't a comforting lie. This was the difficult truth.

But I couldn't do it. Not yet. That moment of reckoning lay ahead.

———

Back home in St. Francisville I avoided calling Mam and Paw to tell them about my trip. I was roiling with emotion from the news that my father and my sister saw me as a charlatan. I was unsure how to act. Julie saw me tailspinning and drove to Starhill one morning to talk to Paw.

She sat with him on his back porch, side by side in the swing, took his hand in hers, and said, "I need your help."

"What is it, baby?" he said tenderly.

"Hannah and Rod had a conversation their last night in Paris and she said some things to him that broke his heart," Julie began. Then she told Paw the whole story, including the parts where Hannah had seen and heard him colluding with her mother in making unkind judgments about me.

Paw took all this in, and fought to suppress his emotions. He said he wouldn't have said or thought those things about his own son, and that he wanted to do what he needed to do to make things right.

Julie returned to town and told me about their conversation.

"He says he wouldn't have said those things?" I sputtered. "That's not true! The words Hannah heard him say about me, I've heard him use about other people."

"Okay, but look, he's hurting, and he wants to see you," Julie said. "Go out there and talk to him."

It took me another day to work up the nerve to drive to Starhill. I was nervous, partly because I hate confrontation and partly because, with his cane leaning against his chair, and with his left hand trembling, he looked so weak and breakable.

I told him that I knew Julie and he had talked, and that I didn't want to go over all that again, but that he had to know how hurt I was by it all. Even to the very last, when I was telling everybody I knew how great my sister was, and how much I admired her heroism, she was tearing me down behind my back, to her children.

Paw shook his head from side to side. His chin trembled, and tears ran down his cheeks.

"I'm so sorry," he rasped. "And now that poor baby is dead in the ground, and she can't make it right."

Suddenly I felt ashamed. This old, sick man buried his daughter. Who am I to inflict my drama on him? Who am I to hold on to this hurt? On the other hand, isn't that part of our family's problem—that we defer difficult conversations out of fear and anxiety, and an unwillingness to risk hurting someone's feelings?

Whatever the truth I lost my stomach for confrontation over his part in this mess. Maybe there would be another day.

After a while I went inside to see Mam. I found her at her sink, and kissed her on the cheek. We made small talk, and then she said, as she had ten thousand times before, how happy she was that we had moved to Louisiana.

"You know," Mam said, "not long before Ruthie died, she said to me, 'Mama, if I don't make it, I believe Rod's going to move home to take care of you and Daddy.'"

I froze.

"She said that?"

"Yes, sitting right there with me on the back porch."

"She really believed I was going to move home?"

Mam looked at me strangely. "Yes. Is something wrong?"

"No. No. Listen, I need to get back to town."

At home on Fidelity Street I motioned for Julie to follow me to our bedroom so we could talk privately.

"So how'd that go with Paw?"

"Not bad, but we didn't have any breakthroughs," I said. "He's so emotional right now. It's too hard to talk to him about this. I think I'm just going to have to let it go. But Mam said something that threw me for a loop."

I told Julie about Ruthie's prophecy. She drew her hand to her mouth. She knew exactly what this meant.

"Family was the most important thing to Ruthie," I said. "This means Ruthie thought that if it came down to it, I would do right by the family. If they needed me, I would sacrifice anything to take care of Mam and Paw."

Julie embraced me.

"It means that deep down my sister believed that I was good." I took my glasses off to wipe away my tears.

That revelation didn't fix everything. But it was a sign, it was a mercy, it was a start. And not long after that things improved between Hannah's sisters and their aunt and uncle.

———

Miss Clophine Toney, whose son I had played Little League with, died in hospice care that spring. She was eighty-two. On the day of her burial I picked Mam and Paw up and we drove to the funeral home in Zachary. James, her son, eulogized his mother. I knew my old friend had become a part-time evangelist, but I had never heard him preach. He stayed up all night praying for the right words to say. He stood behind the lectern next to his mother's open casket, flexed his arms under his gray suit and black shirt, then turned the Spirit loose on the forty or so mourners in the room.

"During the fall, my mother would go out and pick up pecans," he began, in his husky voice. "She wasn't very well educated. Today they tryin' to educate us in everything. Gotta stay with the next game, gotta make sure we go to college. We can't get too far behind, because we might not make enough money, and that would make our lives miserable. My God, we gettin' educated in everything, but we not gettin' educated in morals. We not gettin' educated in sacrifice."

James said his mother was poor and uneducated, but during pecan season, she worked hard gathering nuts from under every tree she could find.

"She was carryin' a cross," he said. "Because let me tell you something, if you don't sacrifice for your brother, if you don't sacrifice for your neighbor, you not carrying your cross."

Miss Clophine, James reminded us, took the money she made selling pecans and went to the dollar store in St. Francisville, where, despite her own great need, she spent it on presents for friends and family. I thought of the tube socks and other small gifts that Miss Clo gave Ruthie and me every Christmas.

"Aunt Grace told me the other day that of all the presents she got from everybody, those meant the most," James said. "Why? Because there was so much sacrifice. She sacrificed everything she made, just to give."

James pointed to Mam and Paw, sitting in the congregation.

"She used to give Mr. Ray and Miss Dorothy presents. And I'll say this about Mr. Ray and Miss Dorothy Dreher, they were so close to my mother and my father. They sacrificed every year, whether my mother and father had enough to give them a gift or not. They gave. We talkin' about sacrifice. We talkin' about whether you're carryin' your cross today."

As a child, James said, he would cross the river into Cajun country to stay with his Grandma Mose, Clophine's mother. There he would eat a traditional dish called couche-couche, an old-timey Cajun version of fried cornmeal mush. Grandma Mose served couche-couche and milk nearly every morning, and little James loved it.

"But every now and then," he continued, stretching his words for effect, "we wouldn't eat couche-couche and milk. We'd eat something called bouille."

Bouille, pronounced "boo-yee," is cornmeal porridge, what the poorest of the Cajun poor ate.

"I didn't like bouille. I frowned up. Mama made me that bouille sometime. Bouille tasted bad. It wasn't good," he said. "But let me tell you something: you may have family members, and you may have friends, that will feed you some bouille. It may not be food. They may not be treating you the way you think you ought to be treated. They may be doing this or doing that. You may be giving them a frown. But we may be talking about real sacrifice."

James's voice rose, and his arms began flying. This man was under conviction. He told the congregation that if a man lives long enough, he's going to see his family, friends, and neighbors die, and no matter what their sins and failings, the day will come when we wish we had them back, flaws and all.

The preacher turned to his mother's body, lying in the open casket on his left, and his voice began to crack.

"If my mama could give me that bouille one more time. If she could give me that bouille one more time. I wouldn't frown up. I wouldn't frown up. I would eat that bouille just like I ate that couche-couche. I would sacrifice my feelings. I would sacrifice my pride, if she could just give me that bouille one more time."

I glanced at Mam, who was crying. Paw grimaced and held on to his cane.

"Let me tell you, you got family members and friends who ain't treating you right," James said, pointing at the congregation. "Listen to me! Sacrifice! Sacrifice!—when they givin' you that bouille. Eat that bouille with a smile. Take what they givin' you with a smile. That's what Jesus did. He took that bouille when they was throwing it at him, when they was spittin' at him, he took it. He sacrificed.

"My mother didn't have much education, but she knew how to sacrifice. She knew that in the middle of the sacrifice, you smile. You smile."

The evangelist looked once more at his mother's body and said, in a voice filled with sweet yearning, "Mama, I wish you could give me that bouille one more time."

James stepped away, yielding the lectern to the hospice chaplain, who gave a more theologically conventional sermon. Truth to tell, I didn't listen closely. The power and the depth of what I had just heard from that Starhill country preacher, James Toney, and the lesson his mother's life left to those who knew her, stunned me. And it made me think of Ruthie, who lived and died as Miss Clophine had done: taking the bouille and giving, and smiling, all for love.

This was true religion. James showed me that. The most gifted preacher who ever stood in the pulpit at Chartres could not have spoken the Gospel any more purely.

The funeral director invited the congregation to come forward and say our last good-byes to Miss Clophine before driving out to the cemetery. I walked forward with my arm around Mam's shoulder. We stood together at Miss Clo's side. Her body was scrawny and withered, and it was clad in white pajamas, a new set, with pink stripes. I felt Mam tremble beneath my arm. She drew her fingers to her lips, kissed them, and touched them to Miss Clophine's forehead.

James buried Miss Clophine at the family cemetery, on a hill overlooking Thompson Creek, in the same graveyard where Roy Dale Craven, who played baseball with James and me, lies. Thousands of cars pass by on Highway 61 every day, and the people inside never know what treasures lay buried on the hilltop, just beyond the trees. Those people have somewhere to get to, and speed along, unaware.

———

One morning that spring a friend texted me from the Bird Man coffee shop: "The Blue Horse is on fire!" Lucas was sitting in the living room watching TV.

"Come on, Luke, there's a fire downtown," I said. "Let's go watch the firefighters put it out."

We motored down Ferdinand Street and parked outside the Ford garage to watch the action. Smoke billowed from the tavern's roof. A group of firefighters crawled up a ladder leaned against the facade, axes in hand, intending to chop a hole in the roof to let smoke out.

"You think Uncle Mike is in there?" Lucas asked.

"I don't know," I told him. In fact Mike was with a group of fire-fighters that had gone in the other side of the building, attacking the flames with hoses.

After a minute or two Lucas and I noticed people rushing into the antique store next to the tavern and hauling furniture, glassware, and paintings out to the parking lot. They were afraid the flames would leap the alley and set the antique store ablaze. Without giving it a second thought, we hustled across the street and into the store, joining the crowd of neighbors helping the shop owner save her inventory.

In the end firefighters extinguished the blaze before it jumped the alley and ignited the antique store, but the tavern and a neighboring gift shop, where the fire started, were total losses. I found Mike standing under an oak tree, covered with sweat. He had been inside the burning tavern when the ceiling collapsed on him and the others. It had been a close call. When I found Lucas and told him that I had seen his uncle, and what his uncle had done to put out the fire, he beamed, and looked as if his heart was going to burst out of his chest.

Back at home I thought about how for the first time in a long time, I had been a participant, not an observer. I had gone downtown to watch the fire and write about it, and ended by doing my part to help a neighbor in distress. For once I was not content to be abstract, ana-lytical, and contemplative. Doing good things instead of thinking good thoughts—that was new to me, and it felt right.

———

About a month after Paw and Julie had that difficult conversation, he and I sat in the shade of his back porch after Sunday dinner, talking about nothing in particular. He had been going through a rough time. One afternoon I found him in his chair, looking at a framed photo of Ruthie he kept on the side table. He was crying.

"It's so hard," he said. "I got her over here, in a picture. And I talk to her two or three times a day. I just tell her what I'm doing, what's on my mind. What my troubles are."

"Do you think she hears you?" I asked.

"I hope she does. I hope she does." He wiped his tears with his hand.

"Do you ask her to help you?"

"Yes," he said, struggling to find his voice. "I ask her to speak to God for me."

He couldn't say anything more. He needed to be alone. I left him there in his chair, talking to his lost little girl, staring at her image, as if it were an icon.

On this Sunday afternoon, though, Paw was in a happier frame of mind. Because he had a cardiologist's appointment later in the week, I had been thinking about his frail health, and pondering big questions about the life he had lived.

"Daddy, you know how Ruthie wouldn't let me record an interview with her when she was sick?" I said. "I hate that, because we don't have anything on video of her talking about her life."

"Yeah, that's a shame," he said.

"I'm wondering if you and Mama would be willing to sit for me interviewing you," I said. "It wouldn't be anything fancy, just me with my iPad camera, having a conversation."

"Well, I reckon we could do that."

I pulled my iPhone out of my pocket and told him that I wanted to do a test question, to show him how easy it would be. I figured this would take about three minutes. Sitting in the chair across from him, I pressed the red button to start recording, then asked: "You have any big regrets in life?"

Paw sat for a moment, rocking in the porch swing, then said yes, he did.

"I should have never gone to college," he said. "I was good with my hands, and wanted to work outside. I should have gone to trade school, or into some kind of technical training. My mother wouldn't have it. Aunt Hilda harassed her constantly about how I should get a college education. So I did. I was the first one in our family to finish college. I did it all for my mother and my family. It was a mistake I have always regretted."

He told me about an agricultural device he invented when he was in college, an innovative plow. Paw shared the idea with an LSU classmate, who drew up the plan and, with his permission, turned it in as a class assignment. The professor took Paw's idea, patented it, and sold the patent to a manufacturer. A couple of years later Paw saw his invention for sale in farm equipment stores.

I knew this story had to be true. When I was a child Paw got tired of swinging an axe to chop firewood, and invented and built a hydraulic woodsplitter. Forty years later the original device still works. He never patented it. I took Paw not so much to be complaining about the unfairness of the world as to be saying that he had a gift for mechanical creativity, but he had been so eager to please his family that he never sought the training that would have allowed him to fully develop his talents.

"There's something I regret even more, he carried on. "I can see now, at the end of my life, that it would have been better if after your Mama and I got married, we had packed up and left here."

I couldn't believe what I had just heard.

"What do you mean?"

"I mean what I said: we should have left this place."

And then Paw told me how he had spent his entire life sacrificing for his mother, his father, his brother, his aunts, and his cousins—all of whom, in his recollection, worked him like a dog and never gave him a moment's thanks. They could always count on Ray to fix anything, to do any job they asked of him, to give up his free time and spend his own money, to help them. They used him up.

"I was a sucker," he said, the bitterness heavy in his voice. "Aunt Lois was the only one of the whole bunch who was ever straight with me. But there was only one of her."

Paw told a jaw-dropping story about the time many years earlier when Aunt Hilda had broken the law to steal land Aunt Lois had promised to sell to him, and instead to convey it under false pretenses to the scoundrel cousin she favored. Paw discovered the ruse, which involved Hilda forging Lois's signature, in courthouse filings long after both the great-aunts were dead. I later confirmed this with someone who had been present when the deed happened.

"How do you think that made me feel, after all I had done for Aunt Hilda?" Paw said. "That right there was a bad woman."

How could I disagree? The hurt in Paw's heart was so raw. It was as if it had all happened yesterday.

"I loved my own mother more than life itself, but she was terrible to your mother," he continued. "She and her sisters, Rita and Ann, they treated your mama like dirt. They thought I had married beneath myself. Aunt Rita disowned me for marrying your mother. But you know Dorothy took it all from them. She served them like a dog, and nobody would help her.

"I should have taken her away from here," he said. "But I was so caught up in my family, and in trying to do the right thing for them. And I was tied down by this place. I was twelve years old when I bought that Farmall Cub tractor with my own money and started planting. Farming was my dream. Aunt Lois saw that, and she helped me. She paid for me to go to Chicago to show my 4-H Club steer. She drove me herself to the State Fair in Shreveport. I bought this place over here from Aunt Em"—Loisie's sister-in-law—"and put cows on it. When I married your mother, I had so much going on here I didn't think I was free to leave."

I sat there across from my father picturing him as a stout boy of twelve, riding high on his little tractor, a shock of fiery orange, cowlicked hair jammed under a straw cowboy hat, dragging a plow across a Starhill field, laying the groundwork for what he thought would be an empire of his own. He would have his family and he would be loved and respected by them all, and everything would work out the way it was supposed to because that's how things turn out for good men who do right, stay loyal, and follow the rules.

Paw's face was tense and pale as he continued to unburden himself. My three-minute interview had turned into half an hour.

"The day finally came when I stood up to my parents," he continued. "I was working in my shop over there behind Daddy's place. A piece of my equipment had broken, and it was a complicated weld to fix it. I had spent four hours that afternoon, working out there in the heat, setting that weld up. Everything was in place, when here comes Daddy out the back door to see what I was doing.

"He always had to have his hands all over whatever I was up to. Lord have mercy, I can't tell you the number of times I would be working on an electrical box, and I would have to slap his hand away—I'm talking about literally slap his hand—because he was about to touch a hot wire and electrocute himself. That's how he was. He thought he knew everything."

Paw said his father ambled over to the weld, tried to pick it up, and caused the three pieces of metal to fall to the ground, destroying an entire afternoon's work. The old man meant no harm; it was only that as usual, he did not understand his son's vision, and when to leave it alone. That afternoon, Paw did what he had never had the courage to do before: tell his father to get the hell out of his business, and stay out. When dark came Paw went into the house to tell his father good-bye and found the old man sitting on the front porch, in good spirits.

"That settled everything. We never had another problem after that," Paw said. "I should have said something like that to him and my mother a long time before. But I didn't, and by then, I was about fifty years old. It was too late for me."

I was speechless. He kept talking.

"Your sister, she was right to stand up to me over marrying Mike," Paw continued. "And so were you, when you went back to Washington to be a writer. I was too strong-willed and stubborn back then. I regret that very much."

We sat in silence for a moment.

"Daddy, I have to tell you, I don't know what to think about all this," I said. "Here I am, a man who turned his life upside down to move back here for the family, and because of the land. And now here you are telling me that you made an idol of family and place, and that you wish you had left it all behind when you were young, just like I did. What am I supposed to make of that?"

His chin trembled, he wrung his hands together, he looked me straight in the eye, and then my father said: "That I'm a sorrier man than you."

Sorrier. It means having regret. But in Southern parlance, it also means morally less worthy.

"But Daddy I hope you understand that I really do want to be back here," I said. "Because I went away all those years ago, I could come back not out of guilt, but out of love, of my own free choice."

"I know, son," he said. "I know. And I appreciate it. What I want to say to you, though, is that I don't want you to feel trapped by this place. When I'm gone, half of it is going to be yours, and the other half will go to Ruthie's children. I want you to do whatever you want with it. Did you know it's the last piece of the old Benjamin Plantation that's still owned by someone in the family? If you want to keep it up, you have my blessing. If you want to sell it, you also have my blessing. You're free."

This conversation was the most graceful thing I have ever experienced. My father, in the twilight of his long life, gave me the greatest gift he could give.

At home that afternoon I told Julie everything that had happened.

She was as stunned as I had been. For myself I had seen the errors one can fall into by placing too much emphasis on career and individual desire at the expense of family and place. But what Paw had done, in part, was to reveal the catastrophic mistake one can make if one makes a false god of family and place.

There has to be balance. Not everyone is meant to stay—or to stay away—forever. There are seasons in the lives of persons and of families. Our responsibility, both to ourselves and to each other, is to seek harmony within the limits of what we are given—and to give each other grace.

"You know," Julie told me later, "you could not have had that conversation with him if we hadn't moved back here."

She was right—and this was an important lesson. Though I talked every day to my mother and father throughout Ruthie's illness, this was not a truth that could have been revealed over the phone. Nor could it have emerged on one of our short fly-in, fly-out visits. It had to work its way to the surface over time, with patience, and, above all, with presence.

———

I was now at peace with my father. On the matter of my sister I still did not have peace, and despaired that I ever would.

The breakthrough happened on a hot Sunday afternoon—once again on Mam and Paw's back porch, after the meal. Matthew provoked a hellacious fight with Lucas, one that ended with us loading the kids into the car and driving home. Back at the house Julie and I stood in the kitchen and laid into Matthew for his constant teasing.

"You can't see this, son, but you are training your little brother to react that way," Julie chastised. "He loves you more than you understand, but you keep picking on him. You've always treated him like this. That's why he blows up at you. That's why he doesn't trust you.

"If you keep this up," she pleaded, "the day is going to come when you're not going to be able to make it right. He's going to remember the way you treated him all those years, and he might not have it in him to believe you when you say you're sorry."

In a flash it became clear. In some sense I must have trained Ruthie to distrust me and my motives. Because I've raised these boys of mine, I knew well how stout and pure Lucas's heart was, and how fiercely he loves his brother. But I also knew well how much Matthew takes that for granted, because of his nature. Both my sons are smart, but Matthew is also clever, in an intellectual and ironic, even sarcastic, way that makes straightforward Lucas feel confused and taken advantage of.

I phoned Mam and Paw later that afternoon to tell them about our disciplinary conversation with Matthew, and how, to our great frustration, Julie and I have been going at this with our older son for years.

"Did you ever have those talks with me about Ruthie?" I asked.

"*Did* we?!" Paw exclaimed. "All the time! You never learned. It broke our hearts to see what was happening between y'all. And you kept on."

"It was just like your uncle Murphy did your daddy," Mam added. "The way he saw it, he was just playing, but it hurt your daddy more than Murphy understood."

That night at bedtime, with the house dark and quiet, Matthew found me sitting in my leather armchair, working. He inclined and gave me a hug.

"Dad, I'm really sorry for what I did to Lucas today," he said, and sounded like he meant it.

"Thank you for saying that, baby," I said. "I need you to think about what Mom said today, about how you're training Lucas to distrust you. The way you are to Lucas, that was the way I was to Aunt Ruthie. I didn't think much of it. I wasn't trying to be mean. But I was mean. Mam and Paw tried to set me straight, but I guess I didn't take them seriously.

"Aunt Ruthie had a lot of trouble understanding me," I continued. "You've heard me talking to Mom. You know how much this bothers me. Watching you and your brother today, I finally understood that a lot of that is on me."

"What do you mean?" my son said.

"You know when Mom told you that the day was going to come when it might be impossible for you to make things right? At some point in our relationship, that's what happened to Aunt Ruthie and me. I can't say for sure when things went bad, or why, but I've got to face the fact that a lot of this is my own doing."

Matthew looked down, his eyes in shadow.

"Honey, Aunt Ruthie is gone, and I can't make it right with her," I said, taking his hand. "She had a chip on her shoulder about me, and she was wrong about that. But your daddy had a lot more to do with putting it there than he realized. Please don't end up like me, with your brother in the grave and you not able to do a thing except feel bad about what you did, and what you didn't do."

"Okay, Dad. Goodnight." He kissed me on the top of the head, and padded off down the hall to bed. I don't know if my words will have done any more good than Mam and Paw's did to me at the same age.

Why did this epiphany about my own culpability in the fate of my relationship with my sister give me so much peace? Because I began life with a sister who loved me so much that she was willing to take the punishment I deserved for being cruel to her. How might things have been different between us if I had been more decent to her when we were children?

I was not an unkind brother in adulthood, but I wasn't around much either to show my sister how I had matured. As our father did, Ruthie saw the world through fixed ideas; once she convinced herself she had someone figured out, she was not open to revising her judgment. With regard to her brother, this was her tragedy.

And with regard to my sister, here is mine: the first fourteen years of her life she spent shared with me, during which time I provided her with ample evidence to justify her verdict on my character. And my decades-long absence allowed that childhood narrative to cloud her judgment and harden her heart.

I spoke to Ruthie in my prayers that evening, confessing my sorrow over the way I treated her as a child, and asking her forgiveness. I have faith that from her place in heaven, with her nature perfected by the love of our merciful God, she gave it to me. And so, I was finally at peace.

———

One day in May the mobile phone in Mike's pocket buzzed. It was the monument company, telling them they were going to deliver Ruthie's headstone the next morning, May 15. It was fitting; had Ruthie lived, that would have been her forty-third birthday.

The two men showed up just before ten a.m., as planned. I drove up right behind them and saw Mike standing in the shade—it was a hot morning—in a T-shirt and jeans, watching the pair turn the earth at the head of his wife's grave, preparing it for the dark granite stone. I walked down the hill toward Mike, careful not to step in one of the fire ant mounds dotting the neatly trimmed grass lawn. The subtropical sun was already so fierce that I broke a sweat in the half a minute it took me to reach Mike.

"Mike, if you'd rather be alone, tell me," I said. "I just didn't want you to be by yourself this morning."

"It's okay," he said.

Mam and Johnette Rettig drove up and joined us, and then Paw stopped by in his pickup, on the way home from his doctor. He stood at the top of the hill, leaning on his cane, and said he didn't think he could stay. We waved him off. Johnette said good-bye as well, leaving just Mam, Mike, and myself, and the workmen.

The two workmen, the younger one black, the older one white, were soaked with sweat by the time they heaved the headstone into place. They wiped their faces, then stood by us at the foot of Ruthie's grave. The monument read:

LEMING

"Ruthie"

LOIS RUTH DREHER

MAY 15, 1969

SEPTEMBER 15, 2011

BELOVED DAUGHTER, SISTER, FRIEND

WIFE, TEACHER, MOTHER

"Today was her birthday," said the young black man. "That's something, ain't it? Sound like she was a good woman."

"She was," said Mike.

I looked at the black man. He was crying. Mike thanked them for their work, they said good-bye, and drove away.

Mike, Mam, and I stood alone at the foot of Ruthie's grave. Then I recited the Lord's Prayer, and Psalm 23. We remained there quietly for a moment, then Mam tapped me to indicate that we should leave.

"I love you, buddy," Mam said to Mike. "Thank you for making her life so happy."

We walked up the hill, got into my car, and drove away, leaving Mike there alone with his grief and loss. By then there was no shade left in the cemetery. How long he remained in the scorching sun that morning before going home, I don't know. For eight months Mike had been in the fire, unreachable. But it had not consumed him. Quietly, faithfully, he endured. Ruthie, who knew what this man was made of better than anyone, would not have been surprised.

Never would I have imagined that I would spend the morning of my little sister's forty-third birthday in the graveyard, watching workmen heave her tombstone into place. But nobody ever thinks about these things when they're young. Nobody thinks about limits, and how much we need each other. But if you live long enough, you see suffering. It comes close to you. It shatters the illusion, so dear to us, of self-sufficiency, of autonomy, of control. *Look, a wife and mother, a good woman in the prime of her life, dying from cancer.* It doesn't just happen to other people. It happens to your family. What do you do then?

The insurance company, if you're lucky enough to have insurance, pays your doctors and pharmacists, but it will not cook for you when you are too sick to cook for yourself and your kids. Nor will it clean your house, pick your kids up from school, or take them shopping when you are too weak to get out of bed. A bureaucrat from the state or the insurance company won't come sit with you, and pray with you, and tell you she loves you. It won't be the government or your insurer who allows you to die in peace, if it comes to that, because it can assure you that your spouse and children will not be left behind to face the world alone.

Only your family and your community can do that.

Because of our own mutual brokenness, the considerable affection Ruthie and I had for each other did not penetrate either of our hearts as it ought to have done. But through Abby, Tim, Laura, Big Show, John Bickham, the barefoot pallbearers, and everyone else in the town who held our family close, and held us up when we couldn't stand on our own two feet, I was able to see the effect of Ruthie's love, given and returned, in steadfast acts of ordinary faith, hope, and charity. The little way of Ruthie Leming is the plainest thing in the world, something any of us could choose. And yet so few of us do.

In the way Ruthie embraced her suffering, and through the compassion of the good people who carried her to the end, I was able to feel for the first time in nearly thirty years a profound and overwhelming affection for this place, and gratitude for what the people who stayed behind held in trust for me. In the quiet drama of my little sister's life and death in a sleepy river town, I experienced the power of love to make the entire world new.

These are my people. This is where I'm from. Ruthie showed me that.

I have wandered in my own way for half my life, and have no regrets. That was my role for a time. Now, though, I want to track, at my own pace and rhythm, the Little Way of Ruthie Leming.

———

If you had driven past the Starhill cemetery late one hot night in May, you might have seen strange figures lingering around a grave in the bottom under the hill. After a year-end meeting at school, Abby Temple, Ashley Harvey, Karen Barron, Jennifer Bickham, Tori Percy, and Rae Lynne Thomas came to be with Ruthie on her birthday. They called Mike, who met them there. They opened a bottle of wine, poured seven glasses, and drank to the memory of their brown-eyed girl. There, where all the dead of Starhill are gathered round, they laughed and told stories, and remembered the good times. Had you been there on that night under the live oaks and the crape myrtles, you would have seen that even from the grave, Ruthie Leming bestows life on those who are willing to receive it.

THE END

Acknowledgments

It is difficult to find people at the very top of the journalism profession who are humble, kind, and generous, but David Brooks is exactly that. His columns in the *New York Times* opened the door for me to tell the story of my sister, my family, and my community. I owe him more than I can ever repay. Gary Morris, my agent, believed in Ruthie's story, and advocated for it beautifully. I thank my editor, John Brodie, for also believing in this story, for making it incomparably better than it would otherwise have been. The man has earned a platter of oysters and a bottle of cold Sancerre—and I promise not to insist that metaphysics is a reliable guide to dinner.

I also owe a debt of gratitude to Steve Waldman, Gary Rosen, and Wick Allison, all of whom at some point gave me the opportunity to write a blog, from which this book was eventually born. Additionally parts of the narrative appeared in an earlier form in a column on *National Review Online*, and in a piece in the *Wall Street Journal*; my thanks, respectively, to Rich Lowry and Erich Eichman for publishing my work. My blog readers, too, have my deep appreciation; their loyalty over the years makes my vocation possible. I also owe a profound debt of gratitude to Howard and Roberta Ahmanson, whose generosity pulled me out of a deep hole and gave me my writing career back.

Ruthie had been dead only four months when I began interviewing her family and friends for this book. It was difficult for some—especially in her family—to speak of her so soon. I am grateful to them for their courage, and in particular want to thank Mike Leming. Mike is a man of strong emotion but few words. Only four months after the love of his life died in his arms, he opened his heart to me for this book. Watching that good man tell of his life and times with Ruthie, and her death, felt to me like standing at the base of a mountain during an avalanche. He knew, though, that sharing his part of the story with the world was both the greatest tribute he could give to Ruthie and an enduring legacy for their children. This book would not have been possible without him. Along these lines, I thank Hannah, Claire, and Rebekah Leming for talking to me about their mother, and for allowing me to invade the privacy of their lives for the sake of telling others about Ruthie's life and legacy. The same is true of Ray and Dorothy Dreher, my parents, who did not find it easy to talk so intimately about their daughter so soon after her death. Their openness and courage have bequeathed to generations of our family yet to be born a priceless inheritance.

The people of Starhill, and of West Feliciana, have my profound thanks, first for what they gave to my family in our time of need; second, for sitting with me for hours, talking about Ruthie; third, for welcoming us so warmly. "I hope you know how special that place is," said a Washington journalist friend. "You come from one of the last real places in America." I do, and I do. I hope they will read this book as a tribute to their own capacity for love and generosity. Ruthie's story is their story too. It is my honor to be able to tell the rest of the world about these fine people.

In part this is a book about the difference in a life a teacher can make. Writing it, and talking to people whose lives were changed for the better by Ruthie's love for them in the classroom, made me more aware of the debt of gratitude I have to my own teachers. First and foremost, there is Nora Marsh, who rescued me. My deepest thanks also goes to the teachers and staff of the Louisiana School for Math,

Science, and the Arts, in Natchitoches, who took a sad, lost kid and gave him a new life.

A number of friends read various pieces of this manuscript during the writing process. I am indebted to them for the gift of their time, and for their advice. I'm thinking in particular of Dewey and Michelle Scandurro, Leroy Huizinga, Erin Manning, Sela Ward, Jason McCrory, Paul Myers, Thomas Tucker, Josh Britton, Frederica Mathewes-Green, Mike Leming, Dorothy Dreher, John and Mia Grogan, Stephanie Lemoine, Abby Temple Cochran, John Bickham, Steve "Big Show" Shelton, James and Ashley Fox-Smith, and Tim and Laura Lindsey. They all helped me to tell this story more truthfully. To the extent I have fallen short of that goal, the fault is my own.

Finally I owe everything to my wife, Julie, and my children, Matthew, Lucas, and Nora. Writing a book is a family affair. Julie made it possible for me to devote long hours to this book. She knew how important it was to our family, and to me personally, to tell this story. She is my best reader, and my best friend. The kids stood every night with their parents before our icons, and prayed for Dad to do a good job on his Aunt Ruthie book. I trust the Lord heard them. Their father loves and cherishes them, and hopes they, along with their Leming cousins of Starhill, will treasure this true story of faith, hope, love, and family—*our* family—take it into their hearts, and build on what they have been given. May they know that wherever they go in this world, their father's love and their father's blessing goes with them. And may they rest assured that they can always, always come home.

Reading Group Guide

Discussion Questions

1. Rod Dreher moves home to be with his family after his sister's lung cancer diagnosis. Do you think a person can ever really go home again?
2. Do you need to live in a small town to experience a sense of community? Why or why not?
3. Ruthie and Rod have very difference experiences deer-stalking. What do these experiences say about them?
4. Teachers are able to shape and guide the lives of their students. How did your favorite teacher most influence you?
5. What kind of values do you associate with Starhill?
6. The idea of Ruthie as "saintly" is a repeated theme. What are some of Ruthie's most "saintly" qualities? What are some of her least "saintly" qualities?
7. What role does faith play in the lives of the Drehers and the Lemings? How does it bind the family together, and in what ways does it also divide them?
8. Have you ever asked a higher power to guide you? Did you receive that guidance and, if yes, how?
9. On page 107, Rod weeps over his sister's diagnosis and then experiences a calming "presence." On page 129 Ruthie similarly encounters "a presence." What do you think this presence was? Have you ever had an experience like Rod's or Ruthie's?

10. Ruthie's motto is "If I tell myself I'm okay, I'm okay." What do you think about this outlook?

11. Do you have a refuge, like Ruthie has in Paw's pond? Where is it and what makes it special?

12. During their ordeal, Rod notes that thanks to the people of St. Francisville, "the Leming family wanted for nothing." Would your community react in a similar way?

13. How do you feel about Rod's choice to honor Ruthie by writing this book? How would you feel about being interviewed about someone you love who had recently passed?

14. How do you want to be remembered after you die?

15. What are the ingredients that one needs to create a community?

16. The author lives many different places and changes his religious denomination several times over the course of the book. Do you think he can ever truly put down roots? Can he ever truly be happy?

17. In what ways did Rod and Ruthie contribute to their mutual estrangement? What should either of them have done differently?

18. What does Ruthie's strategy for facing cancer say about the nature of courage?

19. For Rod, a seeker, faith was primarily a matter of the head; for Ruthie, an abider, faith was primarily a matter of the heart. Discuss the strengths and weaknesses of each approach.

20. The story ends with Ruthie's friends gathering around her tombstone on her birthday. The author writes that, had you been there, you would have seen that "even from the grave, Ruthie Leming bestows life on those who are willing to receive it." What do you think this means?

21. In Paris, was Hannah right to tell the author, her uncle Rod, how her late mother really felt about him? Was Rod right to tell that story in the book? In your opinion, did this make the overall story stronger or weaker?

A Conversation with Rod Dreher, author of

The Little Way of Ruthie Leming

What inspired you to write the book and did it turn out the way you expected? Was it a way to process the grief of losing your sister, or more than that?

This story began on my blog, shortly after Ruthie was diagnosed with lung cancer. I had been writing a blog for four years, and in that time, had written a good bit about certain aspects of my personal life, insofar as they had to do with the kinds of moral, political, and philosophical questions that interested me. I found that the kinds of things Ruthie was going through inspired me and challenged me in dramatic ways.

I expected the book to be a pretty straightforward telling of my sister's life. I began with the intention of exploring how it was that a country girl who married her high school sweetheart and taught school in her tiny hometown had actually lived a life of hidden greatness—and, by extension, how this rural Louisiana community I'd thought small-minded and boring when I was a teenager was in truth a place of remarkable compassion and depth. What did Ruthie know, and what does her community know, that the rest of us missed, or forgot? The book turned out to be just that, but it also took turns I didn't anticipate when I began. Along the way I learned that going home again is a lot more complicated than you think. Returning home was the end of one journey, but it was also the beginning of another one.

To write THE LITTLE WAY OF RUTHIE LEMING, you interviewed many people from your hometown and your immediate family. What was that process like so shortly after Ruthie's passing?

It was difficult. I felt as if I were trying to cross a minefield. It was easier for some than for others, but I don't think it was easy for anybody. She had been gone only three months when I started these interviews. Folks were still dealing with their grief. Nearly everybody I asked for an interview agreed to sit for one, though, and I'll tell you why: they wanted to do it for Ruthie. One way or another, they told me that they wanted the world to know what kind of woman they had loved, and what kind of woman we had all lost.

The hardest interviews, of course, were with my family. During one interview, my father stood behind the couch in his living room talking about Ruthie, and in mid-sentence broke down into sobs, and had to grab the furniture to steady himself. It was heartbreaking to watch the man who had always been the rock of our family reduced to that, and awful too to know that I had forced him into it with my questioning. But I also knew that I couldn't flinch, and neither could he. This story had to be told. Without a doubt the most difficult interview was with Ruthie's husband, Mike, a big, quiet man who doesn't talk much, and never about his feelings. He collapsed emotionally during the interview, but pushed himself on, saying what needed saying. I've done lots of interviews in my career, including talking to 9/11 survivors. But nothing as searing as that one.

You started writing the book very soon after Ruthie passed away in 2011. Did you feel the immediacy was important to the project? Has your perspective changed now that the loss is a little less raw?

Immediacy matters here because I was able to talk to people while their recollections of Ruthie were fresh, and before their poetic memory had turned her into "Saint Ruthie," if you follow me. Writing *Little Way* was, for me, a process of coming to terms with Ruthie's life, her death, and our legacy as brother and sister—it forced me to examine some painful truths, and work through them, or at least start to do so.

In a way, things are more unsettled within me now than when Ruthie died. I've spent the past year and a half learning more about her extraordinary goodness, which has had for me the effect of making the unresolved legacy of our brother-sister relationship even harder to live with. Toward the end of the book, I tell the story about Ruthie's daughter Hannah and me on a trip to Paris together the spring after Ruthie died. On our last night in the city, Hannah revealed a secret that shocked and devastated me. When I came back to Louisiana, I had to face some hard things, and to work through them. That's not over yet, and may never be. The place I ended up, though, was a more truthful one, and therefore, I think, a more hopeful one. In that fateful Paris conversation, I told Hannah that it's wrong to seek happiness at the expense of the truth. It turned out that I had to come home and live that out as I wrestled with Ruthie's legacy. This, though, is the real world. Grace is not cheap. If I hadn't written this book so soon after Ruthie's death, I doubt any of this would have come out. It has been a severe mercy, but a mercy all the same.

What did you learn about your sister over the course of her illness and writing this book that you didn't know before? What did you learn about yourself?

I always knew Ruthie was good, but I didn't know that she was great. Ruthie led a quiet, steady life in our small Southern hometown, doing good for everyone, especially the children in her classes. Everybody here knew who Ruthie was, but the true strength and loving kindness of her character showed itself after her diagnosis. She was unshakable in her cheerfulness, her gratitude, her faith, and her hope. Absolutely steadfast, a joy to be around.

Similarly, I also saw how much I needed what she had. The world looks so different from the perspective of middle age, when you run up hard against limits, and the reality of suffering. I never regretted leaving town; it was what I needed to do. But Ruthie's sickness showed me it was time to come home, and not only that, everything that happened around her suffering helped heal some deep brokenness in me. Ruthie told me that she didn't know why God had allowed her cancer, but she trusted that whatever happened, it would be for the good. I would a million times rather have stayed away for the rest of my life if we could still have had her here. But Ruthie's gift to me was to awaken me to the value of what I had left behind, and to give me the courage to step off the path I had chosen, and take a few steps on her little way.

Ruthie had infinite patience for her students, family, and community, but you two struggled to see eye-to-eye on things. Do you think that was simply typical sibling behavior or did it go deeper than that?

Ruthie loved our family and our land so fiercely that she could not imagine why I did not share her passion. In fact, she interpreted it as a rejection of her and all that she loved. Our father was very much this way. When I was a teenager and young man, he saw that his only son was turning into someone rather different from himself, and he interpreted that as a conscious act of rebellion, rejection, and disloyalty. It hurt him deeply, and he, in turn, hurt me unintentionally by making me feel like a disappointment to him.

Over the years, as I matured and had much wider experience of the world, I came to understand better how it was that my father could love me profoundly, but also reject me at some essential level. Coming to terms with this paradoxical situation didn't make it all okay, but it gave me a perspective that helped me to be more merciful toward him. Ruthie and I had the same problem. Like Paw, she was very traditional, even Confucian, in her outlook: my place in their Starhill hierarchy of value was fixed, and my failure to accept that place was a measure of my lack of virtue. I found it harder to accept from her, though, because she was of my generation, and because she was so naturally empathetic. But that's how she was. For Ruthie, "different" was not a descriptive term, but a pejorative one. And I was different. I thought the advent of her cancer gave us the opportunity to put that behind us once and for all, but it turned out to be a lot more complicated than that. I found myself facing some complex, agonizing truths about love, family, and plain old human brokenness.

Community is a strong theme in the book. How did your idea of community evolve over the course of Ruthie's illness and how did it lead to your decision to leave the "big city" for a tiny country town?

Everybody wants to belong. I grew up in a close-knit place where I belonged, until I got to high school. Suddenly I didn't. I was bullied. This happened at the same time that my father had no idea what to do with me. Paw was, and is, a good and loving man, but as I began to turn out different from what he expected—bookish, nerdy, and intellectual instead of outdoorsy and athletic—the distance between us grew wide. Thank God for Mam, who battled with him on my behalf, so I could leave home and spend my junior and senior years in a public boarding school for gifted kids. I put my hometown behind me and never looked back.

As I grew older and started a family of my own, I found that craving for community, for a place to call home, grew even stronger. I took up themes of place and community in much of my journalism. Yet I never considered the possibility of moving back home. There was the practical matter of what I would do for a living. There was also the matter of what it would be like for my kids to grow up there. Could they have the good things I had without risking the things that drove me away? Could I live with the pressure from Paw and Ruthie? The answer was no. And then Ruthie got sick, and I saw the community in a new way. I also began to see myself in a new way. Ruthie was a healthy woman in the prime of her life and had never smoked—yet she came down with terminal lung cancer. If that could happen to a woman like her, anything was possible. What would I do if it happened to me, or to my wife? We had friends in every place we'd lived, but we hadn't lived in any one place long enough to put down the roots that Ruthie had, not only because she spent her life here, but because she cultivated roots laid down by previous generations of our family. I came to understand that my family needed what Ruthie had, the kind of things that money can't buy. I could have at least some of it, I realized—but only if I sacrificed my own individual desire to follow my career wherever it took me.

The lesson is not that everybody should move to a small town, or should return to their hometown. The lesson is that you need your community more than you think, and that you should practice what the Benedictine monks call "stability." That is, do your best to stay in one place, put down roots, and resist the currents of our culture.

You say that returning to St. Francisville was an unexpected decision, but it felt like what you had to do. What has it been like to come back to the town you grew up in and then left as a young man?

People have been great, really great. I find that some of the ordinary things that I rejected when I was young—the quiet, mostly—are things that I crave now, things that feed my soul. I love the fact that my kids can see their grandparents, and are getting to know a range of cousins they never really knew they had, because we were never able to visit long enough in the past for them to spend time with these people. The familiar used to feel oppressive; now it feels comforting. All that has to do with the way I've changed over the years.

But the town has also changed. When Julie and I were making the decision to move here, Dr. Tim Lindsey, Ruthie's physician, told me that I shouldn't think that this was the same town I left thirty years ago. He was right. It's a more open, tolerant, diverse place now. It's easier to be an outsider—an eccentric, an artist, a weirdo—here than it used to be. The local definition of "acceptably marginal" has become a lot more generous over the last three decades. All to the good!

You've always had a complicated relationship with your father, but over the course of the book that relationship evolves. How did Ruthie's passing and your return home change your relationship?

As long as Ruthie was in Starhill anchoring the family, I felt free to roam the world. I hadn't fully appreciated how much I counted on Ruthie's presence in West Feliciana Parish as key to our family's identity. Not having her made me realize that when my mother and father pass, the concrete link to Louisiana would be lost. I suddenly felt drawn to be closer—physically closer—to my dad, not only to take care of him and my mom as Ruthie was planning to do, but also to guarantee continuity through time of our family's presence there. That stuff didn't matter to me when I was young and could only see the open road ahead.

Paw is 78 now, and is not likely to change much. I didn't expect him to. But he and I had one of the most important conversations of our life together one day on the back porch, after Sunday dinner. He said things to me that he had never said—including a confession that utterly changed the way I saw him. That conversation would likely never have happened if we didn't live here. It emerged from within my dad after months of my presence and couldn't have come out any other way. Because of this, when Paw dies, he will leave me with a peace that I would not have had otherwise—and this, indirectly, is another gift of Ruthie's, to both Paw and me.

Now you're back in St. Francisville. Do you think you will stay or will your love of city life kick back in?

Oh no, we'll stay. We want to stay. We are home. I found what I was looking for here, and the only reason I would leave it is if I could no longer support my family from here, working as a writer. We've got good friends now; we're growing closer with the extended Dreher clan. We helped launch a mission church here. We're putting roots down.

What did your family think of the book? Have you shown it to people in St. Francisville yet and, if so, how did they respond?

My parents love it. When my dad finished it, he called and said, "Son, you told it true. That's just how it happened." That meant the world to me, because some of the things I say in the book about our relationship over the years must have been difficult for him to read. I don't know what Mike thinks of the book, not really, and haven't pressed him on it. He is an extremely private man, and it cannot be easy or pleasant to have his life exposed like this, even in a way that puts his late wife and family in a flattering light. He is still very, very deep in grief, and keeps everything to himself. To my knowledge, none of Ruthie's daughters have read it. Ruthie taught her family to deal with pain and hardship with a stiff upper lip. Their grief has been intensely private. In the end, I think they will be pleased by the reaction to *Little Way*, but it's too much to deal with right now.

I shared versions of the manuscript with the principal characters throughout the writing of the book, because I wanted to make sure I was getting the story right. After it was finished, I tried to make sure everyone who had been kind enough to give me an interview for the book had a chance to read it in advance. The response has been overwhelmingly positive—though one of Ruthie's close friends did caution me. She said that everything I said in the book was absolutely true, but that I should be ready for some people around here to rankle at the fact that Ruthie is portrayed as imperfect.

After decades as a professional journalist, was it difficult to write such a personal story? Were there any unexpected challenges that came up during the writing process?

The chief difficulty came for me in having to recognize that the people I was writing about weren't just subjects, but people I loved and cared about, and among whom I lived. I constantly thought about balancing respect for them and their feelings with respect for the truth. Everybody loves the fun stories about Ruthie, but if I had left it at that, it wouldn't have been the whole story of Ruthie. What I didn't expect were the philosophical challenges that came up as I worked on the book. I was most struck by the nature of Ruthie's courage in facing her cancer. I learned as I reported the book that Ruthie never talked with her husband or her children about the possibility of her death—-this, even though she lived for nineteen months with terminal cancer. She was both accepting of death, and terrified of it. She lived with a lot of denial. In learning more about her, I came to understand that the line between heroic courage and stark terror is far more ambiguous than I thought.

Ruthie's life was deceptively plain, misleadingly simple. It was, in truth, marked by paradoxes like this, and evoked deep questions about life and how to live it. It has always been my nature to analyze things, to break them down for the sake of understanding them, to resolve contradictions. Maybe the main difference between us was that while my nature was to approach the world from a critical stance, she accepted life as it was. She almost always met it with humility, fidelity, and above all, love. It is perhaps the most beautiful paradox of Ruthie Leming's life that in showing us how to die, she showed us how to live.

About the Author

ROD DREHER has been a writer and editor at *The Dallas Morning News* and a columnist and critic for *National Review*, the *New York Post*, and *The American Conservative*. Dreher is a popular writer on issues of religion, culture, and localism. David Brooks called him "one of the country's most interesting bloggers."

The author's first book, *Crunchy Cons*, was published in Crown Forum hardcover in 2006.